AF866205

"This volume brings together important latest research from philosophy and psychology on a topic of significant practical relevance. Highly recommended to researchers, practitioners, and postgraduate students dealing with questions related to suicidality."

Jukka Varelius, *University of Turku, Finland*

Exploring Suicidal Ambivalence

This volume offers a comprehensive interdisciplinary exploration of ambivalence in suicidal agency, a phenomenon that, despite its significance in clinical psychology, remains under-conceptualized.

Philosophers debate what ambivalence amounts to and whether ambivalence undermines practical rationality and agency, yet this discourse has rarely been applied to suicidal ambivalence. This volume examines the structural features of ambivalence in suicidal individuals, focusing, among other things, on the conflicting desires to end one's life versus the desire to live. By analyzing these opposing mental states, it clarifies the psychological and philosophical dimensions of ambivalence and its impact on the transition from suicidal ideation to action. Additionally, it critically evaluates whether ambivalence reflects diminished rationality and whether suicidal ambivalence potentially justifies paternalistic interventions. Bridging psychology and philosophy, this volume provides a nuanced understanding of ambivalence in suicidal agency, with significant implications for clinical practice and ethical decision-making.

Exploring Suicidal Ambivalence will appeal to researchers and graduate students working in philosophy of mind, philosophy of psychology, clinical psychology, medical ethics, and psychiatry.

René Baston is a research fellow at TU Dortmund. He has held positions in Bochum, Düsseldorf, Arizona, Edinburgh, and Boulder. His research focuses on philosophy of mind and psychology, especially suicidology. His dissertation was published as *Implizite Vorurteile – Wie unbewusster Rassismus unser Denken begleitet* (2020).

Martin Weichold is Lecturer in Practical Philosophy at TU Dresden. He previously researched at Göttingen, Berkeley, Vienna, and Regensburg. His work explores links between philosophy of psychology and ethics. His book publications include *Zwischen Reflex und Reflexion* (2015) and *The Autonomous Individual: A Praxeological Enactivist Account* (2024).

Routledge Studies in Contemporary Philosophy

The Essence of History
Edited by Aaron Turner

Neurocognitive Foundations of Mind
Edited by Gualtiero Piccinini

Shifting Paradigms of Evil in Philosophy
Reading the Armenian Genocide with the Shoah
İmge Oranlı

Autobiographical Memory and Moral Agency
Interdisciplinary Perspectives in Philosophy and Psychology
Edited by Daniel Vanello

The Phenomenology of Self-Awareness and the Nature of Conscious Subjects
Edited by Julien Bugnon, Martine Nida-Rümelin, and Donnchadh O'Conaill

Digital Development
Technology, Ethics and Governance
Edited by Mirko Farina, Xiao Yu and Jin Chen

Exploring Suicidal Ambivalence
Philosophical and Psychological Perspectives
Edited by René Baston and Martin Weichold

For more information about this series, please visit: www.routledge.com/Routledge-Studies-in-Contemporary-Philosophy/book-series/SE0720

Exploring Suicidal Ambivalence

Philosophical and Psychological Perspectives

Edited by René Baston and Martin Weichold

Routledge
Taylor & Francis Group
NEW YORK AND LONDON

First published 2026
by Routledge
605 Third Avenue, New York, NY 10158

and by Routledge
4 Park Square, Milton Park, Abingdon, Oxon, OX14 4RN

Routledge is an imprint of the Taylor & Francis Group, an informa business

© 2026 selection and editorial matter, René Baston and Martin Weichold; individual chapters, the contributors

The right of René Baston and Martin Weichold to be identified as the authors of the editorial material, and of the authors for their individual chapters, has been asserted in accordance with sections 77 and 78 of the Copyright, Designs and Patents Act 1988.

All rights reserved. No part of this book may be reprinted or reproduced or utilised in any form or by any electronic, mechanical, or other means, now known or hereafter invented, including photocopying and recording, or in any information storage or retrieval system, without permission in writing from the publishers.

For Product Safety Concerns and Information please contact our EU representative GPSR @taylorandfrancis.com. Taylor & Francis Verlag GmbH, Kaufingerstraße 24, 80331 München, Germany.

Trademark notice: Product or corporate names may be trademarks or registered trademarks, and are used only for identification and explanation without intent to infringe.

ISBN: 978-1-041-01748-6 (hbk)
ISBN: 978-1-041-01747-9 (pbk)
ISBN: 978-1-003-61622-1 (ebk)

DOI: 10.4324/9781003616221

Typeset in Sabon
by Newgen Publishing UK

Contents

Contributors

Lieke Asma is a research fellow at the Leibniz University of Hannover, Germany. Before that, she worked at the Radboud University Nijmegen, the VU Amsterdam, and the Munich School of Philosophy. Her main fields of research are philosophy of psychology, mind, and action, with a focus on free will, acting for reasons, and implicit bias. In 2021, she received a research grant from the Deutsche Forschungsgemeinschaft to study the nature of implicit bias. She published two books: *Mijn intenties en ik. Filosofie van de vrije wil* (2021) and *Blinde vlekken. Hoe impliciete vooroordelen je (mis)leiden* (2024). Both books were shortlisted for the Socratesbeker, the award for the best Dutch philosophy book.

René Baston is a research fellow at the Technical University of Dortmund, Germany. He has previously worked at the Ruhr University Bochum, the Heinrich Heine University Düsseldorf, the University of Arizona, the University of Edinburgh, and the University of Colorado Boulder. His main area of research is the philosophy of mind and the philosophy of psychology, with a particular focus on suicidology. His doctoral dissertation was published as a book under the title *Implizite Vorurteile – Wie unbewusster Rassismus unser Denken begleitet* (2020).

Melanie Bozzay is an assistant professor at the Ohio State University College of Medicine in the United States. Her research focuses on developing strategies to identify who is at risk of suicide, and when that risk is greatest, to inform the refinement of suicide intervention and prevention approaches. She has received grants from the National Institute of Mental Health to develop a sleep-based model of proximal suicide risk, and to identify strategies to optimize brief interventions for patients recently hospitalized for suicide risk.

Peter C. Britton is a clinical psychologist, an associate professor in the Department of Psychiatry at the University of Rochester Medical

Center, and an investigator at the Center of Excellence (CoE) for Suicide Prevention at the Department of Veterans Affairs (VA) Finger Lakes Health Care System. His research work focuses on understanding and preventing suicide in high-risk populations, developing and testing clinical suicide prevention interventions, and evaluating the effectiveness of acute mental health crisis services.

Craig J. Bryan is a board-certified clinical psychologist and professor of psychiatry at the University of Vermont in the United States, where he also serves as the Director of the University of Vermont Health Network's Suicide Care Clinic. His research focuses on developing, testing, and refining treatments and interventions to prevent suicide and promote recovery from trauma. He has published hundreds of refereed scientific articles and multiple books including *Rethinking Suicide: Why Prevention Fails and How We Can Do Better* and *Brief Cognitive Behavioral Therapy for Suicide Prevention.* Considered as one of the world's leading experts in suicide, Dr Bryan is a highly sought speaker and educator.

Michael Cholbi is Professor and Personal Chair in Philosophy at the University of Edinburgh. His books include *Suicide: The Philosophical Dimensions* (2011), *New Directions in the Ethics of Assisted Suicide and Euthanasia* (2nd edition, 2023), and *the Oxford Handbook of the Philosophy of Suicide* (2024). Professor Cholbi is the founder of the International Association for the Philosophy of Death and Dying and serves on the editorial boards of the journals *Ethical Theory and Moral Practice, Journal of Applied Philosophy, Social Theory and Practice,* and *Philosophical Quarterly*.

Sabrina Coninx is Assistant Professor at the Vrije Universiteit Amsterdam, with a specialization in philosophy of mind and philosophy of science. Before that she worked at Ruhr University Bochum as a postdoctoral researcher and scientific coordinator of the Research Training Group "Situated Cognition". Her research lies at the intersection of philosophy, psychology, neuroscience, medicine, and technology, with a particular focus on the multifaceted nature of human suffering. Her work has made significant contributions to the understanding of chronic pains, illuminating how these deeply complex phenomena arise and profoundly influence the lives of those affected. In addition, her work has shaped debates on key concepts within the framework of situated cognition, such as scaffolding and niche construction.

Sanja Dembić is a postdoctoral researcher at the Human Abilities Centre for Advanced Studies in the Humanities, Humboldt-Universität zu Berlin, Germany. Previously, she worked as a research assistant at the Institute of Philosophy at the Friedrichs-Alexander-Universität Erlangen-Nürnberg and she studied psychology and philosophy in Basel and Berlin. Her research focuses on issues in the philosophy of psychiatry, the philosophy of mind, and the philosophy of action. In 2024, she published her book *Philosophy of Mental Disorder: An Ability-Based Approach*. Her article "Defining Addictive Disorder: Abilities Reconsidered" (*Philosophers' Imprint* 2021) was awarded the 2021 Prize for Philosophy and Ethics in Psychiatry and Psychotherapy by the German Society for Psychiatry, Psychotherapy, and Psychosomatics (DGPPN).

Thomas Forkmann is a psychologist, psychotherapist (behavior therapy), supervisor, professor of clinical psychology and psychotherapy, and head of the psychotherapy outpatient clinic at the University of Duisburg-Essen in Germany. He has a research focus on suicidal ideation and behavior, depression, metacognition, and interoception. He has published a large number of scientific articles on suicidal ideation and behavior, clinical psychology, and psychotherapy.

Friedrich Hausen is an independent researcher based in Dresden, Germany. His main areas of interest are value theory, philosophy of religion, aesthetics, and philosophy of mind. In addition to academic philosophy, he is frequently involved in art and contemporary music projects. His academic publications include *Wert und Sinn – Apriorische Hermeneutik des Tuns und Fühlens in der Spur Max Schelers* (2015) and *Philosophie der Psychobiologie – Hans Lungwitz im Kontext neuerer Diskurse* (2020).

Brent M. Kious is Associate Professor of Psychiatry, Adjunct Professor in the Center for Health Ethics, Arts, and Humanities, and Adjunct Professor of Philosophy at the University of Utah. He is Director of the Program in Psychiatric Ethics at the Huntsman Mental Health Institute. He earned his MD and PhD in Philosophy from the University of California, Los Angeles, and completed residency in psychiatry at the University of Utah. He currently practices adult inpatient psychiatry. His research in ethics addresses ethical and conceptual problems in psychiatry, end-of-life care, and suicide prevention. It highlights complexities surrounding concepts like decision-making capacity, suffering, and autonomy in persons with psychiatric illnesses.

Zuzanna Rucińska is a senior postdoctoral fellow of the Research Foundation – Flanders (FWO) at the Centre for Philosophical Psychology, University of Antwerp, Belgium. Her research is on embodied cognition and enactivism as applied to play, imagination, mental health, sport, and VR. In 2022 she edited the special issue "Pretense and imagination from the perspective of 4E cognitive science" for *Phenomenology and the Cognitive Sciences*.

Tobias Teismann is a psychologist, psychotherapist (behavioral therapy), supervisor, and professor of clinical psychology. He is the managing director of the adult psychotherapy outpatient clinic at the Forschungs- und Behandlungszentrum für Psychische Gesundheit (FBZ), Ruhr University Bochum in Germany. His research focuses on depression and suicidality. He has published hundreds of scientific articles as well as various books on clinical psychology, cognitive behavior therapy, depression, and the treatment of suicidal individuals.

Elizabeth Ventham is a research fellow in philosophy at the University of Salzburg, where she is a part of the Salzburg Ethics Group. Before moving to Austria, she worked at the University of Liverpool and Trinity College Dublin. Desire and practical reasoning have been two of her main research interests throughout her career, since she did her PhD on subjective accounts of normativity. Additionally, she has published on topics such as empathy, moral demandingness, the nature of pleasure, depression, and echo chambers.

Martin Weichold is Lecturer in Practical Philosophy at the Technical University of Dresden, Germany. Previously, he has carried out research at the Universities of Göttingen, Berkeley, Vienna, and Regensburg. He is particularly interested in the interconnections between philosophy of psychology and ethics. His book publications include *Zwischen Reflex and Reflexion: Intelligenz und Rationalität im unreflektierten Handeln* (2015) and *The Autonomous Individual: A Praxeological Enactivist Account* (2024).

Preface

We want to gratefully acknowledge that the work on this anthology has been carried out in the context of a research network funded by the German Research Foundation (the *Deutsche Forschungsgemeinschaft*, DFG, BA 6721/3-1). Lieke Asma, René Baston, Daphne Brandenburg, Michael Cholbi, Sabrina Coninx, Sanja Dembić, Thomas Forkmann, Tobias Teismann, Zuzanna Rucińska, Elisabeth Ventham, and Martin Weichold were the network members. The network members met from 2022 to 2026 for five different workshops in Düsseldorf, Bochum, Dresden, Amsterdam, München, and Berlin. We are very grateful to everyone who participated in the workshops, and to the DFG for funding them. Among the guests were Cato Benschop, Dieter Birnbacher, Michael Brady, Peter Britton, Craig and AnnaBelle Bryan, Sarah Conly, Justin Coates, Leon de Bruin, August Gorman, Friedrich Hausen, Brent Kious, Julian Kiverstein, Michael David Rudd, and Borut Škodlar. Also, we thank Jean-Pierre Cyron for preparing the index of this book. We hope that our efforts will ultimately benefit others' research on suicide and, in turn, help individuals who are suicidal.

In editing this volume, we have aimed to adopt a language that remains as value-neutral as possible when discussing suicide. Phrases like *committed suicide*, with their historical connotations of moral or legal wrongdoing, were deliberately avoided. Instead, we use more neutral terms such as *suicidal behavior* or *death by suicide* in order to keep the discussion free of normative prejudices.

Introduction

The Relevance of Ambivalence in Suicidal Behavior

René Baston and Martin Weichold

The Phenomenon of Suicidal Ambivalence

A suicidal person self-reports:

> […] but I found a lot of the time I was kind of in a "should I, shouldn't I?" You know like I need a reason why I shouldn't kill myself today, and you know it's really looking like a good idea right now, but I really need to know why I shouldn't do this right now. So I had a lot of internal discussion with myself.
>
> (Bergmans et al., 2017, p. 639)

The philosopher Clancy Martin, who used to be suicidal and wrote a book about this state of mind, explains,

> That challenge—*after all these attempts, why aren't I dead yet?*—stays with me. Is it possible that I don't really want to die? Of course. You can want both things. On many days I did want both things: to die, so I didn't have to live this life anymore, so that I could stop struggling, stop suffering, stop failing, stop disappointing—in an instant, all my problems, gone; and to live […].
>
> (Martin, 2023, p. 18)

A person who jumped from the Golden Gate Bridge and survived reported: "I instantly realized that everything in my life that I'd thought was unfixable was totally fixable—except for having just jumped" (Joiner, 2007, p. 53). There are several reports about agents who survived their suicide attempt by jumping from high places and said that they regretted the act in midair. A similar case is the case of Tina Zahn, who describes in her memoir *Why I Jumped* how she was about to jump from a high bridge. Yet immediately before jumping, her desire to die and her fearlessness

DOI: 10.4324/9781003616221-1

waned a bit and let her hesitate, which gave a law enforcement officer the necessary seconds to catch her (Joiner, 2010, p. 62).

These reports express a phenomenon called "suicidal ambivalence" or "ambivalence in suicidal behavior." Many suicidal agents are torn between taking their lives and go on with living. They may have the intention to kill themselves, while they look at the same time for rescue and hope to not succeed. In a broader conceptualization of suicidal ambivalence, suicidal individuals have a desire to live and a desire to die. Suicidal ambivalence is a complex phenomenon with various facets, and it is the topic of this book.

The Importance of Investigating Suicidal Ambivalence

Suicide remains a significant public health issue. For example, according to the Centers for Disease Control and Prevention (CDC), in the United States, suicide was the 12th leading cause of death overall in 2020, accounting for over 45,000 deaths. In 2022, the suicide rate in the United States stood at approximately 14.3 per 100,000 individuals, the highest since 1941. In Europe, the scenario varies widely among countries, but the World Health Organization (WHO) reports suicide rates ranging from around 5 to 25 suicides per 100,000 people. Countries in Eastern Europe tend to report higher rates, reflecting broader socioeconomic and mental health service disparities. Both regions show a higher prevalence of suicide among men compared to women, and increasing efforts are focused on improving mental health services and prevention strategies.

Beyond all epidemiological assessments, being suicidal is dramatic for those who are struggling to continue living. Behind these outlined statistical numbers lies enormous suffering. Edwin Shneidman (1998), a pioneer in the field of suicidology, posited that suicide often results from an individual's unbearable psychological pain. He emphasized that this intense suffering, which he termed "psychache," is the critical factor driving individuals toward considering suicide as a solution to end their distress. Moreover, families, friends, and communities that lose loved ones to suicide suffer intensely. Furthermore, there is even more suffering visible when considering that for each completed suicide, it is estimated that there are 10 to 25 suicide attempts and 100 people with suicidal thoughts.

Yet despite this importance of suicide, it is still unclear to researchers why individuals kill themselves (Heeringen, 2018), notwithstanding some progresses in suicide research. Only a fraction of those sincerely considering suicide or desiring death actually commit suicide—what exactly accounts for the difference between wanting and doing in this case is still unclear. This is indicated by the fact that predicting suicidal behavior is challenging for clinical psychology. A meta-study (Franklin et al., 2017) showed that no known risk factors can predict suicide far above chance levels, and the predictive ability has not improved across 50 years of research. Arguably, understanding the role of suicidal ambivalence for suicidal action contributes to our understanding of why some individuals who consider self-killing actually act on it.

To be sure, the existence and importance of suicidal ambivalence has long been acknowledged in the literature. The psychologist Shneidman (1998) thinks that ambivalence is one of the ten Communalities of Suicide, and he calls it the "common cognitive state" of a suicidal agent,

> I believe that people who are actually committing suicide are ambivalent about life and death at the very moment they are committing it. They wish to die and they simultaneously wish to be rescued. […] To feel that one has to do it, and, simultaneously, to yearn for intervention.
>
> (Shneidman, 1998 p. 133)

Leenaars (2010) summarizes ambivalence as follows: "The prototypical psychological picture of a person on the brink of suicide is one who wants to and does not want to. He makes plans for self-destruction and at the same time entertains fantasies of rescue and intervention" (p. 8). The *Encyclopedia of Suicide* states that ambivalence

> is perhaps the single most important psychological concept in the understanding of suicide. Ambivalence can be seen in the person who wants to commit suicide but doesn't want to, who simultaneously wishes to die even while fantasizing rescue. The ambivalence is so strong that often suicide victims have been found dead, the telephone clutched in their hand.
>
> (Evans & Farberow, 2003, p. 9)

However, although ambivalence is a well-known phenomenon among suicidal individuals in clinical psychology, the structural characteristics of suicidal ambivalence and its role in actions remain unclear. The phenomenon has neither been systematically conceptualized nor evaluated, neither in philosophy nor in psychology.

The complexity of suicide, coupled with a current gap in comprehensive understanding, underscores the need for more focused research. This is where this book comes in. It is the first book-length attempt to systematically understand suicidal ambivalence from an interdisciplinary perspective, encompassing both philosophy and psychology. This edited volume delves into the concept of suicidal ambivalence to explore this critical aspect of the suicidal experience. By examining the nature of ambivalence, the contributions in this book seek to enhance our understanding of suicidality and inform more effective interventions. Additionally, this book investigates ethical topics related to suicidal ambivalence, including the role suicidal ambivalence can play in justifying paternalistic suicide interventions.

This is important for several reasons. First, understanding the specific phenomenon of suicidal ambivalence can help us better understand suicide. Being able to understand and explain suicide supports any practical method of preventing it. Second, understanding the mental state of suicidal ambivalence can foster empathy and compassion for those who are suicidal. Third, understanding this specific phenomenon can help improve existing interventions for suicidal behavior. For example, certain psychotherapeutic interventions (such as "motivational interviewing," as discussed later in this book) can help individuals deal with suicidal ambivalence and, hopefully, resolve it with a commitment to life. Moreover, psychotherapeutic interventions might help suicidal individuals transform unwholesome states of ambivalence into more wholesome ones. Fourth, understanding suicidal ambivalence can be crucial for the rationality and ethics of suicide interventions. Some clinical psychologists, such as Edwin Shneidman, view suicidal ambivalence as a justification for paternalistic suicide interventions: "It is this omnipresent ambivalence that gives us the moral imperative for clinical intervention" (Shneidman, 1998, p. 133).

Shneidman's intuition can be fleshed out with the philosophy of Harry Frankfurt, who argued that ambivalence undermines an agent's practical rationality and autonomy, making paternalistic interventions less problematic. Arguably, intervening in a person's choice, such as the choice to take one's own life, is not acceptable if the person made their choice autonomously and rationally, but is acceptable if the choice was made in an irrational way. Against this background, reflecting on suicidal ambivalence might provide new justifications for the permissibility or even duty of intervening in suicidal behavior—or, conversely, it might reveal that ambivalence does not actually undermine a person's autonomy, in which case it would not constitute a reason for intervention.

Outline of the Following Chapters

This book is structured as follows. The first three chapters present the basics to the reader, before the subsequent chapters explore new lines of research. In Chapter 1, Tobias Teismann, René Baston, and Thomas Forkmann present the state of the art of research on suicidal ambivalence in psychology. The authors provide a detailed overview of existing empirical studies on suicidal ambivalence. At the same time, they highlight numerous shortcomings in these studies and identify gaps in our empirical knowledge of suicidal ambivalence. This suggests that while the importance of suicidal ambivalence for suicidality is empirically supported, much more research is needed. This includes not only empirical work but also conceptual analysis, as undertaken in the other chapters in this book.

This book includes contributions from different fields. For instance, in Chapter 2, René Baston and Sanja Dembić move from psychology to the field of philosophy. Within philosophy, there is some work on ambivalence, but none on suicidal ambivalence in particular. The authors concentrate on discussing the seminal work of Harry Frankfurt on this topic, as well as recent criticisms of his view by Justin Coates. Importantly, they highlight that analytic philosophers such as Frankfurt and Coates use the notion of ambivalence in ways that have both similar and dissimilar elements compared to how psychologists use it. Baston and Dembić investigate in detail how philosophical discussions of ambivalence can enrich psychological discussions of suicide and suicidal ambivalence. In particular, philosophers discuss the potential rationality of ambivalence as well as the role identification plays, while these two crucial ideas do not play a crucial role in existing empirical work on suicidal ambivalence.

In the third chapter, Martin Weichold and Friedrich Hausen provide a taxonomy of different cases of ambivalence. They start from an observation that becomes clear when just considering the first two chapters: the notion of ambivalence is used very differently in different contexts. However, Weichold and Hausen argue that this should not be taken to mean that only one usage is correct while the others are false. Instead, different notions of ambivalence can serve different theoretical and practical functions. It is only important to not confuse them and to be clear about what one means by "ambivalence" in each context.

In the second part of the book, encompassing Chapters 4, 5, 6, and 7, the authors reflect on how suicidal ambivalence might be explained, thus contributing to a better understanding of the suicidal mind. In Chapter 4, Lieke Asma analyzes suicidal ambivalence from the perspective of analytic philosophy of action. She does so by investigating what it means to have reasons for action, and in particular the action of intentional self-killing. Asma examines the nature of acting for reasons and applies it to three key aspects of suicide: its unpredictability, fluctuations between the wish to die and the wish to live, and ambivalence. She also proposes a shift in focus from predicting suicide to understanding it, emphasizing how self-understanding can play a crucial role in prevention, especially since suicidal ideation may hinder this process and increase risk for ambivalent individuals.

In Chapter 5, Tobias Teismann, Peter C. Britton, and Thomas Forkmann develop a psychological model of suicide according to which suicidal ambivalence is central for understanding the phenomenon of suicide in its entirety. The model suggests that suicidal behavior encompasses an uncertainty phase, a transition phase, and an action phase. Ambivalence plays a role in all phases, even in the action phase. The authors argue that this model, with its emphasis on ambivalence, makes important practical differences for clinical contexts.

In Chapter 6, Craig J. Bryan and Melanie Bozzay provide another psychological approach to suicidal ambivalence. They critically scrutinize the assumption that the desire to die and the desire to live lie on a continuum. According to them, ambivalence has historically been viewed as a unidimensional continuum, with each end defined by a distinct motive, such that people who are ambivalent about suicide potentially move back and forth along the continuum through various states of wanting to live, experiencing ambivalence, and wanting to die. In contrast to this received view, Craig Bryan and Melanie Bozzay describe, from a psychological perspective, how the emergent phenomenon of suicide arises from the dynamic interplay between the desire to die and the desire to live, drawing on the framework of dynamical systems theory. Understanding the temporal patterns of the wish to live and the wish to die could therefore reveal critical information about the emergence of suicidal behavior and clues for promoting recovery after someone experiences a suicidal crisis.

In Chapter 7, Zuzanna Rucinska, Lieke Asma, and Sabrina Coninx approach the topic of suicidal ambivalence and of decision-making in the actions of the suicidal agents from another perspective rooted in cognitive science, namely, the perspective of situated cognition. They aim to better understand why some suicidal agents, but not others, try to die by suicide, even when they do not resolve their suicidal ambivalence. To shed new light on this question, the authors highlight the role of the situation and the context the suicidal person is in, aiming to understand how it actively shapes their suicidal behaviors. The authors investigate in detail the notion of suicidal affordances, and discuss how it can have implications for interventions into suicidal behavior.

In the third part of the book, encompassing Chapters 8, 9, and 10, the authors move from the theoretical explanation of suicidal ambivalence to the practical evaluation of ambivalence. This part of the book lays the normative groundwork for ethical questions on how one should deal with suicidal ambivalence. Traditional assumptions have been that ambivalence is something bad—Harry Frankfurt has prominently argued for this position in philosophy. Additionally, the term "ambivalence" was introduced by Eugen Bleuler (1911) to analyze schizophrenic patients. However, more recent thinkers, such as Justin Coates (2017, 2022), have argued for the positive value of ambivalence, pointing out that certain cases of ambivalence do not undermine agency and can indeed be an adequate attitude when facing conflicting reasons.

In this spirit, in Chapter 8, Elizabeth Ventham and Sabrina Coninx argue for the importance and potentially beneficial effects of ambivalence for agency. Not only can ambivalence be warranted, it can—they argue—even be necessary for a functional, rational agent. The authors aim to demonstrate a useful two-way relationship: that the literature on ambivalence can teach us something important about the ethics of suicide intervention, and that the psychological literature about suicidal intervention is a valuable source of cases that can teach us about the nature and importance of ambivalence.

Chapters 9 and 10 present the opposing side of the dialectic. While acknowledging the valuable contribution of Elizabeth Ventham and Sabrina Coninx in emphasizing the bright sides of ambivalence, in Chapter 9, Friedrich Hausen and Martin Weichold present many cases, particularly from psychopathological contexts where ambivalence can take extreme forms and make the lives of those who suffer from it worse. Here, the authors do not only investigate suicidal ambivalence but also suggest that extreme forms of ambivalence in many areas of life can motivate suicidal behavior. Hausen and Weichold then offer a hypothesis about what distinguishes acceptable or even rational cases of ambivalence from those where ambivalence is an unbearable state of mind: namely, whether the ambivalence is mastered or unmastered. In particular, they argue that unmastered ambivalence is harmful because it threatens the integrity of those who suffer from it. Thus, the connection between ambivalence and integrity is crucial for evaluating whether an instance of ambivalence is harmful or beneficial.

A similar, compatible argument is made in Chapter 10 by Sanja Dembić. She also argues that ambivalence threatens human agency in certain cases. In contrast to Hausen and Weichold, who are more interested in existential, organic, and psychopathological dimensions of ambivalence, Dembić focuses on the notions of reasons and intentions. She distinguishes between two "faces" of ambivalence and argues that one of these faces necessarily threatens our agency. These are cases in which the agent needs to make an important, unavoidable life decision by committing to a stable intention for going on, but is—due to their ambivalence—unable to form such a stable intention. Furthermore, Dembić discusses how ambivalence might be resolved in such cases: she argues that one should *create* for oneself new reasons for acting.

In the fourth and final part of the book, authors investigate the ethical implications of the previous examinations of suicidal ambivalence. In particular, in Chapter 11, Michael Cholbi investigates the implications of ambivalence in suicidal behavior for the ethics of paternalistic suicide interventions. Cholbi critically scrutinizes the idea that the existence of ambivalence can offer a new justification for paternalistic interventions into suicidal behavior. According to Cholbi, the role of ambivalence in interventions is equivocal. At least in some cases of genuine ambivalence, Michael Cholbi argues, ambivalence does justify paternalistic interventions, but there are ethical limitations even in these cases.

In Chapter 12, Brent Kious explores the role of ambivalence for medical aid in dying. Since many countries are about to change their legislations on this topic, the chapter shows the relevance of suicidal ambivalence particularly well. Kious starts with a recent real-life case of a doctor who provided medical aid in dying in Germany and was subsequently convicted of manslaughter. The fact that the person who received the medical aid in dying was ambivalent about her decision played a crucial role in the court judgement. So, does the presence of suicidal ambivalence make medical aid in dying illegitimate? Kious investigates several arguments to this effect. However, against the background of his investigation of ambivalence and related phenomena, he argues that the presence of suicidal ambivalence is compatible with the legitimacy of medical aid in dying. Still, Kious argues, in cases of medical aid in dying, suicidal ambivalence should be resolved for instrumental reasons.

Defining Key Terms

Before ending this introduction, we want to define a few key terms, to provide more orientation for the reader for the following chapters.

- The term "suicide" refers to the result of intentional self-killing (Cholbi, 2011). However, it is often meant to refer to the act of intentional self-killing itself. Intentional self-killing excludes acts that accidentally result in one's death. Moreover, the term "suicide" should be understood in a value-neutral way. It is an open question whether there are some suicides that are rational and morally permissible, or even morally obligatory (Battin, 1995; Cholbi, 2011; Cosculluela, 1995). While suicide is not inherently bad, many cases of suicide should be prevented.
- The term "suicidal behavior" can be taken to refer to everything from thoughts about suicides ("suicidal ideation"), to considering, imagining, planning, to attempts, to completed suicides. Suicidal behavior does not necessarily meet the criteria of "full-blown agency" as defined in the theory of action.
- "Ambivalence" means, in first approximation, the co-existence of opposing desires, attitudes, reasons, or emotions toward something. An ambivalent person is of two minds (Railbley, 2021). However, this characterization is very broad and still not uncontroversial. We do not want to define "ambivalence" from the outset, because exploring its meaning

is the very purpose of the chapters in this book. As the reader will see, there are many different, interrelated phenomena that can be meant by "ambivalence." A better understanding of these phenomena, their interrelations, and the dynamics between them is precisely what leads to a deeper understanding of the many facets of suicidal ambivalence.

References

Battin, M. P. (1995). *Ethical issues in suicide* (pp. xiv, 240). Prentice-Hall, Inc.

Bergmans, Y., Gordon, E., & Eynan, R. (2017). Surviving moment to moment: The experience of living in a state of ambivalence for those with recurrent suicide attempts. *Psychology and Psychotherapy*, 90(4), 633–648.

Bleuler, E. (1911 / 2014). *Dementia praecox oder Gruppe der Schizophrenien* (Unchanged New Edition). Psychosozial-Verlag.

Cholbi, M. (2011). *Suicide: The philosophical dimensions*. Broadview Press Ltd.

Coates, D. J. (2017). A wholehearted defense of ambivalence. *The Journal of Ethics*, 21(4), 419–444.

Coates, D. J. (2022). *In praise of ambivalence*. Oxford University Press.

Cosculluela, V. (1995). *The ethics of suicide* (1st edition). Routledge.

Evans, G., & Farberow, N. L. (2003). *The encyclopedia of suicide* (2nd edition). Facts On File.

Franklin, J. C., Ribeiro, J. D., Fox, K. R., Bentley, K. H., Kleiman, E. M., Huang, X., Musacchio, K. M., Jaroszewski, A. C., Chang, B. P., & Nock, M. K. (2017). Risk factors for suicidal thoughts and behaviors: A meta-analysis of 50 years of research. *Psychological Bulletin*, 143(2), 187–232.

Heeringen, K. van. (2018). *The neuroscience of suicidal behavior* (Illustrated edition). Cambridge University Press.

Joiner, T. (2007). *Why people die by suicide* (1st edition). Harvard University Press.

Joiner, T. (2010). *Myths about suicide*. Harvard University Press.

Leenaars, A. A. (2010). Lives and deaths: Biographical notes on selections from the works of Edwin S. Shneidman. *Suicide and Life-Threatening Behavior*, 40(5), 476–491.

Martin, C. (2023). *How not to kill yourself: A portrait of the suicidal mind*. Pantheon.

Raibley, J. R. (2021). Ambivalence, well-being, and prudential rationality. In B. Brogaard & D. E. Gatzia (Eds.), *The philosophy and psychology of ambivalence: Being of two minds* (pp. 269–293). Routledge.

Shneidman, E. S. (1998). *The suicidal mind* (reprint edition). Oxford University Press.

Part 1

The Basics

1 Psychological Perspectives on Suicidal Ambivalence

Tobias Teismann, René Baston, and Thomas Forkmann

1.1 Introduction

Suicidal ideation is common in the general population as well as among psychotherapy patients: Serious suicidal ideation during the past two weeks was reported by 8% of respondents in a German representative study (Forkmann et al., 2012) and by 16–67.5% of outpatients starting psychotherapy in Germany (Teismann et al., 2024a). Suicidal ideation is a significant risk factor for suicidal behavior (Franklin et al., 2017) and exerts a high mental burden on affected persons (Jobes & Joiner, 2019). Even though suicidal thoughts typically show a strongly fluctuating course (Hallensleben et al., 2018), about 20–30% of suicidal individuals suffer from suicidal thoughts that persist over years (Teismann & Koban, 2022). The fact that a decision to die by suicide is of the utmost gravity suggests that many of those thinking about suicide will go through a phase of cognitive-affective ambivalence before making the decision to act on a suicide wish (cf. Buttlar et al., 2024).

In line with this reasoning, Shneidman (1996) states that suicidal ambivalence is the common cognitive state "that occurs in almost every case of suicide" (p. 129) and Evans and Farberow (1988) refer to ambivalence as "perhaps the single most important psychological concept in our understanding of suicide" (p. 12). In contrast to the significance of suicidal ambivalence expressed in these statements, there is comparatively few research that has dealt with suicidal ambivalence scientifically (Teismann et al., 2024b).

This chapter summarizes the existing empirical studies on suicidal ambivalence: the psychological understanding and assessment of suicidal ambivalence is explained; the frequency and nature of suicidal ambivalence is described; and associations between suicidal ambivalence, markers of positive and negative mental health, as well as suicidal thoughts and suicidal behavior are discussed.

DOI: 10.4324/9781003616221-3

1.2 Definitions, Conceptualization, and Operationalization of Suicidal Ambivalence

The term "ambivalence" was introduced into psychology and psychiatry by the Swiss psychiatrist Eugen Bleuler (1911). Bleuler understood ambivalence as the simultaneous occurrence of incompatible emotions, cognitions, or intentions within one person. Freud (1943) later adopted the term ambivalence into his psychoanalytic theory: according to him, ambivalence refers mainly to inconsistencies between emotions, such as love and hate. More contemporary psychological definitions of ambivalence refer to *the simultaneous existence of positive and negative (implicit or explicit) evaluations regarding a given person, experience, or other (sets of) objects* (cf. Connor & Sparks, 2002). Gardner (1987, p. 241), for example, defined ambivalence as "a psychological state in which a person holds mixed feelings (positive and negative) towards some psychological object". Emmons (1996, p. 326) defined ambivalence as "an approach-avoidance conflict – wanting but at the same time not wanting the same goal object". Other authors added a distinction between *diachronic* and *synchronic* ambivalence: As such, ambivalence may not only reflect "mixed feelings" toward something at a particular moment in time (*synchronic ambivalence*) but might also include changes in the dominance of competing motives at different points in time (*diachronic ambivalence*; cf. Connor & Sparks, 2002).

In the context of suicidality, ambivalence often refers to the experience of being torn between a wish to die (WTD) on the one hand and a wish to live (WTL) or fears of dying or being dead, on the other hand (Teismann et al., 2024b). However, there has been a lack of formal definitional work in this specific field to date: As such different terms are used (interchangeably) to refer to suicidal ambivalence, for example, internal suicide debate (Harris et al., 2010), internal struggle (Kovacs & Beck, 1977), WTD vs. WTL (Bryan et al., 2016), or reasons for living (RFL) vs. reasons for dying (RFD) (Fox et al., 2021). This inconsistency in terminology is problematic because, at face value, RFL and RFD measure something different from the existence and intensity of a WTD or a WTL. These concepts consider different factors in understanding ambivalence – and it remains unclear to what extent these reasons are linked to suicidal wishes.

In line with this lack of a formal definition and uniform conceptualization, suicidal ambivalence – as well as ambivalence more generally (Jonas & Ziegler, 2007) – is operationalized and measured in a variety of different ways. The most common approach consists in instructing individuals to provide separate ratings of their positive and negative reactions toward an attitude object. In the context of suicidal ambivalence persons are therefore asked to separately rate their current WTD and their current

WTL, or they are asked separately to indicate their RFL and their RFD (Teismann et al., 2024b). In many studies, these positive/life-affirming and negative/death-affirming reactions are then combined according to a mathematical formula. This type of measure has been called "objective ambivalence" or "indirect measure of ambivalence" (Jonas & Ziegler, 2007). In some studies (e.g., Bonewyn et al., 2017; Brown et al., 2005; Kochanski et al., 2018), a WTL/WTD index has, for example, been calculated by reversing the WTL score and by subtracting this score from the WTD score. Subsequently this or other kinds of index scores are used to create distinct groups. Some studies (e.g., Bonewyn et al., 2017; Kovacs & Beck, 1977; O'Connor et al., 2012a; Ring et al., 2019), for example, trichotomized the score into three groups: One group called "Wish to Die, WTD", consisting of participants who display a stronger WTD than a WTL, an "Ambivalent" group, consisting of participants who showed an even WTD and WTL, and a "Wish to Live, WTL" group, consisting of participants who displayed a stronger WTL than a WTD. In other studies (Corona et al., 2013; Fox et al., 2021), the total number of RFD became subtracted from the total number of RFL to create three groups: Life-motivated, Ambivalent, Death-motivated.

A frequent problem with the WTL/WTD index is that only those persons are classified as "ambivalent" who have an equally strong WTD and WTL. In fact, however, this group could include people who are indifferent (rather than ambivalent) toward their lives (cf. Schneider & Schwartz, 2017), and this group does furthermore not include people who are possibly more inclined to live or more inclined to die, but are still ambivalent at the same time (Teismann et al., 2024b). In general, the unidimensional approach to the WTL and WTD may obscure important distinctions in understanding suicidal ambivalence. In this vein, different authors (Bryan, 2020; Ernst et al., 2024) recommend treating WTL and WTD as independent constructs, as this allows for a more nuanced understanding of ambivalence.

A problem with the RFD/RFL index is that it regularly lacks a weighting of the significance of the various reasons (e.g., Fox et al., 2021), meaning that a subjective experience and intensity of ambivalence cannot be depicted in this way. In consequence, the RFD/RFL index oversimplifies how these reasons actually function in decision-making (Baston, 2024): In decision-making, pro and con arguments are often asymmetrical – some reasons carry more weight than others, and their relevance can shift depending on the context. A person might list multiple RFD, yet one meaningful reason for living could outweigh them all. A more nuanced approach would need to account for how individuals prioritize and emotionally process their reasons rather than reducing them to a simple numerical difference.

Measures of "felt ambivalence", that is, measures that directly ask participants, if they feel torn or divided regarding an attitude object (Jonas & Ziegler, 2007) have rarely been used in suicide research. There are only a few studies that directly asked, for example, if participants "ever had an internal debate about whether to live or die?" (Harris et al., 2010) or that asked people after they tried to kill themselves, whether they did intend to die, did not intent to die, or partially intended to die by the attempt (Gromatsky et al., 2022).

All of the studies mentioned so far do not do sufficient justice to the potentially dynamic nature of suicidal ambivalence. A small number of recent studies therefore used smartphone-based ecological momentary assessment (EMA) designs, in which participants are repeatedly asked about suicidal ideation and WTD/WTL within shorter periods of time, in order to assess trajectories of suicidal ambivalence and associations with suicidal desire (Ernst et al., 2024; Oakey-Frost et al., 2023). This method permits capturing moment-to-moment variations in psychological and behavioral variables in the participants' natural environment. It prevents hindsight biases and allows calculating relations between constructs within and across sampling moments (Trull & Ebner-Priemer, 2009). In these studies, WTD/WTL are generally considered separately or in interaction (see also Bryan et al., 2016). Despite all the advantages of such an EMA approach, the extent to which participants actually experience themselves as ambivalent and/or suffer from feeling ambivalent regularly remains unclear. By now, there are only a few qualitative studies that focus on the experience of feeling ambivalent regarding suicide and that try to understand how suicidal individuals deal with suicidal ambivalence (e.g., Bergmans et al., 2009, 2017; Galasinski & Ziolkowska, 2024).

In sum, there are various ways in which suicidal ambivalence has been operationalized, some of which may be too broad to understand the role of suicidal ambivalence in the escalation of a suicidal crisis. These different operationalizations may, however, capture entirely different aspects of ambivalence. Moreover, there is ongoing debate about how exactly the measured data – such as wishes for or against suicide – should be interpreted and calculated to determine ambivalence. There is therefore an urgent need to develop and test different measures to assess facets of suicidal ambivalence. Measures to assess ambivalent experiences in general (van Harrefeld et al., 2015) might offer suggestions for future research on the assessment of suicidal ambivalence.

1.3 Prevalence of Suicidal Ambivalence

In studies in which a group affiliation is determined based on a one-time assessment of the WTL /WTD or RFL/RFD, 17% to 57% of suicidal persons have been classified as being ambivalent about suicide at the time of the assessment (Teismann et al., 2024b). However, most studies assigned participants to the Ambivalent-group – as has already been described – if they displayed a balanced strength of the WTD/WTL (Corona et al., 2013; Lento et al., 2013; Oakey-Frost et al., 2023; O`Connor et al., 2012a; Ring et al., 2019) or equal numbers of RFL/RFD (Corona et al., 2013; Fox et al., 2021). In consequence, these studies might underestimate the incidence of suicidal ambivalence. This is all the more true as a one-time assessment certainly does not do justice to the dynamic nature of suicidal ambivalence (Ernst et al., 2024; Fartacek et al., 2024). Accordingly, in an online study lifetime experiences with suicidal ambivalence are reported by 94% of suicidal participants – 37.6% indicated to frequently engage in an internal debate about the pros and cons of suicide (Harris et al., 2010).

Of those participants who survived a suicide attempt, 41% to 50% stated that they felt ambivalent about dying by suicide at the time they attempted (Ammerman et al., 2020; Gromatsky et al., 2022; Kovacs & Beck, 1977) and 36% to 43% felt ambivalent about having survived the suicidal act (Bhaskara et al., 2014; Henriques et al., 2005). In sum, suicidal ambivalence is a common experience in persons contemplating suicide and suicidal ambivalence seems to be present before, during, and after a carrying out the suicidal act.

1.4 Characteristics of Suicidal Ambivalence

In qualitative studies on suicidal ambivalence, various characteristics of ambivalent experiences become highlighted (Teismann et al., 2024b), such as:

- First of all, ambivalence seems to be something that does not take place exclusively in an (explicit) internal debate, but also finds expression in the fact that apparently clear intentions ("I want to die") appear in conjunction with behavior that seems to comprehensively undermine this objective, for example, going to a psychiatrist after having overdosed (Brooke & Horn, 2010), or postponing the implementation of a suicide decision because of rather mundane reasons (van Wijngarden et al., 2021). Ambivalence may also be revealed when people respond to the question surrounding suicidal intent with words such as "maybe", "not yet", and "probably" (van Wyk & Gibson, 2022).
- Second, participants stress that it is physically and attitudinally demanding to hold the tension between the desire to end life while being not convinced that this was the right choice (Bergmans et al., 2017). Participants describe the state of ambivalence about life and death as torturous.

- Third, suicidal ambivalence becomes characterized as a fragile and fluid state that can react quickly to "tipping and turning points" (Bergmans et al., 2009). The rapidly changing nature of suicidal ambivalence has also been documented in EMA studies in which participants report on their WTD and WTL within short time-intervals (Ernst et al., 2024).
- Fourth, suicidal ambivalence needs not to be resolved with one side winning or prevailing when persons show a transition from suicidal thoughts to suicidal behaviors. Rather, it seems that some of those affected set ambivalence aside and show a sudden shift from an ambivalent thinking mode to an action mode in which there is no place for ambivalence (Galasinski & Ziolkowska, 2024).

The characteristics described here complement study findings on attitudinal ambivalence in general: As such a distinction between implicit and explicit ambivalence has been made (Schneider & Schwartz, 2017) and ambivalence has been shown to cause discomfort, anxiety, and tension (van Harreveld et al., 2009a,b).

1.5 Association of Suicidal Ambivalence with Markers of Positive and Negative Mental Health

In studies in which a group affiliation was determined based on a single assessment of the WTL/WTD or RFL/RFD, the extent to which the mental state of ambivalent persons differs from that of persons who were assigned to either the WTD group or the WTL group was studied repeatedly. With a view at markers of negative mental health, ambivalent participants were shown to have lower self-hate (Corona et al., 2013), hopelessness (Heniques et al., 2005; Lento et al., 2013; O`Connor et al., 2012a), depression (Heniques et al., 2005; Lento et al., 2013), and symptom burden scores (O`Connor et al., 2012a) than participants with a firm WTD and higher self-hate (Corona et al., 2013) as well as hopelessness scores (Corona et al., 2013; Lento et al., 2013) than participants with a stronger WTL. Furthermore, it was shown that compared to WTD groups, ambivalent participants scored higher in social support (Bonewyn et al., 2017) as well as in RFL compared to both a WTD group (O'Connor et al., 2012b) and a WTL group (O`Connor et al., 2012a).

The findings are not completely consistent, but it appears that ambivalent persons are in the middle range between persons with a firm WTD and those with a stronger WTL with regard to their general well-being. Again, however, it must be emphasized that this is a very static approach that does not adequately consider the dynamic nature of being suicidal and potentially disregards the ambivalence of persons with unbalanced WTD and WTL who still feel ambivalent.

1.6 Association of Suicidal Ambivalence with Suicidal Ideation, Plans, Attempts, and Suicide

In studies on attitudinal ambivalence, it was shown that high ambivalence is associated with a weaker attitude–behavior relationship than low ambivalence (Jonas & Ziegler, 2007); that means it is less clear and predictable in which way an ambivalent person will behave. Suicidal ambivalence might, therefore, add to the unpredictability of suicidal behavior (Teismann et al., 2022).

From the perspective of clinical psychology, the question of whether suicidal ambivalence is something good or something bad is fundamentally relative: on the one hand, it is of course good if a person is still ambivalent, as this means that the decision to die by suicide has not yet been made (and that there are still RFL or against dying). On the other hand, suicidal ambivalence naturally also means that the person no longer feels firmly committed to life, and that a transition to suicidal behavior might rapidly take place. In line with this reasoning, it has been shown that a firm WTD – compared to an ambivalent position and/or a firm WTL – was associated with future suicides (Brown et al., 2005) and that suicide attempters who wished they had died in a recent suicide attempt were twice as likely to die by suicide in the future compared to those who felt ambivalent and/or glad to have survived a recent suicide attempt (Henriques et al., 2005). Yet, in a recent study, a firm WTD and suicidal ambivalence at baseline both were associated with an increased likelihood of suicide attempts compared with the reference category WTL (Höller et al., 2024). In a similar vein, persons who felt ambivalent about having survived a recent suicide attempt had a comparable risk of future suicide attempts than persons who wished to be dead after a recent attempt (Bhaskara et al., 2014), and patients with a suicide attempt history had higher ambivalence scores than participants from a healthy control group (Del-Monte & Graziani, 2020; see also Ernst et al., 2024). Further studies found that ambivalent participants scored similar (Lento et al., 2013) or lower (O'Connor et al., 2012b) on suicidal ideation than WTD groups. In a recent EMA study, a relatively equal WTL and WTD – as an indicator of ambivalence – was found to predict suicidal desire; even after controlling for suicidal desire at the previous assessment (Oakey-Frost et al., 2023; see also Ernst et al., 2024). Further studies found that ambivalence was associated with suicidal ideation/behavior (Harris et al., 2010) and heightened overall suicide risk compared to a WTL group (Corona et al., 2013; O'Connor et al., 2012a), as well as lowered suicide risk compared to a WTD group (O'Connor et al., 2012a).

In sum, there are heterogeneous findings on the association between suicidal ambivalence and suicidal ideation and behavior and the number of available empirical studies is generally limited. Findings differ depending on the respective comparison group: in comparison to people with a predominant desire to live, the presence of suicidal ambivalence represents a risk factor; in comparison to people with a predominant desire to die, the presence of suicidal ambivalence is to be understood as rather protective.

1.7 Discussion

The aim of this chapter was to summarize the empirical literature on suicidal ambivalence. Suicidal ambivalence is considered to be a central characteristic of suicidal patients (Shneidman, 1996); nevertheless, comparatively few studies have dealt with suicidal ambivalence by now (Teismann et al., 2024b). The study situation lacks a clear definition and conceptualization of suicidal ambivalence and despite the knowledge that ambivalence can be subject to rapid changes (Bryan et al., 2016; Oakey-Frost et al., 2023), ambivalence is assessed rather statically in most studies, that is, people are classified as ambivalent or nonambivalent in relation to their WTL/WTD on the basis of one single assessment. An additional difficulty is that in various studies participants are classified as ambivalent only if the same strength of WTD and WTL (Corona et al., 2013; Lento et al., 2013; Oakey-Frost et al., 2023; O`Connor et al., 2012a; Ring et al., 2019), or the same number of RFD/RFL (Corona et al., 2013; Fox et al., 2021), is assessed. Prevalence rates must, therefore, be regarded as potentially underestimating the true prevalence of suicidal ambivalence. Nevertheless, the prevalence figures – even if they are only regarded as rough estimates – indicate that many suicidal persons know ambivalent experiences before, during, and after a suicidal act.

Studies on the association between suicidal ambivalence and negative/positive mental health as well as suicidal ideation and behavior indicate that ambivalent individuals regularly fall between those with a strong desire to die and those with a strong desire to live in terms of markers such as hopelessness, self-hate, suicidal ideation, and suicide risk. Yet, ambivalent persons are sometimes more similar to persons with a WTD and sometimes resemble persons with a WTL. This potentially indicates that the assignment to the ambivalence group is often a snapshot and that there is sometimes an area of overlap between the different groups. From the perspective that ambivalence can be a transitional stage, the question also arises as to in which direction those affected are moving: from a firm WTD to a WTL or from a WTL to a firm suicidal intention. Depending on this, different levels of stress and risk regarding suicidal thoughts and suicidal behavior should become apparent. This also indicates that suicidal ambivalence cannot be clearly classified as a protective or a risk factor (Teismann et al., 2024b). In general, a more fine-grained understanding of the consideration process leading up to a suicide decision is urgently needed. A more in-depth scientific study of (implicit and explicit) suicidal ambivalence (including context factors), therefore, seems urgently needed.

In contrast to studies on general attitudinal ambivalence, it is striking that, on the one hand, the immediate emotional effects of suicidal ambivalence have only rarely been investigated and that, on the other hand, there is a lack of studies that investigate how people deal with suicidal ambivalence. It is known from studies on attitudinal ambivalence – as already mentioned – that ambivalence is associated with negative emotional states and increased physiological activity (Buttlar et al., 2024). Yet, it is still unclear to what extent this also applies to suicidal ambivalence and whether suicidal ambivalence in consequence might contribute to an escalation of emotional turmoil in suicidal persons (cf. Teismann & Forkmann, 2024). With regard to attitudinal ambivalence, it is also assumed that the aversive state of feeling ambivalent motivates people to employ emotion- and problem-focused strategies to cope with ambivalence-induced negative affect (Buttlar et al., 2024): The Model of Ambivalent Induced Discomfort (van Harreveld et al., 2009b) outlines that emotion-focused coping is aimed at reducing ambivalent discomfort, for instance, by postponing a decision or obviating the responsibility for a decision. One might speculate that postponing a decision could also contribute to a chronification of suicidal thoughts. However, studies on these issues are missing at the moment. In contrast to emotion-focused coping, problem-focused coping is aimed at the root of the problem and reduces ambivalence and discomfort by changing inconsistent evaluations underlying an ambivalent attitude. In an attempt to change their inconsistent evaluations, people can either process and seek information or persuade themselves even without enquiring new information (Buttlar et al., 2024). By now, it is unclear if people use strategies like these to deal with suicidal ambivalence. Still, one prominent therapeutic approach for treating suicidal patients called Motivational Interviewing (MI) for suicidal patients (Britton et al., 2008, 2011) tries to help suicidal patients to do just that. Within this counselling approach, motives pro and contra dying are explored in a nonjudgmental manner and counsellors aim to bring patients into cognitive and emotional contact with motives and reasons pro living and/or against dying, that is, they help patients to process information that run against a death wish. MI for suicidal patients (Britton et al., 2016, 2020) and MI-strategies have been evaluated in a variety of studies on adolescent (Czyz et al., 2019, 2021; Grupp-Phelan et al., 2019) or adult (Britton et al., 2012, 2020) suicidal patients – either as an adjunct to other treatment strategies or as a stand-alone treatment. However, in none of these studies the impact of MI on suicidal ambivalence has been assessed or reported. Therefore, it is unclear whether problem-focused coping with suicidal ambivalence underlies the effect of MI for suicidal patients.

Taken together, the study results point to the particular relevance of suicidal ambivalence for the understanding of the suicidal process. At the same time, there are large gaps in our knowledge about the development, impact, and therapeutic responsiveness of suicidal ambivalence. The development of better measurement methods, the implementation of high-quality longitudinal (EMA) studies, and the development of a deeper theoretical and therapeutic understanding of suicidal ambivalence is therefore urgently needed (see Teismann & Forkmann, 2024).

References

Ammerman, B.A., Fahlgren, M.K., Sorgi, K.M., & McCloskey, M.S. (2020). Differences in suicidal thoughts and behaviors among three racial groups. *Crisis*, *41*(3), 172–178. https://doi.org/10.1027/0227-5910/a000621

Baston, R. (2024). Beyond prediction: A new paradigm for understanding suicide risk. *Synthese, 204*, 35. https://doi.org/10.1007/s11229-024-04689-7

Bergmans, Y., Gordon, E. & Eynan, R. (2017) Surviving moment to moment: The experience of living in a state of ambivalence for those with recurrent suicide attempts. *Psychology and Psychotherapy, 90*, 633–648.

Bergmans, Y., Langley, J., Links, P. & Lavery, J.V. (2009). The perspective of young adults on recovery from repeated suicide-related behavior. *Crisis, 30*, 120–127.

Bhaskara, J., Wang, Y., Roos, L., Sareen, J., Skakum, K. & Bolton, J.M. (2014). Method of suicide attempt and reactions to survival as predictors of repeat suicide attempts: A longitudinal analysis. *Journal of Clinical Psychiatry, 75*, e802–e808.

Bleuler, E. (1911). Vortrag über Ambivalenz [Lecture on ambivalence]. *Zentralblatt für Psychoanalyse*, *1*, 266–268.

Bonewyn, A., Shah, A., Bruffaerts, R. & Demyttenaere, K. (2017). Factors determining the balance between the wish to die and the wish to live in older adults. *International Journal of Geriatric Psychiatry, 32*, 685–691.

Britton, P.C., Williams, G.C. & Conner, K.R. (2008). Self- determination theory, motivational interviewing, and the treatment of clients with acute suicidal ideation. *Journal of Clinical Psychology*, *64*(1), 52–66. https:// doi.org/ 10.1002/ jclp.20430

Britton, P.C., Patrick, H., Wenzel, A. & Williams, G. (2011). Integrating motivational interviewing and self- determination theory with cognitive behavioral therapy to prevent suicide. *Cognitive and Behavioral Practice*, *18*, 16–27.

Britton, P.C., Conner, K.R. & Maisto, S.A. (2012). An open trial of motivational interviewing to address suicidal ideation with hospitalized veterans. *Journal of Clinical Psychology*, *68*(9), 961– 971. https:// doi.org/ 10.1002/ jclp.21885

Britton, P.C., Bryan, C.J. & Valenstein, M. (2016). Motivational Interviewing for means restriction counseling with patients at risk for suicide. *Cognitive and Behavioral Practice*, *23*, 51–61

Britton, P.C., Conner, K.R., Chapman, B.P. & Maisto, S.A. (2020). Motivational Interviewing to address suicide ideation: A randomized controlled trial I veterans. *Suicide and Life- Threatening Behavior*, *50*, 233–248.

Brooke, S. & Horn, N. (2010). The meaning of self-injury and overdosing amongst women fulfilling the diagnostic criteria for "borderline personality disorder". *Psychology and Psychotherapy*, *83*, 113–128.

Brown, G.K., Steer, R.A., Henriques, G.R. & Beck, A.T. (2005). The internal struggle between the wish to die and the wish to live: A risk factor for suicide. *American Journal of Psychiatry*, *162*(10), 1977–1979. https://doi.org/10.1176/appi.ajp.162.10.1977

Bryan, C.J. (2020). The temporal dynamics of the wish to live and the wish to die among suicidal individuals. In A.C. Page & W.G.K. Stritzke (Eds.), *Alternatives to suicide: Beyond risk and toward a life worth living* (pp. 71–88). Elsevier Academic Press. https://doi.org/10.1016/B978-0-12-814297-4.00004-2

Bryan, C.J., Rudd, M.D., Peterson, A.L., Young-McCaughan, S. & Wertenberger, E.G. (2016). The ebb and flow of the wish to live and the wish to die among suicidal military personnel. *Journal of Affective Disorders, 202*, 58–66.

Buttlar, B., Pauer, S. & van Harreveld, F. (2024). The model of ambivalent choice and dissonant commitment: An integration of dissonance and ambivalence frameworks. *European Review of Social Psychology*. Advance online publication. https://doi.org/10.1080/10463283.2024.2373547

Conner, M. & Sparks, P. (2002). Ambivalence and attitudes. *European Review of Social Psychology, 12*, 37–70. https://doi.org/10.1080/14792772143000012

Corona, C.D., Jobes, D.A., Nielsen, A.C., Pedersen, C.M. Jennings, K.W., Lento, R.M. & Brazaitis, K.A. (2013). Assessing and treating different suicidal states in a Danish outpatient sample. *Archives of Suicide Research, 17*, 302–312.

Czyz, E.K., King, C.A. & Biermann, B.J. (2019) Motivational interviewing-enhanced safety planning for adolescents at high suicide risk: A pilot randomized controlled trial. *Journal of Clinical Child & Adolescent Psychology*, *48*, 2, 250–262.

Czyz, E.K., King, C.A., Prouty, D., Micol, V.J., Walton, M. & Nahum-Shani, I. (2021). Adaptive intervention for prevention of adolescent suicidal behavior after hospitalization: A pilot sequential multiple assignment randomized trial. *Journal of Child Psychology and Psychiatry*, *62*(8), 1019–1031. https://doi.org/10.1111/jcpp.13383

Del-Monte, J. & Graziani, P. (2020). Anticipatory, relief-oriented and permissive beliefs in patients with suicidal behaviors: An exploratory case-control study. *Archives of Suicide Research, 5*, 629–640.

Emmons, R.A. (1996). Strivings and feeling: Personal goals and subjective well-being. In P.M. Gollwitzer & J.A. Bargh (Eds.), *The psychology of action: Linking cognition and motivation to behavior* (pp. 313–337). Guilford.

Ernst, M., Gemke, T.J., Olivi, L.J. & O'Connor, R.C. (2024). Ambulatory assessment of suicidal ambivalence: The temporal variability of the wish to live and the wish to die and their relevance in the concurrent and prospective prediction of suicidal desire. *Suicide & Life-Threatening Behavior*, *54*, 831–843. https://doi.org/10.1111/sltb.13120

Evans, G. & Farberow, N.L. (1988). *The encyclopedia* of *suicide*. Facts on File.

Fartacek, C., Fartacek, R., Schiepek, G.K., Sturm, J., Aichhorn, W. & Plöderl, M. (2024). Dynamic association between suicidal ambivalence and suicide risk among individuals with a history of suicide attempts. *Suicide & Life-Threatening Behavior*, *54*, 860–868. https://doi.org/10.1111/sltb.13096

Forkmann, T., Brähler, E., Gauggel, S. & Glaesmer, H. (2012). Prevalence of suicidal ideation and related risk factors in the German general population. *The Journal of Nervous and Mental Disease*, *200*, 401–405. https://doi.org/10.1097/NMD.0b013e31825322cf

Fox, A.M., LaCroix, J.M., Bond, A.E., Perera, K.U., Luk, J.W., Goldston, D., Weaver, J., Soumoff, A. & Ghahramanlou-Holloway, M. (2021). Evaluating suicide risk using the Reasons for Dying-Reasons for Living (RFD-RFL) Index in a military psychiatric inpatient setting. *Psychiatry Research*, *295*, 113576. https://doi.org/10.1016/j.psychres.2020.113576

Franklin, J.C., Ribeiro, J.D., Fox, K.R., Bentley, K.H., Kleiman, E.M., Huang, X., Musacchio, K.M., Jaroszewski, A.C., Chang, B.P. & Nock, M.K. (2017). Risk factors for suicidal thoughts and behaviors: A meta-analysis of 50 years of research. *Psychological Bulletin*, *143*(2), 187–232. https://doi.org/10.1037/bul0000084

Freud, S. (1943). Zur Dynamik der Übertragung. In S. Freud (Ed.), *Gesammelte Werke chronologisch geordnet* [*Collected works chronologically arranged*] (pp. 364–374). Imago.

Galasiński, D. & Ziółkowska, J. (2024). The end of ambivalence. A narrative perspective on ambivalence in the suicidal process. *Suicide & Life-Threatening Behavior*, *54*(5), 888–899. https://doi.org/10.1111/sltb.13101

Gardner, P.L. (1987). Measuring ambivalence to science. *Journal of Research in Science Teaching*, 24,241–7.

Gromatsky, M., Edwards, E.R., Sullivan, S.R., van Lissa, C.J., Lane, R., Spears, A.P., Mitchell, E.L., Armey, M.F., Cáceda, R. & Goodman, M. (2022). Characteristics of suicide attempts associated with lethality and method: A latent class analysis of the Military Suicide Research Consortium. *Journal of Psychiatric Research*, *149*, 54–61.

Grupp-Phelan, J., Stevens, J., Boyd, S., Cohen, D.M., Ammerman, R.T., Liddy-Hicks, S., Heck, K., Marcus, S.C., Stone, L., Campo, J.V. & Bridge, J.A. (2019). Effect of a motivational interviewing-based intervention on initiation of mental health treatment and mental health after an emergency department visit among suicidal adolescents: A randomized clinical trial. *JAMA Open*, *2*(12), e1917941.

Hallensleben, N., Spangenberg, L., Forkmann, T., Rath, D., Hegerl, U., Kersting, A., Kallert, T.W. & Glaesmer, H. (2018). Investigating the dynamics of suicidal ideation. *Crisis*, *39*, 65–69.

Harris, K.M., McLean, J.P., Sheffield, J. & Jobes,D. (2010). The internal suicide debate hypothesis: Exploring the life versus death struggle. *Suicide and Life-Threatening Behavior*, *40*, 181–192.

Henriques, G., Wenzel, A., Brown, G.K. & Beck, A.T. (2005). Suicide attempters´ reaction to survival as a risk factor for eventual suicide. *American Journal of Psychiatry*, *162*, 2180–2182.

Höller, I., Forkmann, T., Glaesmer, H., Teismann, T., Hallensleben, N., Schreiber, D. & Krais, J.T. (2024). Torn between living or dying – Analyses of influencing factors on suicide ambivalence and its longitudinally impact on suicidal ideation and behavior in a high-risk sample. *Suicide and Life-Threatening Behavior, 54*, 869–877.

Jobes, D.A. & Joiner, T.E. (2019). Reflections on suicidal ideation. *Crisis, 40*, 227–230.

Jonas, K. & Ziegler, R. (2007). Attitudinal ambivalence. In M. Hewstone, H. A. W. Schut, J. B. F. De Wit, K. Van Den Bos & M. S. Stroebe (Eds.), *The scope of social psychology: Theory and applications* (pp. 29–42). Psychology Press.

Kochanski, K., Lee-Tauler, S.Y., Brown, G.K., Beck, A.T., Perera, K.U., Novak, L., LaCroix, J.M., Lento, R.M. & Ghahramanlou-Holloway, M. (2018). Single versus multiple suicide attempters. *Journal of Nervous and Mental Disease, 206*, 657–661.

Kovacs, M. & Beck, A.T. (1977). The wish to die and the wish to live in attempted suicides. *Journal of Clinical Psychology, 33*, 361–365.

Lento, R., Ellis, T.E., Hinnant, B.J. & Jobes, D.A. (2013). Using the suicide index score to predict treatment outcomes among psychiatric inpatients. *Suicide and Life-Threatening Behavior, 43*, 547–561.

O`Connor, S.S., Jobes, D.A., Yeargin, M.K., FitzGerald, M.E., Rodriguez, V.M., Conrad, A.K. & Lineberry, T.W. (2012a). A cross-sectional investigation of the suicidal spectrum. *Comprehensive Psychiatry, 53*, 461–467.

O`Connor, S.S., Jobes, D.A., Comtois, K.A., Atkins, D.C., Janis, K., Chessen, C.E. & Landes, S.J. (2012b). Identifying outpatients with entrenched suicidal ideation following hospitalization. *Suicide and Life-Threatening Behavior, 42*, 173–184.

Oakey-Frost, N., Moscardini, E.H., Cowan, T., Cohen, A. & Tucker, R.P. (2023). The temporal dynamics of wish to live, wish to die, and their short-term prospective relationships with suicidal desire. *Behavior Therapy, 54*, 584–594.

Ring, M., Walther, S., & Gysin-Maillart, A.C. (2019). The association between therapeutic alliance and individuals' wish to die or live. *Psychology, 10(*12), 1711–1725. doi.org/10.4236/psych.2019.1012112

Schneider, I.K. & Schwarz, N. (2017). Mixed feelings: The case of ambivalence. *Current Opinion in Behavioral Science, 15*, 39–45.

Shneidman, E.S. (1996). *The suicidal mind.* Oxford University Press.

Teismann, T. & Forkmann, T. (2024). Ambivalenzmodell der Suizidalität (ABS-Modell): Ein Verstehens- und Orientierungsmodell für die Behandlung suizidaler Personen. *Verhaltenstherapie, 34*, 85–92.

Teismann, T., Forkmann, T., Glaesmer, H., Alpers, G.W., Brakemeier, E.L., Brockmeyer, T., Christiansen, H., Fehm, L., Glombiewski, J., Heider, J., Hermann, A., Hoyer, J., Kaiser, T., Klucken, T., Lincoln, T.M., Lutz, W., Margraf, J., Pedersen, A., Renneberg, B., Rubel, J., Rudolph, A., Schöttke, H., Schwartz, B., Stark, R., Velten, J., Willutzki, U., Wilz, G. & In-Albon, T. (2024a). Prevalence of suicidal ideation in German psychotherapy outpatients: A large multicenter assessment. *Journal of Affective Disorders, 351*, 971–976.

Teismann, T., Hilbert, K. & Forkmann, T. (2022). Prädiktion suizidalen Verhaltens: Von der klinischen Urteilsbildung zur künstlichen Intelligenz. *Nervenheilkunde*, 41, 253–257.

Teismann, T. & Koban, C. (2022). Chronische Suizidgedanken: ein Behandlungsvorschlag. *Verhaltenstherapie*, *32*, 222–229.

Teismann, T., Siebert, A. & Forkmann, T. (2024b). Suicidal ambivalence: A scoping review. *Suicide and Life-Threatening Behavior, 54*, 802–813.

Trull, T.J. & Ebner-Priemer, U.W. (2009). Using experience sampling methods/ecological momentary assessment (ESM/EMA) in clinical assessment and clinical research: Introduction to the special section. *Psychological Assessment, 21*, 457–462. https://doi.org/10.1037/a0017653

van Harreveld, F., Nohlen, H.U. & Schneider, I.K. (2015). The ABC of ambivalence: Affective, behavioral, and cognitive consequences of attitudinal conflict. *Advances in Experimental Social Psychology*, 52, 285–324. https://doi.org/10.1016/bs.aesp.2015.01.002

van Harreveld, F., Rutjens, B.T., Rotteveel, M., Nordgren, L.F. & van der Pligt, J. (2009a). Ambivalence and decisional conflict as a cause of psychological discomfort: Feeling tense before jumping off the fence. *Journal of Experimental Social Psychology, 45*(1), 167–173. https://doi.org/10.1016/j.jesp.2008.08.015

van Harreveld, F., van der Pligt, J. & de Liver, Y.N. (2009b). The agony of ambivalence and ways to resolve it: Introducing the MAID model. *Personality and Social Psychology Review*, *13*(1), 45–61. https://doi.org/10.1177/1088868308324518

van Wijngarden, E., Merzel, M., van den Berg, V., Zomers, M., Hartog, I. & Leget, C. (2021). Still ready to give up on life? A longitudinal phenomenological study into wishes to die among older adults. *Social Science and Medicine, 284*: 114180.

Van Wyk, J. & Gibson, K. (2022). An analysis of young clients' communications about their suicidality on a text message helpline: "I`m scared of what I might do to myself". *Frontiers in Psychiatry, 13*, 925830.

2 Philosophical Perspectives on Suicidal Ambivalence

René Baston and Sanja Dembić

2.1 Philosophical Perspectives on Suicidal Ambivalence

Suicidal individuals are often described as "ambivalent", a term that suggests that they have conflicting attitudes, such as desires, toward life and death. However, the psychological research discussed in the first chapter does not offer a clear, unified understanding of what ambivalence entails, leaving the concept somewhat vague. Philosophers, while largely silent on the specific topic of suicidal ambivalence, have examined ambivalence more generally. In the absence of a philosophical literature on *suicidal* ambivalence, we aim to explore how insights from general philosophical discussions of ambivalence can be adapted to the context of suicidality. In what follows, we will show that the philosophical work on ambivalence offers valuable insights for psychology, in particular by clarifying what it means to hold conflicting attitudes and how they might impact decision-making and action in life-or-death situations. These insights, we argue, also have potential for therapeutic means.

There are many philosophical discussions about ambivalence that examine different aspects of ambivalence, e.g. its nature, its function, its value, its rationality, or its resolution. However, there is little philosophical work on the topic of suicidal ambivalence. In this chapter, we aim to advance some discussions on suicidal ambivalence by focusing on two aspects of the general philosophical discussion of ambivalence – those that concern the concept of ambivalence and its relation to autonomy and rationality – and relating them specifically to the case of suicidal ambivalence. More specifically, we will argue that the impact of ambivalence on research and practical responses to suicidal ambivalence depends on how one defines "ambivalence" and evaluates its relationship to autonomy and rationality.

Before starting the investigation, it is helpful to clarify some terms in advance. When we talk about agency, we talk about *human agency*. Philosophers typically understand human agency as the capacity of

DOI: 10.4324/9781003616221-4

individuals to make choices and act intentionally, guided by reasons, desires, and rational deliberation. It involves the ability to form intentions and commit to actions, rather than being merely driven by external forces or impulses like urges (Paul, 2020). *Practical rationality* is central to human agency because it allows individuals to act for reasons rather than simply reacting to impulses. Through rational deliberation, agents can evaluate desires, form and revise beliefs and intentions, and commit to actions. Although human beings possess capacities of practical rationality (they are not *arational*), they do act *irrationally* from time to time. Sometimes "irrationality" is understood as internal incoherence (Broome, 1999), e.g. when a person intends to φ, believes that ψ-ing is a necessary means to φ-ing, but does not intend to ψ. Often, however, it is understood as failing to respond adequately to one's reasons, e.g. when a person has decisive reason to φ, but does not intend to φ (Kiesewetter, 2017). We aim to make explicit which sense of "irrationality" is used in the views discussed. *Autonomy* is the capacity to make one's own decisions independently, guided by one's own reasons, rather than external control or situational coercion (Barvosa, 2007; Ekstrom, 1993; Paul, 2020). It involves the ability to self-govern and act in accordance with one's own principles.

Concerning the concept of ambivalence, an important distinction can be found in the literature between "ambivalence" in the sense of (a) conflicting first-order desires or (b) conflicting second-order attitudes. The target of first-order desires are *not* mental states; they can target external objects, like the desire to travel. In contrast, second-order desires have other desires as their targets, such as the desire to have the desire to travel. There are many different views on how to make sense of this distinction or how to conceive of the conflict-type (b) (see Frankfurt, 1971, 1988, 1992; Korsgaard, 1986; Watson, 1975). But for the purposes of this chapter, the details of these views do not matter as much as the general conceptual distinction. Because of that we will focus on Harry Frankfurt's seminal work on the topic. We will argue that the aforementioned conceptual distinction is relevant for psychological research on suicidal ambivalence. This is because, as we will argue, what the psychological research actually measures are first-order desires, but what they should focus on to adequately grasp and explain the phenomena of suicidal ambivalence are second-order desires.

Concerning the autonomy and rationality of ambivalence, some people hold that ambivalence is necessarily irrational and a threat to a person's autonomy (Ekstrom, 1993, 2010; Frankfurt, 1971, 1988, 1992, 2004; Korsgaard, 2009; Velleman, 1989) while others hold that it is not (Barvosa, 2007; Coates, 2017, 2022; Gunnarsson, 2014; Kekes, 2011; Rössel, 2008). Again, for the purposes of this chapter, the details of these views do not matter as much as the fact that there are basically two competing views. As the most elaborated views are those by Frankfurt (1971, 1988, 1992, 2004) and Justin Coates (2017, 2022), we will focus on their accounts. We will argue that the issues of autonomy and rationality are relevant to questions of practical responses to suicidal ambivalence. This is because the view that suicidal ambivalence is necessarily irrational and a threat to a person's agency suggests that the practical response to suicidal ambivalence should be to resolve it, whereas the view that suicidal ambivalence is not necessarily irrational and not a threat to a person's agency suggests that sometimes the practical response should be to maintain it, because it might actually be a reasonable response.

We will proceed as follows: In Section 2.2, we will describe Frankfurt's and Coates' general views on the concept of ambivalence and its relation to autonomy and rationality. We will discuss how suicidal ambivalence can be understood in light of their general views. In Section 2.3, we will discuss the implications of these different views for questions of research and for questions of practical responses to suicidal ambivalence. Section 2.4 concludes.

2.2 Two Philosophical Views of Ambivalence

In Section 2.2.1, we will describe Frankfurt's and Coates' view of the concept of ambivalence and its implications for how to understand suicidal ambivalence. In Section 2.2.2, we will elaborate on their respective views on how ambivalence relates to rationality and autonomy. With respect to the concept of ambivalence, Frankfurt's and Coates' views are broadly similar, but their views differ significantly when it comes to the rationality of ambivalence.

2.2.1 The Concept of Ambivalence

Frankfurt defines "ambivalence" as follows:

> Ambivalence is constituted by conflicting volitional movements or tendencies, either conscious or unconscious, that meet two conditions. First, they are inherently and hence unavoidably opposed; that is, they do not just happen to conflict on account of contingent circumstances. Second, they are both wholly internal to a person's will rather than alien to him; that is, he is not passive with respect to them.
>
> (Frankfurt, 1992, p. 8)

On this view, "ambivalence" refers to a particular type of *volitional* conflict (in contrast to, say, an emotional or cognitive conflict); i.e. it relates to the will or an action. To better understand the particular type, one needs to know what volitions are and what it means that two volitions are "inherently and unavoidably" in conflict with each other and "wholly internal to the person's will". In what follows, we reconstruct Frankfurt's views on these issues.

Frankfurt (1971) argues that, in contrast to other creatures, persons have a complex desire and will structure. People can have many desires, and not all desires determine their actions. The action-determining desires constitute the person's will. People can have "first-order desires" that are related to an action; but they can also develop higher-order attitudes and take a stand on their first-order desires. In particular, persons can have "second-order desires": "Besides wanting and choosing and being moved *to do* this or that, men may also want to have (or not to have) certain desires and motives" (Frankfurt, 1971, p. 12). More specifically, "someone has a desire of the second order either when he wants simply to have a certain desire or when he wants a certain desire to be his will [that is, to be effective]" (1971, p. 16). For example, a person can have a (second-order) desire to have the desire to stop drinking alcohol, or a desire for their desire to stop drinking alcohol to be effective (i.e. to be such that it moves them to act accordingly). The latter is what Frankfurt calls "second-order volitions".[1]

On Frankfurt's view, conflicts that relate to first-order desires – such as the desire to drink alcohol (because of its positive effects) and the desire to not drink alcohol (because of its negative effects) – do not constitute a conflict of the will (as these desires need not be action-determining) and are hence not a case of ambivalence at all. In his view, this is just a conflict of one's impulses, and only conflicts that relate to second-order volitions are conflicts of the will (because second-order volitions are action-determining desires). A creature who does not *care* about which of their desires should be effective and simply gets pushed around by their first-order desires is not a person, but what Frankfurt calls a "wanton" (1971, p. 16).

However, not all conflicts in which the will is involved are cases of ambivalence. For example, cases in which there are "psychic forces" (Frankfurt, 1992, p. 9) which are not "wholly internal to the person's will" in the sense that the person does not *identify* with them are not cases of ambivalence. Frankfurt's example is "the unwilling addict", a person with an addictive disorder who does not want to be moved by their addictive desire but who struggles to defeat it effectively. This person is not ambivalent, but stands "wholeheartedly on one side of the conflict" (Frankfurt, 1992, p. 9), even though the person may ultimately fail to act according to their will.

When are two volitions "inherently and unavoidably" in conflict with each other? Some volitional conflicts are such that the competing desires cannot be fulfilled simultaneously, but only one after the other. For example, a person may have a desire to solve the relationship problems with their partner and a desire to overcome the addiction (but not the resources to tackle both problems at the same time). In principle, such conflicts can be resolved by placing them in a certain *order* and are, therefore, not "inherently and unavoidably" in conflict with each other. Frankfurt calls this kind of resolving a conflict "integration" (1988, p. 170).

By contrast, consider "someone who is moved to commit himself to a certain career, or to a person, and also moved to refrain from doing so" (Frankfurt, 1992, p. 99). In such cases, the volitions are "inherently and unavoidably" in conflict with each other, because the person has contrary desires to the same object. The solution in these cases cannot lie in integration, but rather: "Resolving a conflict of [this] kind involves a radical *separation* of the competing desires, one of which is not merely assigned a relatively less favored position but extruded completely as an outlaw" (Frankfurt, 1988, p. 170).

To sum up, according to Frankfurt, cases of ambivalence are cases in which a person has two second-order volitions (desires for some of their first-order desires to be effective) with which the person identifies and which are in conflict with each other, where the conflict cannot be resolved through integration. More formally, we propose the following reconstruction of Frankfurt's view:

Amb S is ambivalent about whether to φ or to ψ if and only if,

1. φ-ing and ψ-ing are mutually incompatible (at time *t* or within a relevant period of time);
2. S has the desire to φ and the desire to ψ; and
3. S *identifies* with their desire to φ and their desire to ψ in the sense that S has the *second-order volition* to φ and the second-order volition to ψ, i.e. S has the desire that both their desire to φ and their desire to ψ be effective.

Coates (2022, p. 1 and p. 37) has a similar view of the concept of ambivalence, but his third condition is slightly different:

3* S *cares deeply* about φ-ing and about ψ-ing, in the sense that,

a. S *identifies* to a significant degree with their desire to φ and their desire to ψ; and
b. by not φ-ing or not ψ-ing, S would be failing to honor an important aspect of their practical identity, i.e. who they are.

One of Coates' (2022, p. 1) examples is Erica: she has a new job offer on the other side of the country, which she regards as the "culmination of years of very hard work on her part" (p. 1), and two aging parents for whom she is the primary caregiver. Erica cannot take the job and continue to be the primary caregiver for her parents, but she desires both of these options and cares deeply about them.

Now, what does it mean to "identify" with one's desire in Coates' view? According to Coates (2022, p. 37), to identify with one's desire is to "regard it as having some authority to move us to action". As such it is similar to Frankfurt's view, according to which one identifies with one's desire if one has a second-order volition that the first-order desire be effective, i.e. such that it moves one to act accordingly. However, Coates (2022) highlights that there might be other psychological states that could play the same authoritative role as second-order volitions, namely, attitudes of care (Frankfurt, 1988; Jaworska, 2007),[2] what we take to be valuable (Watson, 1975; Korsgaard, 1986), or what we love (Frankfurt, 2004).

To continue with Coates' own view, he does not define what he means by "practical identity". But what he seems to suggest by this term is that people have a practical identity in the sense of having certain core commitments or values. Of course, people have many things they value, love, or care about. But some things are more important to them than others. In this sense, they are part of their (present) practical identity. A consequence of this view is that in cases of ambivalence, the person "must [...] regard her conflict as being one that cannot be resolved without significant *value remainder* or *value residue*" (Coates, 2022, p. 44). In other words, whichever way the ambivalent person proceeds, it will be at significant cost to them, because they will have to give up something that they care about deeply.

It is worth noting that, according to Coates (2022), to be *undecided* or *uncertain* about whether to φ or to ψ is neither necessary nor sufficient for being ambivalent. It is not sufficient for ambivalence, because a person may lack good evidence about what to do or may not have thought it through yet (Coates, 2022, p. 23). It is not necessary for ambivalence, because a person may decide to φ and be certain that φ-ing is the right course of action, but still be ambivalent (Coates, 2022, p. 21). In contrast to Frankfurt's view, Coates' view of ambivalence is compatible with being decided and certain about a particular course of action: A person decides to φ and is certain that φ-ing is the right course of action, but still *cares deeply* about ψ-ing, in the sense that they identify with their desire to ψ to a significant degree; and by not ψ-ing, they would not fail to honor an important aspect of their practical identity. At its core, then, ambivalence is to care deeply about two incompatible actions both of which one desires to pursue.

What insights for the concept of suicidal ambivalence can we gain from these views? Given Frankfurt's and Coates' views of ambivalence, cases of suicidal ambivalence are cases in which a person (1) has a (first-order) desire to die by suicide and a (first-order) desire to live on, and (2) wants both of them to be effective (Frankfurt); or alternatively (2*) regards both of them as having some authority to move them to action, and by not pursuing one of the competing courses of action, the person would fail to honor an important aspect of their practical identity (Coates). In both versions, we would argue, the fear of death alone, as the opposite motivation to the desire for death, is not sufficient to make it a case of ambivalence. Only when the person identifies (in one of the elaborated senses) with the desire to die by suicide is it a case of ambivalence.[3]

2.2.2 *Ambivalence, Autonomy, and Rationality*

Let us now turn to the question of rationality. Frankfurt (1988, 1992, 2004) argues that ambivalence necessarily threatens our autonomous and rational agency. According to Frankfurt (1988, 1992, 2004), autonomous agency necessarily requires (1) wholeheartedness and (2) unity of the will on the part of the agent, because only then is the agent's will, according to which they act, "their own". However, ambivalence consists essentially in having a divided will. This, in turn, renders the agent unable to be wholehearted and to form a unified (i.e. coherent and integrated) will. Therefore, ambivalence necessarily threatens autonomous agency. Other authors (Velleman, 1989; Ekstrom, 1993, 2010; Bratman, 2007; Korsgaard, 2009) argue similarly that ambivalence necessarily threatens autonomy, because it threatens the agent's coherence or their diachronic stability.

Furthermore, Frankfurt (2004, p. 96) argues that ambivalence necessarily threatens rational agency, because it necessarily moves the agent "to act in contrary directions at the same time". This either precludes agential effectiveness completely or it makes the agent's actions incoherent and, therefore, irrational. More generally, one might worry, as Coates (2022, p. 105) puts it, "that a sufficiently robust *pattern* of ambivalence—a regular or frequent inability to settle your will—does seem like it might threaten your ability to live your life in the way you see fit".

In contrast, Coates (2022) holds that ambivalence is not necessarily a threat to our agency.[4] He agrees that an ambivalent person may lack wholeheartedness and unification. But in his view, this does not tell us anything about whether the person is a well-functioning agent. More specifically, Coates (2022) objects to the view that ambivalence necessarily threatens autonomous agency by arguing that an agent's action can be in the relevant sense "their own" even if they do not stand unified and wholeheartedly behind that action. For example, an agent's promise to help a friend move may have an "action-guiding authority" (Coates 2022, p. 61), even if the agent is still ambivalent about the promised action. The agent's ambivalence does not have to impede their ability to overcome obstacles to help the friend move, and it cannot excuse them from their promissory obligation. A person can resolve their ambivalence by deciding on the basis of reasons that they should pursue one action over the other. But this does not require that the person wholeheartedly identifies with the motives that are responding to those reasons (Coates 2022, pp. 65–66).

Coates (2022, p. 112) also objects to the view that ambivalence necessarily threatens rational agency by arguing that in some cases of ambivalence, the competing motives are "responsive to something that is genuinely worthy of the agent's concern". In these cases, ambivalence is not irrational, but, to the contrary, that is what rationality demands. Erica's ambivalence is a case in point. Both her profession and her role as a caregiver for her parents are central to her practical identity. If she were not ambivalent, she would fail to respond adequately to some of her reasons. In light of this Coates (2022) argues that what matters instead is whether the person possesses normative competence in the sense that they respond adequately to their reasons. And crucially, ambivalence can indicate that we are responding adequately to our reasons.

In sum, Frankfurt argues that ambivalence necessarily threatens our autonomous and rational agency, because in being ambivalent we necessarily are not unified (i.e. incoherent) as agents and not wholehearted in our decisions. In his view, unity of the will (or coherence) and wholeheartedness are the hallmarks of autonomous and rational agency. Coates, however, denies this and argues that the hallmark of autonomous and rational agency is that the person's actions are exercises of their ability to respond adequately to their reasons.

In Frankfurt's view, cases of suicidal ambivalence are cases in which the ambivalence necessarily threatens the person's autonomous and rational agency, because it renders the agent unable to be wholehearted and to form a unified will and it moves the agent to act in contrary directions at the same time. In contrast, Coates would argue that cases of suicidal ambivalence are *not* cases in which the ambivalence necessarily threatens the person's autonomous and rational agency, because the person may still retain and exercise their ability to respond adequately to their reasons for acting.

2.3 Implications

In this section, we will discuss some implications of the aforementioned philosophical views on suicidal ambivalence. In Section 2.3.1 we will discuss some implications for empirical research, and in Section 2.3.2 we will discuss implications for questions of practical responses to suicidal ambivalence by those affected and those who treat them.

2.3.1 Implications for Research

To understand the implications of the philosophical views of ambivalence for research on suicidal ambivalence, we first need to highlight some of this research (for a detailed discussion, see Chapter 1). One of the most influential psychological theories of suicide is Joiner's Interpersonal-Psychological Theory of Suicidal Behavior (IPT; Joiner, 2007; Van Orden et al., 2010). The desire for death is a crucial component of the IPT. The theory posits that if individuals perceive themselves as disconnected or a burden to others, they develop a passive desire for death, such as "I wish I were dead". If individuals see themselves as both disconnected *and* a burden, then an active desire for death develops, like "I want to kill myself". The emergence of the active desire for death is an explanatory element of the theory and plays an explanatory role for how suicide ideation translates through the passive desire for death to intentional self-killing.

Clinical psychologists often assess suicidal ambivalence by measuring the desire for death (or wish to die) and the desire to live (or wish to live). Briefly speaking, being ambivalent in this sense means to be torn between the desire to die and the desire to stay alive (Shneidman, 1998). Traditionally, the concept of suicidal ambivalence has been viewed as a continuum with the desire to live and the desire to die at opposite ends. Researchers typically measure an individual's desire to live and desire to die on separate scales, and then calculate the difference to derive an ambivalence index. In this index, negative scores suggest a predominant desire to live, positive scores suggest a predominant desire to die, and a score of zero indicates ambivalence. For instance, the first two questions of the Scale for Suicide Ideation developed by Beck, Brown, and Steer (1997), are often used to assess ambivalence. This scale evaluates the intensity of the desire to live and die, yielding an index that ranges from +2 (indicating a strong desire to live and no desire to die) to -2 (indicating no desire to live and a strong desire to die). A zero score, then, indicates suicidal ambivalence, according to this view (see the scoping review on suicidal ambivalence, Teismann et al., 2024).

As outlined in Section 2.2, philosophical views assume that ambivalence involves conflicting motivations, such as desires, intentions, or volitions. Ambivalent agents are torn between different options for action. This perspective narrows the phenomenon down to the practical dimensions of an agent, while the focus is on the agent's motivations. According to both Frankfurt (1992) and Coates (2022), ambivalence is only possible if an agent has conflicting motivations with which they identify or which are truly their own. In contrast, a case in which an agent experiences a fleeting urge to do something but recognizes that this urge is alien to their self and does not align with their sense of purpose is not considered a case of ambivalence. The state of ambivalence is thus a complex mental state, as it depends on how agents *identify* with their mental states.

Considering the philosophical views on ambivalence, it makes a difference whether an agent just happens to have a desire but feels alienated from it, or whether they acknowledge this desire as their own. We draw two lessons from these philosophical approaches to ambivalence for research.

First, theory building. While IPT suggests that the desire for death plays a crucial role in understanding suicidal action, it does not take into account how an individual relates to this desire. It is possible that some suicidal individuals have a desire for death but do not identify with it. They may wish to be free of this desire or even be indifferent to it. It is also possible that some individuals may gradually develop a sense of identification with the desire for death, and this developmental process may play an important role in understanding suicide ideation and its relation to suicidal action. This is, of course, an empirical question – but one that, to our knowledge, has been overlooked. In any case, a theory of suicidality should be complex enough to include different metacognitive attitudes (non-/identification, indifference) toward the individual's desire for death.

Second, measurement. To date, self-report measures of suicidality have only captured the intensity of an agent's desire to die (and desire to live) and arguably only their first-order desires. This, however, does not seem to do justice to the complexity of agents, as it does not reflect the fact that agents can relate in different ways to their (first-order) desires. With this in mind, suicidal ambivalence may be more complex than many clinical psychologists assume. If it is important for suicidal action that an agent actually identifies with their desire to die, then it is not sufficient to measure self-reported desires, as agents may only self-report first-level desires. Therefore, an assessment of second-order desires may also be necessary.

2.3.2 Implications for Practical Responses

How should one respond to suicidal ambivalence given the different philosophical views of ambivalence outlined in Section 1?

The answer will depend, among other things, on the perspective from which the question is asked. In Section 2.3.2.1, we focus on the first-person perspective, i.e. on perspective of the person experiencing suicidal ambivalence. In Section 2.3.2.2, we focus on the third-person perspective of a therapist who is confronted with a person experiencing suicidal ambivalence.

2.3.2.1 Implications for the Suicidal Person

In light of Frankfurt's view, cases of suicidal ambivalence are cases in which the ambivalence necessarily threatens the person's autonomous and rational agency, because it renders the agent unable to be wholehearted and to form a unified will, since it moves the agent to act in contrary directions at the same time. On this view, the ambivalent person should resolve their ambivalence either by integrating their second-order volitions or by separating themselves from one of them. Applied to the case of suicidal ambivalence, the person has (at least in theory) the following options:

1 live on now and die by suicide later;
2 live on and disidentify from the desire to die by suicide; or
3 to die by suicide now and to dissociate from the desire to live on.

Here, the question arises: How should the person decide between their options? Frankfurt does not give an explicit answer to this question. However, Frankfurt's (1988) view of the importance of what we care about – a question that is distinct from the question of what is morally right – can be used to suggest a way forward. According to Frankfurt (1988), caring consists in "guiding oneself in a distinctive course or in a particular manner" (p. 83); as such, it necessarily involves an activity that "is essentially a reflexive one" (p. 83) and "some degree of persistence" (p. 84). More specifically, he states:

> A person who cares about something is, as it were, invested in it [in the sense that] he makes himself vulnerable to losses and susceptible to benefits depending upon whether what he cares about is diminished or enhanced.
>
> (Frankfurt, 1988, p. 83)

One way of caring is to love. And loving is a personal matter in the sense that the person who loves "does not thereby commit himself to supposing that anyone who fails to love what he does has somehow gone wrong" (Frankfurt, 1988, p. 90). As such, caring differs from (objective) rationality, which is impersonal in the sense that in claims about what is (objectively) rational "it is implicit that anyone who disagrees with the claims must be mistaken" (Frankfurt, 1988, p. 90). In light of Frankfurt's view, then, one could argue that the person should decide what to do by recognizing what they (most) care about.

On Coates' view, cases of suicidal ambivalence are *not* cases in which the ambivalence necessarily threatens the person's autonomous and rational agency, because the person can still retain and exercise their ability to respond adequately to their reasons for acting. On this view, the person should exercise their normative competence by deciding what to do on the basis of their reasons. Coates does not give us a range of options, but the following three are at least theoretically possible. The person has

1 sufficient reason to live on, but not sufficient reason to die by suicide;
2 sufficient reason to die by suicide (now), but not sufficient reason to live on; or
3 sufficient reason to live on and sufficient reason to die by suicide.

Given Coates' view, one could argue that the person in option (1) should decide to live on and the person in option (2) should decide to die by suicide (now). Importantly, option (1) does not have to dissociate from their desire to die by suicide. At least in theory, a suicidal agent can decide to live on for reasons, while still caring deeply about the (reasons for the) option not taken.

There are two important differences between Frankfurt's and Coates' views when applied to cases of suicidal ambivalence. Given Frankfurt's view, the suicidal person's goal should be to resolve their suicidal ambivalence (because it threatens their autonomy and rationality), and a good way to do this is to find out what they care about. In contrast, given Coates' view, the suicidal person's goal should be to exercise their normative competence, and the way to do this is to identify their reasons and decide accordingly. While what the person cares about is personal, what the person has reason to do is impersonal.

For both views, the question arises: What should the person do if they have sufficient reason to live on and sufficient reason to die by suicide or if they care about both options equally? Neither Frankfurt nor Coates give us an answer to this question (but see Chapter 10 for a discussion of such cases).

While Frankfurt and Coates leave open the question of how one should act when there are sufficient reasons for both options, existential philosophy might offer a different perspective, emphasizing action as a way to resolve such conflict. Sartre (2000) believes that *acting*, despite being ambivalent, is the key to resolving it. Sartre argues that individuals often face ambivalence because they are fundamentally free to choose their own path, but they often try to escape this freedom by deceiving themselves about their own nature and the nature of their situation. Resolving ambivalence, from an existentialist perspective, involves embracing this freedom by *making* a choice. It requires individuals to make *authentic* choices that reflect their deepest values, even in the face of uncertainty and conflicting motivations. While not explicitly speaking about ambivalence,

Sartre develops an approach to resolving ambivalence through action, rather than through consideration of reason or emotion.

From an existentialist perspective, action can resolve cases of ambivalence for which the agent cares equally about both options. Instead of considering what agents have the most reason to do or which option they care the most for, agents can ask themselves "Which option is more authentic to my true self"? From here, although reasons and values might be equally powerful, one of both actions potentially is more authentic. Authenticity requires a deeper level of self-reflection from the agent. An authentic decision is one that is deeply considered and stems from an individual's self-reflection. In contrast, inauthentic judgments often result from conforming to societal expectations or external influences without significant personal conviction or reflection. For authenticity, the agent must consider not just the alignment with core values but also which action resonates with their past experiences, their life narrative, and their future aspirations.

Regarding future aspirations, an authentic decision involves envisioning the kind of person one wants to be. This projection into the future helps to reframe the decision in terms of personal development. The individual asks, "Which choice aligns with the person I want to be in the future?" The decision should be consistent with one's personal narrative. This means considering how each option fits into the broader context of one's life, (authentic) plans, and (authentic) past choices. By aligning decisions with a coherent personal narrative, individuals ensure that their actions reflect their true self. Thereby, existential philosophy might give guidance to those whose decision is about options they care equally about.

2.3.2.2 Implications for Therapists

For clinical psychologists, the fact that an individual is ambivalent about suicide allows for therapeutic strategies to resolve the ambivalence in favor of life. In contrast, if a person is not ambivalent but wholeheartedly committed to self-killing, the range of possible interventions would be narrow. For the latter type of individual, a reasonable initiation of suicidal ambivalence may be helpful in certain circumstances.

One way in which clinicians treat (or induce) suicidal ambivalence is the Motivational Interviewing (MI; Miller & Rollnick, 2012) approach, in which, for the case of treating suicidality, a therapist talks with an agent about reasons for living and reasons for dying. MI is a client-centered, directive method of therapy that enhances an individual's motivation to change by helping them explore and resolve suicidal ambivalence (Britton et al., 2011). In MI, therapists guide in a careful and empathetic way the exploration of the person's *own* motivations, while the therapist encourages the person to verbalize their thoughts about the pros and cons for living. This process can be understood as an examination of the reasons behind conflicting motivations. Also, MI involves discussions that help clarify the person's values and priorities. The therapist guides the person to consider how their suicidal thoughts align (or do not align) with their deeper values and long-term goals.

For MI, ambivalence is a decisive factor. The ambivalent individual already has the motivation and reasons in favor of a positive change at hand. The idea of MI is to reconnect the individual to those reasons and motivations, which is why MI is not a manipulation strategy. No solutions, motivations, or reasons come from the therapist; rather, the way of interviewing helps the patient appreciate the powers they have for change. One part of the interviewing strategy is to ask open questions, leading the patient to elaborate on reasons for living and reasons for dying while talking about them. People talk themselves into change when they, together with the therapist, explore their ambivalence. Therefore, the therapist is especially interested in "change talk", which is the patient speaking about the reasons in favor of change. Miller and Rollnick (2012) summarize how a therapist using MI should deal with the patient's ambivalence:

1 That you [as a therapist] want to help the person explore the dilemma [state of ambivalence] that has him or her stuck.
2 That you intend to remain neutral yourself with regard to what the person should do until they decide.
3 That exploring a dilemma like this can be uncomfortable or upsetting, which is one reason people get stuck in ambivalence.
4 That you want to help them work through the dilemma and discomfort, make their own decision, and move on as they choose. (p. 270)

A possible approach to solve ambivalence is to establish a hierarchy of values in order to determine what is most important to someone. Establishing a hierarchy of one's values is a cognitive strategy that requires the individual to settle what is most important to them. During MI, the therapist asks open questions to make the patent elaborate on what they value. From the therapist's perspective, the agent has motivation to change but may be unsure about what they value the most. For instance, if someone values family over personal ambition, this hierarchy will help resolve ambivalence in scenarios where these two are in conflict. Such an approach aims to ensure that the resolution of ambivalence is thoughtful, consistent with one's values, and justified by a rational assessment of the underlying motivations.

In the handbook for MI, there is the subsection "The Forest of Ambivalence". Here, the authors highlight that "[b]eyond the logical arguments, ambivalence can involve passionate emotion as well. Choices about specific behavior may be linked to deeper issues of meaning and identity" (Miller & Rollnick, 2012, p. 193). So, a different approach to revolve ambivalence is to understand one's *emotions* regarding one's ambivalence to better understand the roots of one's ambivalence. By understanding emotions, agents understand their desires more deeply and recognize what merely appears to be desirable due to external influences or momentary impulses. Accordingly, responding with self-hate to suicidal ambivalence sheds light on the agent's negative self-schemas as well as internalized negative beliefs. From understanding emotions, then, we can gain an understanding about problematic self-conceptions. Arguably, from here, agents can resolve ambivalence adequately.

For clinical settings, this perspective encourages therapists to help patients explore not just the cognitive, but also the emotional aspects of suicidal ambivalence that underpin them. We believe that this road of exploring ambivalence is underrepresented in the latest handbook on MI. So far, only sidenotes recognize the relevance of working through one's emotions for resolving ambivalence in a satisfying way. But recognizing these emotions can contribute to self-knowledge (Kramer & Pascual-Leone, 2018; Lambie, 2009; Mackenzie, 2002) and lead to a deeper understanding of why a patient may feel torn between different courses of action. While being ambivalent probably feels aversive, does it lead to emotions, such as anger, self-hate, or sadness? For instance, if a person values decisiveness and views their ambivalence as an inability to make clear choices, this might lead to feelings of inadequacy or self-criticism. Each emotional reaction offers insight into what aspects of their personality are most salient to the individual at that time. These responses are not just passive experiences but can actively shape how a person resolves their ambivalence, by indicating what they care about most, prompting action or causing further hesitation.

Finally, according to Coates (2022), remaining in a state of ambivalence can be a legitimate response to practical problems that present both pro and con reasons. Contra Frankfurt, Coates argues that ambivalence does not necessarily indicate irrationality or impaired agency. Instead, it can reflect the complex nature of practical problems where conflicting reasons can coexist on both sides of an issue. This perspective acknowledges that individuals can navigate their lives effectively even when ambivalent. Therefore, ambivalence should not be seen as a failure of will or clarity but as a nuanced and often appropriate stance in the face of multifaceted problems. The clinical approach of MI, however, does not take this perspective into account. The theory of MI suggests that resolving ambivalence is always the right thing to do, aiming to guide individuals toward a positive change. According to Coates, this is simply not true, as ambivalence itself can be a rational state. Thus, MI might benefit from considering ambivalence not as an obstacle to be overcome but possibly as a desired state of mind. Through MI, the therapist could support clients in recognizing that staying ambivalent can be a justified response, thus empowering them to make decisions at their own pace without feeling pressured to resolve their ambivalence.

2.4 Conclusion

In this chapter, we have argued that research on and practical responses to suicidal ambivalence can benefit from the philosophical discussions concerning the concept and rationality of ambivalence.

Suicidal ambivalence is typically assessed by measuring the competing desires to live and to die and calculating an ambivalence index. However, philosophical perspectives, such as those of Frankfurt and Coates, highlight the importance of how individuals relate to their desires, distinguishing between fleeting desires and those that an individual cares deeply about. Current measures capture only first-order desires, ignoring how individuals identify with these desires. We argue that research should expand to include second-order desires, which reflect deeper metacognitive attitudes and provide a more nuanced understanding of suicidal ambivalence and ideation.

We also explored how individuals and therapists might respond to suicidal ambivalence, drawing on Frankfurt's and Coates' views of ambivalence. For individuals, Frankfurt's view suggests resolving ambivalence to restore autonomy by integrating or rejecting conflicting desires. Suicidal individuals can decide on the basis of what they deeply care about, reflecting on their values through their cognitions and emotions. In contrast, Coates argues that ambivalence doesn't necessarily undermine rational agency. His view suggests that individuals should evaluate their reasons for living and their reasons for dying, and make a decision based on those reasons. Existentialist philosophy (e.g. Sartre) advocates action as a resolution, emphasizing authenticity by aligning choices with one's true self and life narrative.

For therapists, suicidal ambivalence opens opportunities for intervention, notably through MI. MI involves exploring reasons for living and dying, reconnecting individuals with their motivations without imposing solutions. Techniques include open-ended questions, clarifying values, and creating a hierarchy of priorities. We argue that exploring emotions to resolve ambivalence is underexplored but crucial, as emotions reveal deeper self-understandings and values. Furthermore, we argue that therapists should seriously consider the possibility that ambivalence can be rational and an appropriate stance toward complex problems. This broader perspective could empower clients and promote authentic choices.

Notes

1 Frankfurt's approach to identification with one's desires has not remained without criticism or alternative proposals from other philosophers (for an overview, see chapter 9 in McKenna & Pereboom, 2016). Watson (1975), Velleman (1992), and Bratman (2000, 2007) have developed different criteria for understanding identification with one's desires.
2 Ambivalence arises only with respect to options that we genuinely care about. Notably, caring does not necessarily require explicit mental states such as judgments or desires; it can exist in a more implicit or unconscious form. As Jaworska (2007) points out, caring can persist even against our best judgements or higher-order desires. Therefore, ambivalence could arise between options that we outwardly reject but remain conflicted about because of a deep-seated, perhaps involuntary, concern. That is, it is possible to experience ambivalence about options that we consciously reject but cannot stop caring about.
3 See Chapter 3 of this book for a defense of the opposite position.
4 Other authors who object to the view that ambivalence necessarily threatens autonomy or rationality are, e.g. Calhoun (1995), Wolf (2002), Velleman (2002), Benson (2005), Barvosa (2007, 2008), Kekes (2011), Rössler (2009, 2017), Poltera (2010), Marino (2011), Gunnarsson (2014), Razinsky (2016), Brunero (2021), and Feldman and Hazlett (2021).

References

Barvosa, E. (2007). Mestiza Autonomy as Relational Autonomy: Ambivalence & the Social Character of Free Will. *Journal of Political Philosophy*, *15*(1), 1–21. https://doi.org/10.1111/j.1467-9760.2007.00249.x

Barvosa, E. (2008). *Wealth of Selves: Multiple Identities, Mestiza Consciousness, and the Subject of Politics*. Texas A&M University Press.

Beck, A. T., Brown, G. K., & Steer, R. A. (1997). Psychometric Characteristics of the Scale for Suicide Ideation with Psychiatric Outpatients. *Behaviour Research and Therapy*, *35*(11), 1039–1046. https://doi.org/10.1016/S0005-7967(97)00073-9

Benson, P. (2005). Taking Ownership: Authority and Voice in Autonomous Agency. In J. Anderson & J. Christman (Eds.), *Autonomy and the Challenges to Liberalism: New Essays* (pp. 101–126). Cambridge University Press.

Bratman, M. E. (2000). Reflection, Planning, and Temporally Extended Agency. *The Philosophical Review*, *109*(1), 35–61.

Bratman, M. E. (2007). *Structures of Agency: Essays*. Oxford University Press.

Britton, P. C., Patrick, H., Wenzel, A., & Williams, G. C. (2011). Integrating Motivational Interviewing and Self Determination Theory with Cognitive Behavioral Therapy to Prevent Suicide. *Cognitive and Behavioral Practice*, *18*(1), 16–27.

Broome, J. (1999). Normative Requirements. *Ratio*, *12*(4), 398–419. https://doi.org/10.1111/1467-9329.00101
Brunero, J. (2021). Instrumental Rationality: The Normativity of Means-Ends Coherence. *Ethics*, *132*(1), 243–248. https://doi.org/10.1086/715282
Calhoun, C. (1995). Standing for Something. *Journal of Philosophy*, *92*(5), 235–260.
Coates, D. J. (2017). A Wholehearted Defense of Ambivalence. *The Journal of Ethics*, *21*(4), 419–444.
Coates, D. J. (2022). *In Praise of Ambivalence*. Oxford University Press.
Ekstrom, L. W. (1993). A Coherence Theory of Autonomy. *Philosophy and Phenomenological Research*, *53*(3), 599–616. https://doi.org/10.2307/2108082
Ekstrom, L. W. (2010). Ambivalence and Authentic Agency. *Ratio*, *23*(4), 374–392. https://doi.org/10.1111/j.1467-9329.2010.00474.x
Feldman, S. D., & Hazlett, A. (2021). Fitting Inconsistency and Reasonable Irresolution. In D. Gatzia & B. Brogaard (Eds.), *The Philosophy and Psychology of Ambivalence: Being of Two Minds* (pp. 131–146). Routledge.
Frankfurt, H. G. (1971). Freedom of the Will and the Concept of a Person. *The Journal of Philosophy*, *68*(1), 5–20.
Frankfurt, H. G. (1988). *The Importance of What We Care About*. Cambridge University Press.
Frankfurt, H. G. (1992). The Faintest Passion. *Proceedings and Addresses of the American Philosophical Association*, *66*(3), 5–16. https://doi.org/10.2307/3130658
Frankfurt, H. G. (2004). *The Reasons of Love*. Princeton University Press.
Gunnarsson, L. (2014). In Defense of Ambivalence and Alienation. *Ethical Theory and Moral Practice*, *17*(1), 13–26. https://doi.org/10.1007/s10677-013-9464-x
Jaworska, A. (2007). Caring and Internality. *Philosophy and Phenomenological Research*, *74*(3), 529–568.
Joiner, T. (2007). *Why People Die by Suicide* (1st edition). Harvard University Press.
Kekes, J. (2011). Doubts about Autonomy. *Philosophy*, *86*(337), 333–351.
Kiesewetter, B. (2017). *The Normativity of Rationality*. Oxford University Press.
Korsgaard, C. M. (1986). Skepticism about Practical Reason. *Journal of Philosophy*, *83*(1), 5–25. https://doi.org/10.2307/2026464
Korsgaard, C. M. (2009). *Self-Constitution: Agency, Identity, and Integrity*. Oxford University Press.
Kramer, U., & Pascual-Leone, A. (2018). Self-Knowledge in Personality Disorders: An Emotion-Focused Perspective. *Journal of Personality Disorders*, *32*(3), 329–350. https://doi.org/10.1521/pedi.2018.32.3.329
Lambie, J. A. (2009). Emotion Experience, Rational Action, and Self-Knowledge. *Emotion Review*, *1*(3), 272–280. https://doi.org/10.1177/1754073909103596
Mackenzie, C. (2002). Critical Reflection, Self-Knowledge, and the Emotions. *Philosophical Explorations*, *5*(3), 186–206. https://doi.org/10.1080/10002002108538732
Marino, P. (2011). Ambivalence, Valuational Inconsistency, and the Divided Self. *Philosophy and Phenomenological Research*, *83*(1), 41–71. https://doi.org/10.1111/j.1933-1592.2010.00459.x

McKenna, M., & Pereboom, D. (2016). *Free Will: A Contemporary Introduction* (Annotated Edition). Routledge.
Miller, W. R., & Rollnick, S. (2012). *Motivational Interviewing, Third Edition: Helping People Change* (3rd edition). Guilford Publications.
Paul, S. (2020). *Philosophy of Action* (1st edition). Routledge.
Poltera, J. (2010). Is Ambivalence an Agential Vice? *Philosophical Explorations, 13*, 293–305.
Razinsky, H. (2016). *Ambivalence: A Philosophical Exploration.* Rowman & Littlefield Publishers.
Rössel, J. (2008). Radikale Mikrosoziologie versus soziologische Erklärung: Der Makro-Mikro-Makro-Link in der Theorie des rationalen Handelns und in der Theorie der Interaktionsrituale. In J. Greve, A. Schnabel, & R. Schützeichel (Eds.), *Das Mikro-Makro-Modell der soziologischen Erklärung* (pp. 285–310). VS Verlag für Sozialwissenschaften. http://link.springer.com/chapter/10.1007/978-3-531-91774-0_12
Rössler, B. (2009). Autonomie und Ambivalenz. In R. Forst (Ed.), *Sozialphilosophie und Kritik*. Suhrkamp Taschenbuch.
Rössler, B. (2017). *Autonomie: Ein Versuch über das gelungene Leben*. Suhrkamp Verlag.
Sartre, J.-P. (2000). *Der Existentialismus ist ein Humanismus: Und andere philosophische Essays 1943 – 1948* (Trans. by W. Bökenkamp, H. G. Brenner, M. Fleischer, T. König, G. Scheel, H. Schöneberg, & V. von Wroblewsky, 12th edition). Rowohlt Taschenbuch.
Shneidman, E. (1998). *The Suicidal Mind* (Reprint Edition). Oxford University Press.
Teismann, T., Siebert, A. M., & Forkmann, T. (2024). Suicidal Ambivalence: A Scoping Review. *Suicide & Life-Threatening Behavior*, *54*(5), 802–813. https://doi.org/10.1111/sltb.13092
Van Orden, K. A., Witte, T. K., Cukrowicz, K. C., Braithwaite, S., Selby, E. A., & Joiner, T. E. (2010). The Interpersonal Theory of Suicide. *Psychological Review*, *117*(2), 575–600.
Velleman, J. D. (1989). *Practical Reflection*. Princeton University Press.
Velleman, J. D. (1992). What Happens When Someone Acts? *Mind*, *101*(403), 461–481. https://doi.org/10.1093/mind/101.403.461
Velleman, J. D. (2002). Identification and Identity. In S. Buss & L. Overton (Eds.), *Contours of Agency* (pp. 91–123). Cambridge. http://archive.nyu.edu/handle/2451/34657
Watson, G. (1975). Free Agency. *Journal of Philosophy*, *72*(4), 205–220.
Wolf, S. (2002). *The True, the Good, and the Lovable: Frankfurt's Avoidance of Objectivity*. In S. Buss & L. Overton (Eds.), *Contours of Agency* (pp. 227–244). https://direct.mit.edu/books/edited-volume/2429/chapter/64290/The-True-the-Good-and-the-Lovable-Frankfurt-s

3 Ambivalence

Some Conceptual Distinctions

Martin Weichold and Friedrich Hausen

3.1 Methodological Introduction

Ambivalence is a fundamental aspect of human experience – timeless in its presence, yet particularly pronounced in today's world, where individuals navigate an overwhelming array of choices and perspectives shaped by contemporary social practices. Understanding ambivalence is crucial for grasping both the complexities of the human mind and the nuances of human agency, both of which are deeply influenced by these practices. A striking example is ambivalence in suicidal behavior, where it is not only pervasive (Shneidman, 1998) but also central to understanding the suicidal mind. Gaining deeper insights into the nature of ambivalence can significantly enhance our ability to interpret suicidal tendencies and ethically inform interventions where appropriate. However, research on ambivalence remains in its early stages (see Otscheret, 1988; Brogaard & Gatzia, 2021; Coates, 2022). This chapter aims to contribute to this emerging field by introducing key conceptual distinctions, with a particular focus on the unique case of suicidal ambivalence – the central theme of this book.

Let us be clear about the mission of this chapter. "Ambivalence" is a term of art. The technical term has been invented by Eugen Bleuler for characterizing often-observed conflicting states of persons with schizophrenia (Bleuler 1911 / 2014). Today, "ambivalence" is used in very different ways in different contexts. Jason Raibley observes (2021, p. 271):

> It is doubtful that use of the term 'ambivalence' among philosophers and psychologists tracks any single, unified phenomenon. Rather, the term has been used to pick out a range of phenomena related to the metaphor of being of two minds.

Against this background, in this chapter, we will *not* provide a linguistic analysis of "ambivalence." We will not attempt to develop definitions with necessary and sufficient conditions that capture the intuitions of the person

DOI: 10.4324/9781003616221-5

on the street about what the term "ambivalence" means. Everyone has different intuitions, because the term is used in a variety of ways. Instead, what we are interested in is the multifaceted phenomenon, or more accurately, the phenomena of ambivalence. Yet to grasp those phenomena well, concepts matter. What we want to do in this chapter is developing conceptual tools that help us to differentiate between the many phenomena of ambivalence as clearly as possible. In other words, we are engaging in conceptual engineering. The aim is to help cutting nature at its joints by making explicit distinctions that are really there. On top of that, our distinctions might be helpful on a pragmatic scale by enhancing self-understanding and coping, and, in particular, psychotherapeutic treatment of suicidal clients.

This chapter will proceed as follows. In the next section, we will start with presenting a real case of suicidal ambivalence, in the form of published suicide notes. The focus on this case will ensure that our subsequent development of conceptual tools is able to precisely target real-world phenomena. In Section 3.3, we will briefly discuss why existing analyses of the term "ambivalence" are helpful, but why we should still move on to develop additional conceptual tools. In the remaining sections, we will propose new conceptual tools for talking about ambivalence. After some preliminary considerations (Section 3.4), we will develop a taxonomy that distinguishes different varieties of ambivalence, based on differences in the object of ambivalence (Section 3.5), its scope (Section 3.6), its timeframe (Section 6.7), its modality (Section 3.8), its strength (Section 3.9), its level (Section 3.10), the quality of coping with it (Section 3.11), and its ontology (Section 3.12). Finally, we will end with a conclusion (Section 3.13).

3.2 A Real Case of Ambivalence

Here is our real case. What follows are notes by a 23-year-old man in Germany. He has written them down in the last hours of his life. He died by gas after having written his suicide notes. The notes were found next to his dead body and a detailed suicide letter. The notes have been published, in anonymized form, of course, by the Dresden suicidologists Helmut Kulawik and Dieter Decke in 1973. In 2004, the notes have been re-published in a German collection of suicide letters entitled "*Ich möchte jetzt schließen. Briefe vor dem Freitod*" ("I Want to Close Now: Letters Before Suicide"), edited by Udo Grashoff (Grashoff 2004: 37–38). For the purposes of this chapter, we have asked the artificial intelligence *DeepL* to translate the text from German into English, while we subsequently checked and improved the translation. Here are the notes, which we quote in full, because they express many subtle nuances of the multi-facetted phenomena of ambivalence.

"It has to be done, and yet I can't. – It has to be done! I'm scared. It's not easy to overcome fear, and yet I have to. Fear is weakness! I wish I knew what I was afraid of, when everything is so easy and beautiful. Sleep, sleep forever. Death. – How that sounds. It must be beautiful. It must, it must. Farewell, farewell! Take care! N. N.

Still can't help it. I love R., but it's too late.

3 o'clock. The gas will release me in a few minutes. I smoke another cigarette. The gas is flowing loudly, I am scared of it. I really am. Although I know it will all be over then, I'm scared. Sorry, I'm weak … It has to be. Farewell, go your way. Farewell! Your dear brother, to whom you were everything. Don't tell mom anything … Accident N. N.

I'm a coward. I wouldn't have dared. How the gas hisses monotonously. It makes you dread. I felt incredibly sick. A roaring in my ears. I felt the fear of death, and yet I know I have to get through it. My head is buzzing, my ears are still numb. Now I'm really scared. At least I imagine I am. And yet it has to be done. If I had another cigarette, I'd smoke. So I go back under the covers. I've become heavy. Quite strange. Everything seems to be controlled. If I'd had the courage to take my hand off the tap, I would have done it long ago. Now it starts all over again. If it weren't for the hissing and the fear, everything would be half as bad. And yet it's not fear. Fear? That I could die? Honestly, now I feel like laughing. I want to die and I'm afraid of it. My heart aches. Now I'm going one more time. For good. Now I'm going to lie down. Bye, wave, wave. N. N.

5 o'clock. Must puke. I am a cowardly dog, afraid, afraid of redemption. Maybe I should have stayed sober. Is the alcohol irritating? The gas? Doesn't matter, I feel sick. Dog misery. What now? Must die and I'm too … careful. But no. I'm really hot. It's almost over. H., goodbye, I'm scared, I'm a coward. Not my style. Now I'm leaving. Now. Now. Now. Never thought dying would be so hard. And yet I have to. Farewell. Farewell. N. N.

I'm not a coward, but dying so young ... I'm a coward. No perspective and then the fear. Now I'm going to pee and then. I can't help it, I must, must, must, must die now. Slowly, slowly, slowly. Hopefully I can hold out now. Third attempt. My head. The roaring. Do you know what it's like when you pull the covers over your head and turn them up? Not a nice feeling. Once again I'm scared. But now I'm going. Smiling, because he's waiting for me with a smile. The gas is disgusting. Disgusting. But now I pull myself together. Hard, hard, but it has to be done. I tell myself: it's hard, and yet it's easy. Never see the sun again. Another smoke ... Should I live one more time? No! No! No! To be dead. Gone forever. Take care. My cigarette is out. Here we go. I'm scared. Farewell! Forever. Farewell! N. N."

These notes indicate ambivalence in suicidal behavior very clearly. In what follows, we want to investigate whether the notes allow for not only seeing ambivalence in a very clear way, but also for perceiving it in a very nuanced manner.

3.3 Prospects and Limitations of Existing Conceptualizations of Ambivalence

Let us start with discussing the conceptualizations of "ambivalence" in psychology, before moving to philosophy. Tobias Teismann, Annika Maria Siebert, and Thomas Forkmann (2024) have recently created a scoping review about the research on suicidal ambivalence in psychology and related fields. While the authors find the great significance of studying ambivalence for better understanding suicidal behavior confirmed, they still have to conclude (Teismann et al. 2024, p. 1):

> The study situation lacks a clear definition, conceptualization and operationalization of suicidal ambivalence. Nonetheless, suicidal ambivalence is a common experience in persons contemplating suicide and suicidal ambivalence seems to be present before, during and after a suicide attempt.

In more detail, Teismann et al. (2024, p. 4) summarize existing research as follows:

> In none of the included studies a formal definition of suicidal ambivalence is given. One study stated that suicidal ambivalence is "characterized by contradictory thoughts about suicide" (Del-Monte & Graziani, 2020, p. 3). Bergmans et al. (2009) understand suicidal ambivalence as a kind of transitional stage between a stronger desire to die and a resurgent will to live. The idea that suicidal ambivalence marks an undecided state that lies between the poles of an unconditional will to live or to die is inherent in all studies. Along these lines, Harris et al. (2010) speculate that "before becoming acutely suicidal, a person might, with some degree of rationality, debate whether their life is worth living or not. An internal debate could be part of early suicidal ideation, a stage where death by suicide first becomes an acceptable choice.
>
> (p. 182)

On the one hand, these characterizations are helpful for analyzing some of the phenomena of suicidal ambivalence, which are manifested in the quoted suicide notes. A first aspect is that psychologists define suicidal ambivalence as involving "contradictory thoughts about suicide." This is evident in the notes, where NN expresses both a desire to die and significant fear or hesitation. For instance, phrases like "It has to be done, and yet I can't," and "I want to die and I'm afraid of it" highlight this internal conflict. Second, the concept of ambivalence as a transitional stage between a stronger desire to die and a resurgent will to live is seen in the notes. Statements such as "Should I live one more time? No! No! No!" suggest moments of reconsideration or a back-and-forth struggle. Third, NN might be seen as having an internal debate about whether his life is worth living, as indicated also by the just quoted statement.

On the other hand, the characterizations offered by the psychologists are too coarse-grained to capture all the nuances in the notes. First, the NN's ambivalences have many facets. It is not only an ambivalence between contradictory thoughts. Rather, what stands out clearly here is a tension between the intention to die and the emotion of fear to die. It is primarily a conflict between an intention and an emotion, and not between two thoughts. For instance, NN writes: "I want to die and I'm afraid of it." To be sure, this does not mean that contradictory thoughts do not also play a role. When NN writes "Should I live one more time? No! No! No!," that can be taken to express contradictory thoughts. But his overall ambivalence is far more complex. Secondly, the psychological characterizations appear to describe ambivalence in intellectualist, cognitivist language, using terms like "contradictory thoughts" and "internal debate." However, NN's case suggests, at least if it is paradigmatic, that there is a rich emotional and embodied dimension to – some types of – ambivalence. For instance, the notes describe physiological sensations like sickness, numbness, and a buzzing head. Thirdly, by characterizing ambivalence as an "undecided *state*," one might overlook the detailed fluctuations. At some points in time, NN is basically decided, at others he is ambivalent in one particular moment, and his overall assessment and emotions fluctuate dramatically over time. For example, NN shows a dramatic fluctuation by writing: "If it weren't for the hissing and the fear, everything would be half as bad. And yet it's not fear. Fear? That I could die? Honestly, now I feel like laughing." These are just some of the points which the psychological definitions cannot capture well. Thus, while they are helpful, it might also be helpful to refine and complement them.

Before doing so, let us have a look into philosophical characterizations of ambivalence (see Chapter 2). Looking into the philosophical characterizations is important to make clear that it will be helpful to refine and enrich them as well. Harry Frankfurt (1992, p. 8) famously defines ambivalence in this way:

> Ambivalence is constituted by conflicting volitional movements or tendencies, either conscious or unconscious, that meet two conditions.

> First, they are inherently and hence unavoidably opposed; that is, they do not just happen to conflict on account of contingent circumstances. Second, they are both wholly internal to a person's will rather than alien to him; that is, he is not passive with respect to them.

A more recent, different but related definition of ambivalence has been developed by philosopher Justin Coates. According to Coates (2022, p. 37) an agent S is ambivalent about whether to φ or to ψ if and only if,

1. φ-ing and ψ-ing are mutually incompatible (at time *t* or within a relevant period of time);
2. S has the desire to φ and the desire to ψ; and
3. S *cares deeply* about φ-ing and about ψ-ing, in the sense that
   a. S *identifies* with their desire to φ and their desire to ψ to a significant degree; and
   b. not φ-ing or not ψ-ing would radically change S's *practical identity*.

In some respects, these characterizations are helpful for focusing our attention on aspects of real-world cases of suicidal ambivalence such as NN's case. As both Frankfurt and Coates can help to articulate, there is a conflict in NN between the two incompatible options of dying now and staying alive.

However, there are also several respects in which Frankfurt's and Coates's analyses are too coarse-grained to offer a very nuanced analysis of cases like NN's. First, as already discussed, NN's conflict is more a conflict between an intention and an emotion, namely between the intention to end his life and the emotion of fear of dying. By contrast, NN's conflict is not, at heart, a conflict between two desires, such as the desire to be dead and the desire to stay alive. That would only be a rather superficial analysis of what NN is struggling with. Again, the phrases "It has to be done, and yet I can't" and "I want to die and I'm afraid of it" are examples. Second, NN appears to identify himself only with the wish to die, but not with the wish to live, nor with his fear of death. For example, he writes: "I am a cowardly dog, afraid, afraid of redemption." Often, after reporting his fear to die, NN describes himself as a coward. The context makes clear that NN despises himself for being a coward. This suggests that he feels alienated from the fear of death. And this, in turn, suggests that he does not identify with his fear to die, which he views as a manifestation of his cowardice. Yet, we think that Frankfurt and Coates would not want to deny that NN's case is a case of genuine ambivalence, even if he fully identifies only with one of the two options. Third, one might argue that Frankfurt and Coates do not capture the rapid fluctuation of emotions, nor the embodied dimensions of ambivalence, such as the physiological sensations of sickness, numbness, and a buzzing head.

There are even more facets of ambivalence that might not become visible by means of the conceptual tools discussed in this section. Against this background, we will proceed from now on in a constructive way by proposing new conceptual tools for analyzing the many phenomena of ambivalence. As it will become clear, there are many facets of ambivalence present in NN's complex case. However, our new conceptual distinctions are needed in order to make those facets explicit.

3.4 A New Start

To get a starting point for developing new conceptual tools for analyzing the phenomena of ambivalence, we have asked the AI Chat-GPT4o to define ambivalence, which has led, after some discussion, to this characterization:

Ambivalence (GPT): The coexistence of opposing or conflicting attitudes, beliefs, emotions, or reactions toward a particular entity or situation, leading to mixed or contradictory feelings and responses.

To our mind, this is a good starting point. The AI does not reduce ambivalence only to a conflict between cognitive states, as some of the discussed psychologists did, nor reduce ambivalence to a conflict between volitional states or desires, as the discussed philosophers did. Moreover, it leaves out the problematic aspects of identification, which we have found troublesome in Frankfurt's and Coates' analyses.

Against this background, we want to follow the AI analysis, but define it more technically. Starting with our revisionary conceptual engineering, we suggest that "ambivalence" should be taken to describe a *relation*. It describes a relation between a subject S and an object X. In other words, ambivalence is always an ambivalence *for someone*. And there is always *something* that is ambivalent for her. The relation is a relation concerning *values*. The relevant values are *opposed* to each other. Thus, we can write:

Ambivalence: Subject S is ambivalent about X if and only if S values X both in a positive and in a negative way.

The notion of "valuing" is crucial here. We emphasize that we understand this concept in a broader sense than it is often understood within analytic philosophy.[1] In our understanding, valuing something means to consider it good in some way such as considering it beneficial, wholesome, satisfactory or of worth – or, in the negative case, as unwholesome or harmful. It is inherent in attitudes like preferring, affirming, liking or loving something, being glad of something, being satisfied with something, or, in the negative case, avoiding, fearing, or hating something. This valuing can be both described in terms of implicit attitudes or in terms of processes. It might be done consciously or unconsciously, and intellectually or emotionally. For example, if someone feels only a slight, unconscious feeling of emotional resistance when meeting a neighbor, this already indicates a (soft) negative valuing. One might at the same time consciously and intellectually value the neighbor positively in light of the activities they have done for the community, and still feel an unconscious, emotional resistance toward them, and thus value them (also) negatively. This illustrates that valuing, as we understand it, has bodily, affective, and unconscious dimensions. Thus, it is not reducible to cognition (at least according to many meanings of "cognition"). Rather, it is a ubiquitous, embodied way of relating to the world.

Now, this technical notion of ambivalence does not run into the same problems as the previously discussed characterizations, because it can be used as a basis for fine-grained conceptual distinctions between different facets of ambivalence, which are not appreciated by those previously discussed characterizations. Before moving on by using this new notion as a basis for engineering such new conceptual distinctions, we want to clarify three points.

First, we have analyzed ambivalence as a *binary* relation between a subject S and an object X. By contrast, several philosophers, such Coates and Frankfurt discussed above, implicitly analyze ambivalence as a *ternary* relation. According to them, ambivalence is a relation between a subject S and an option O1 and an option O2, where O1 and O2 are mutually exclusive. We have deliberately avoided such an analysis. For, the basic idea of ambivalence is that one subject has conflicting attitudes toward one object. This is already manifested in the AI definition, which summarizes common knowledge. This definition is also reasonable. A first reason in favor of it is that the term "ambivalence" literally expresses the synchronicity of contradicting valences, what seems instantiated paradigmatically where a subject is ambivalent about exactly one object. An example would be loving and hating one particular person. Many paradigmatic examples may be directly or indirectly tied to conflicting options, but this implies that, in light of the situation, both are experienced ambivalently. So, these examples can be analyzed as instances of double ambivalences. What makes the state ambivalence are the conflicting value-attitudes toward each of the two options. A second reason for analyzing ambivalence as a binary relation is that not all cases of ambivalence are ambivalences about decisions and conflicting options for actions, which would adequately be analyzed in a ternary relation. They can, for instance, also be about persons, as just illustrated (see also Section 3.5). It would be a bias of philosophers if they assumed that all that matters in life is choosing between different options. Our mental life is more complex than that. Furthermore, here is the third reason for analyzing ambivalence as a binary relation. If we followed those philosophers in assuming that there can be situations with two options, then it suggests itself to think that there are also situations with three, four and many more options. So, why should ternary relations be the crucial case? To illustrate, consider a fictive variation of the famous case of Sophie's choice: A Nazi officer in Auschwitz forces the imprisoned Sophie to decide which two of her five children would live and which three would be sent to the gas chamber. If she refuses to choose, all five would die. Here, Sophie has 10 options. But that shouldn't make us analyze ambivalence as an 11-ary relation.[2] Consequently, analyzing ambivalence as a binary relation seems preferable to analyzing it as higher-arity relation.

Second, it is noteworthy that our technical notion of ambivalence does not entail an identity-criterion: according to our notion, if a subject is ambivalent about X, this ambivalence can, but need not be central to the (evaluative) identity of the subject. We have intentionally chosen to conceptually engineer "ambivalence" in this less demanding way in order to allow both for more and for less important and existential cases of ambivalence. When authors such as Frankfurt speak of a subject as being ambivalent, this might suggest that the ambivalence is a threat to the (evaluative) identity of the subject and to its unification by consistent affirmation. However, we have intentionally chosen the formulation of "being ambivalent *about* X," to allow that a subject might be ambivalent just about a minor detail in their life. Of course, our formulation allows also for the more extreme cases where the "X" a subject is ambivalent about is indeed central to their (evaluative) identity (see Section 3.10).

A third point we want to clarify concerns the fact that our new notion of ambivalence is rather abstract. Apparently, this is the opposite from what we wanted. We wanted very fine-grained conceptual tools for grasping a large spectrum of the nuances of the phenomena of ambivalence that are present in cases like NN's. Yet this is what we are going to develop now. Based on the just developed abstract conceptualization of ambivalence, we will now conceptually engineer conceptual tools that allow for grasping much more nuances of the phenomena of ambivalence. Step by step, we will introduce different distinctions, starting with different possible objects of ambivalence, that is, things one can be ambivalent about.

3.5 Object of Ambivalence

Let us start with a simple set of distinctions. In our definition of ambivalence, we said that a subject can be ambivalent about an object X. When talking about "an object X," we mean an intentional object. We can now distinguish more carefully what this X can be. It can be 1) a person, 2) a thing, 3) a situation, or 4) a set of options when making a choice. Thus, we can say:

Person-related ambivalence: Subject S is ambivalent about a person P if and only if S values P both in a positive and in a negative way.

Thing-related ambivalence: Subject S is ambivalent about a thing T if and only if S values T both in a positive and in a negative way.

Situation-related ambivalence: Subject S is ambivalent about a situation SI if and only if S values SI both in a positive and in a negative way.

Option-related ambivalence: Subject S is ambivalent about a set of options SO if and only if S values SO at the same time both in a positive and in a negative way.

Even if there is not always a sharp line between those four types of ambivalence, making these distinctions can be helpful to appreciate the multi-facetted nature of ambivalence, and for targeting different aspects of it in different contexts. For example, in psychotherapy it might be important to decide which aspect of a complex, entangled, multifaceted state that contains many ambivalences should be in the center of attention – should it, for example, be a person-related ambivalence or an option-related ambivalence?

NN's case manifests all of these kinds of ambivalence, showing how multifaceted real-world cases of ambivalence are. We can start with person-related ambivalence. For example, NN writes "I love R., but it's too late." Here, NN sees R. to be worthy of his love, and yet any attempt of living out this love again to be hopeless. At the same time, NN also manifests thing-related ambivalence. For instance, he writes: "The gas is disgusting. Disgusting. But now I pull myself together." Here and at other places, NN shows disgust of the gas. And yet, for him it is the necessary means to his chosen end, according to the way of ending his life which he has chosen for himself. Furthermore, NN manifests situation-related ambivalence. He writes: "Third attempt. My head. The roaring. Do you know what it's like when you pull the covers over your head and turn them up? Not a nice feeling. Once again I'm scared. But now I'm going. Smiling, because he's waiting for me with a smile." NN considers the whole situation of his approaching death both welcome and repulsive.[3] Finally, NN manifests, of course, option-related ambivalence, having to decide between the mutually excluding options of staying alive or of dying now. For instance, he writes: "Should I live one more time? No! No! No!" For a brief moment, he reconsiders the option of staying alive, before excluding it vehemently.

3.6 Range of Ambivalence

A subject might be ambivalent toward something in its entirety. For example, someone might be ambivalent about whether she likes her life as a whole. However, a subject might also break this down, and become clear that she likes one aspect of her life, while she dislikes another aspect. In other words, the object of ambivalence can be more or less specific. We can distinguish:

Global ambivalence: Subject S is globally ambivalent about X if and only if S values X, in its entirety, both in a positive and in a negative way.

Local ambivalence: Subject S is locally ambivalent about X if and only if S values at least one aspect of X in a positive and at least one aspect of X in a negative way.

For example, if someone loves and hates her partner at the same time, they are in a state of person-related global ambivalence. If, by contrast, they can specify that they value this one particular characteristic of their partner positively and that one particular characteristic negatively, they are in a state of local ambivalence. NN is globally ambivalent about what he should do at all. When he writes, nearly at the end of his suicide notes "Should I live one more time? No! No! No!," this shows that he contemplates for a short moment the thought of not dying now. This indicates that even at the end, he was unsure how to view his entire situation. At the same time, NN appears to be locally ambivalent concerning the gas. He writes "If it weren't for the hissing and the fear, everything would be half as bad." He appears to be clear that he hates one aspect of the gas, the sound, but positively values another, namely, that the gas is, for him, the necessary means to his goal of dying.

This distinction is important for several reasons. One reason lies in the hypothesis that it is global ambivalence that makes people suffer so much. They are what makes a situation so confusing and overwhelming. One might speculate that therapeutic interventions, like motivational interviewing, help patients to reduce cases of global ambivalence to cases of local ambivalence. Then, the inner conflict might be attenuated, one understands one's situation more clearly, and one can adopt a metacognitive stance toward one's own situation. We leave the question open whether all cases of global ambivalence can be broken down to cases of local ambivalence.

As the reader will have noticed, our taxonomy of different facets or kinds of ambivalence is modular: the different distinctions can be combined with each other in all logically possible ways. For example, there can be global situation-related ambivalence, or local person-related ambivalence.

3.7 Timeframe of Ambivalence

Another distinction concerns the timeframe in which subject S values X in a positive and a negative way. It might be the case that the positive and negative valuing happens simultaneously. We can now call this "synchronic ambivalence." However, it might also happen that a subject oscillates over time between valuing X in a positive and in a negative way. We can write:

Synchronic ambivalence: Subject S is synchronically ambivalent about X if and only if S values X at the same time both in a positive and in a negative way.

Diachronic ambivalence: Subject S is diachronically ambivalent about X if and only if S oscillates within a relevant timeframe between valuing X in a positive and in a negative way.

The notion "relevant timeframe" is crucial. If Emma values puppets at the age of 4, and hates them at the age of 37, this does not constitute a case of diachronic ambivalence. Suicidal agents can experience both kinds of ambivalence. However, in particular the philosophical definitions discussed above appear to define ambivalence exclusively in terms of synchronous ambivalence. Yet the case of NN shows that there are rich fluctuations of emotions over time in ambivalent behavior.

NN manifests both kinds of ambivalence. At some specific moments, he clearly expresses synchronic ambivalence. For example, he says: "I want to die and I'm afraid of it. My heart aches." Both the desire to die and the fear of it occur at the same time. However, NN also manifests an oscillation over time. For example, he writes "Farewell, NN" very often, having apparently made a final decision. However, four times he revises or postpones that decision. This distinction between synchronic and diachronic ambivalence might be important because it entails that even if a suicidal person appears to have made up her mind at one point in time, this does not necessarily mean that she is not (diachronically) ambivalent.[4]

3.8 Modality of Ambivalence

A further distinction concerns what kind of attitude ambivalence is. In other words, the distinction concerns what the "valuing" consists in. We have already seen that "valuing" has been defined intentionally as a very broad notion. The discussed psychologists have used cognitivist, intellectualist notions to describe the kinds of attitudes that humans have when they are ambivalent. By contrast, the discussed philosophers have used volitional notions like "desire" or "volitional movements." At the same time, the case of NN suggests that the attitude is one of emotions, or feeling, or of experience (see also Maiese, 2016). All of these characterizations are appropriate for certain phenomena: they all describe one kind of ambivalence, or one facet of the multi-dimensional realm of phenomena of ambivalence. In other words, they each describe one way how one can positively and negatively value something. We can distinguish:

Affective ambivalence: Subject S is affectively ambivalent about X if and only if S feels both a positive and a negative value of X.

Cognitive ambivalence: Subject S is cognitively ambivalent about X if and only if S has a reflective attitude of valuing X both in a positive and in a negative way.

Volitional ambivalence: Subject S is volitionally ambivalent about X if and only if S desires X and desires non-X.

This threefold distinction has to be taken with care. Real-world cases of ambivalence often entail affective ambivalence, cognitive ambivalence, and volitional ambivalence at the same time, sometimes in a complex and entangled way. Still, it is helpful for theoretical clarity and for practical coping to clearly distinguish between these different facets of ambivalence. It is crucial that real-world ambivalences cannot be reduced to just one of the three types.

For instance, NN manifests all three kinds of ambivalence in his suicidal behavior. He is affectively ambivalent when he writes "I'm scared. It's not easy to overcome fear, and yet I have to." He fears death, yet hopes for it. But NN also manifests cognitive ambivalence on some occasions. For example, he writes "Honestly, now I feel like laughing. I want to die and I'm afraid of it." The phrase "Honestly, now I feel like laughing" shows a detached, almost ironic reflection on his situation, which indicates a cognitive ambivalence about his own death. Moreover, NN also manifests volitional ambivalence, for instance when he writes "If I'd had the courage to take my hand off the tap, I would have done it long ago." He desires to not take his hand off the tap, and he desires to take his hand off the tap, meaning that he desires dying now and staying alive at the same time. Importantly, as discussed earlier, there can be *mixed cases*. For instance, NN writes: "I felt the fear of death, and yet I know I have to get through it." Here, we find an opposition of a feeling and a cognitive attitude, paired with a resolution to do what he takes to be necessary.

It is once again important to appreciate the complexity of the phenomena of ambivalence, in particular with hindsight to interventions. By contrast, the semantic fields that are used in different disciplines might make it harder for some researchers to see all the different kinds of ambivalence – for instance, if some psychologists are used to analyze the mind in terms of cognitive states, while many analytic philosophers of actions always work with concepts such as "volition" or "desire."

3.9 Strength of Ambivalence

Often, ambivalence is characterized by a felt inner conflict. We can use this feature in order to define "strong ambivalence," as a contrast term to "weak ambivalence":

Strong ambivalence: Subject S is strongly ambivalent about X if and only if S values X both in a positive and in a negative way, resulting in a strong inner conflict.

Weak ambivalence: Subject S is weakly ambivalent about X if and only if S values X both in a positive and in a negative way, resulting only in a weak or in no inner conflict.

Obviously, "strong" and "weak" lie on a continuum, so there is no clear cut-off point between strong and weak ambivalence. Still this distinction between strong and weak ambivalence is crucial for appreciating different ways of talking about ambivalence. If someone says, in a light-hearted mood on a summer's day, that they are ambivalent about whether they should choose chocolate or vanilla ice-cream, then it is fair to talk like this. They can simply be taken to mean that they are in a state of weak ambivalence. However, this is entirely different from the existential pain that can come with cases of strong ambivalence, such as in NN's case. We can acknowledge all the different kinds of ambivalence, from the light-hearted value conflict to the tormenting existential nightmare, by distinguishing between weak and strong ambivalence.

Clearly, NN only manifests types of strong ambivalence. This is evident, for instance, when he writes "I'm not a coward, but dying so young ... I'm a coward." He is in a maximally strong, inner conflict.

3.10 Levels of Ambivalence

Some philosophers, such as Frankfurt and Coates discussed earlier, view ambivalence as a matter of second-order attitudes. For them, ambivalence is not simply constituted by the fact that a subject values something in a positive and a negative way. Rather, Frankfurt and Coates emphasize that the subject must also identify themselves both with the positive and the negative valuing. It is not merely the case that a subject finds themselves to value something in a positive and a negative way. Rather, they stand behind the positive and the negative valuing as the person they are. The ambivalence concerns the subject's evaluative identity. In other words, ambivalence is a matter of second-order attitudes, or of second-level attitudes, that is, of identifying oneself as a person with both the positive and the negative valuing one happens to have.[5] By contrast, psychologists – as seen in Section 3.3 – usually view ambivalence as a first-order – or first-level – phenomenon. To psychologists, ambivalence only demands that a subject values something positively and negatively. It is possible, but not required, that the subject identifies with their valuing the object in a positive and a negative way. The AI definition discussed above, summarizing common knowledge, also works without referring to a second-order identification. It is reasonable to suppose that both ways of characterizing ambivalence are legitimate and refer to different types of ambivalence:

First-order ambivalence: Subject S is ambivalent about X on a first-order level if and only if S values X both in a positive and in a negative way.
Second-order ambivalence: Subject S is ambivalent about X on a second-order level if and only if (S values X both in a positive and in a negative way, and S identifies with their valuing X in a positive way, and S identifies with their valuing X in a negative way).

As we argued in Section 3.4, first-order ambivalence is the basic case, and we have intentionally designed our basic characterization of ambivalence to not entail second-order level identification. If an agent intellectually appreciates what their neighbor has done for the community, but always has a slight, half-conscious bad feeling in the company of her neighbor because the neighbor's skin color, then the agent is (first-order, person-related) ambivalent about the neighbor – even if the agent understands intellectually that their bad feelings about their neighbor are shaped by an implicit racism which the agent hates themselves for having, instead of identifying with it. While first-order level ambivalence is very common, there are also the subtle, more existentially relevant second-order cases. A subject might value their new child positively and negatively at the same time, and identify both with their love for this particular living being as well as with their now lost ability for living an independent, creative life with less daily responsibilities. These cases entail a stronger existential conflict than the first-order level cases.

There can also be *asymmetrical* cases. In those asymmetrical cases, the subject identifies on a second-order level with one valuing (e.g., valuing X positively), but does not identify with the other valuing (e.g., valuing X negatively). NN's case is a case in point. As already discussed in Section 3.3, NN identifies himself only with the wish to die now, but not with the wish to continue living. As discussed, this becomes clear by NN's affirmations of his wish to die, and by his disidentification with his hesitance to die, for instance when he writes "I am a cowardly dog, afraid, afraid of redemption."

These distinctions are important to show that real-life cases of ambivalence are sometimes more complex than some psychologists assume, that not all real-life cases are cases of second-order level ambivalence, as some philosophers think, and that there can also be asymmetrical cases, which neither philosophers nor psychologists have yet talked about.

3.11 Quality of Coping with Ambivalence

Subjects can cope with ambivalence differently. On the one hand, there can be mastered ambivalence. On the other hand, there can be unmastered ambivalence:

Mastered ambivalence: Subject S manifests mastered ambivalence about X if and only if S values X both in a positive and in a negative way, and copes with this in a way that preserves well-functioning agency.

Unmastered ambivalence: Subject S manifests unmastered ambivalence about X if and only if S values X both in a positive and in a negative way, but does not cope with this in a way that preserves well-functioning agency.

One may master ambivalence, or be mastered by ambivalence. To be sure, mastered ambivalence is still ambivalence: one might still value something in both a positive and a negative way, but doing so mindfully and skillfully diminishes most of the extreme suffering that can be caused by ambivalence. Often, meta-cognitive awareness is decisive (though not always sufficient) for mastering ambivalence. Consider, for example, the case of Sophie's choice again. A Nazi officer in Auschwitz offers Sophie to choose which of her two children should be killed in the gas chamber, and which one should live. If Sophie does not pick one child, both will be killed. Here, Sophie clearly manifests second-order level option-related ambivalence: Saving one of her beloved children means sacrificing the other. There are three possibilities for how Sophie could cope with the situation, now and in the rest of her life. First, she could be tormented for her entire life by nightmares because her choice led to the death of one of her children. At the same time, she might be glad to have saved the other. Sophie would forever be tormented by her ambivalence. She could not continue to live like this. She would permanently need help from others. This would be a case of unmastered ambivalence.

Second, Sophie could just shrug her shoulders and say to herself: "Well, that's life. I did the best I could by saving at least one child. Nothing to feel sorry about." The Sophie of this second option would be able to continue living well and manifest well-functioning agency. However, her attitude would not be a morally appropriate response to what has happened – to echo Coates (2022). Sophie would have dissolved her ambivalence entirely, while she should have remained ambivalent in light of both the good and bad aspects of the situation.

Third, Sophie might master the ambivalence. She might remain ambivalent: she might still be glad to have saved one child and regret the death of the other. And she might sometimes even be tormented by memories of the sacrificed children and her decision. However, she would not be broken by this ambivalence. Instead, she would understand and accept her dispositions, needs and evaluative states involved in the inner dissonance and pain. She would understand and accept that this ambivalence is now part of her life. She would be able to see the ambivalence from some distance, and integrate its existence coherently into her life, instead of pushing it away, or being carried away by it. She would cope with it mindfully and retain her well-functioning agency. She would be able to raise her remaining child with love, care and responsibility.[6]

NN clearly manifests unmastered ambivalence most often. For example, he writes: "I'm a coward. I wouldn't have dared." The overwhelming fear and inability to resolve it show unmastered ambivalence. There are no instances of mastered ambivalence in his case. Even at the very end, he writes: "Take care. My cigarette is out. Here we go. I'm scared. Farewell! Forever. Farewell! N. N." The inclusion of the "I'm scared" makes clear that he did not simply resolve and master the ambivalence at the end, or even overcome it (as some of the discussed psychologists might suggest when speaking of a transitory ambivalence phase). NN remained ambivalent until the end, without mastering his ambivalence.

As we will argue in Chapter 9 entitled "Unmastered Ambivalence," this distinction between mastered and unmastered ambivalence is crucial for distinguishing the acceptable or even rational cases of ambivalence from those cases where ambivalence is harmful.

3.12 Ontology of Ambivalence

A final distinction concerns the ontology of ambivalence. So far, we have analyzed ambivalence as a *relation* between a subject S and an object X. Mind and (understood) situation are always related to each other. However, the way ambivalence is often talked about by philosophers and psychologists suggests thinking of ambivalence exclusively in terms of mental states and attitudes of a subject. In other words, being ambivalent is often analyzed as a characteristic of a *subject's mind*. However, it is also possible to analyze ambivalence as a characteristic of a subject's *situation*. We can say that *a situation* is ambiguous, or ambivalent. It can provide several affordances, or solicitations, that would pull every human being in that situation into different directions, that is, invite contradictory responses. Against the background of shared human needs, the objective features of a situation can pull the subject in different directions. To be clear, ambivalence is always a relation. But still, we can talk about mental ambivalence and about situational ambivalence. Talking of situational ambivalence highlights the objective side of the relation. Talking of mental ambivalence highlights the subjective side. In other words, talking of mental ambivalence and of situational ambivalence is consistent with the fact that "ambivalence" describes a relation. However, there is a tendency in some literature to neglect the situational side. Against this background, it is crucial to point to it with the concept of situational ambivalence. It is important to emphasize the objective side of ambivalence as well, since social and physical realities often present decision problems and dilemmas that exist largely independent of the particular individual's attitudes. Individuals may face conflicting normative demands.

Here are three examples for situational ambivalence: (1) A soldier patrolling an occupied city encounters a civilian carrying an unidentified object. The situation itself is ambivalent: it affords both the interpretation that the civilian is an innocent non-combatant and the possibility that they are concealing a weapon. The soldier must respond, but the objective ambiguity of the situation generates a pull toward conflicting actions – caution and restraint versus preemptive defense. (2) A refugee hears that peace has been restored in their home country. The situation provides two opposing affordances: the opportunity to return home and reclaim a lost sense of belonging, but also the risk of instability, economic hardship, or lingering violence. Any refugee in this scenario would be drawn between these conflicting responses by the objective features of the situation itself. (3) A parent stands at the airport as their child departs for college in another country. The situation affords two conflicting responses: pride and joy at their child's success and independence, but also sorrow and loss at their departure. Any loving parent in this position, regardless of personality, would feel pulled between celebrating and grieving.

Against this background, we can distinguish:

Mental ambivalence: Subject S is mentally ambivalent about X if and only if S desires, thinks, or feels concerning X both in a positive and in a negative way.

Situational ambivalence: A situation is situationally ambivalent for a subject S, if and only if the solicitations of the situation itself push S in radically different directions.

Mental ambivalence is ubiquitous in NN's example, as analyzed above. For example, when NN says "I want to die and I'm afraid of it," this is an ambivalence where a desire and an emotion toward the same event collide. Yet at the same time, there are also passages that might be well analyzed by speaking of situational ambivalence. For example, NN writes: "3 o'clock. The gas will release me in a few minutes. I smoke another cigarette. The gas is flowing loudly, it scares me." Here, the cigarette is – against the background of NN's dispositions – a solicitation for smoking it, and for staying alive a little longer. The gas and its sounds solicit, on the one hand, the release from the pains of living, but its scaring sound also solicits turning it off. There are thus multiple contradicting solicitations in this situation.

We understand that the idea of situational ambivalence might be viewed as controversial. At this place, we do not want to defend this concept in great detail. Our point is only that the *façon de parler* of speaking of situational ambivalence should not simply be ignored, and that there might even be an ontological elaboration of it, using concepts like "solicitations" and "affordances." However, this is something that will have to be explored on another occasion.[7]

3.13 Conclusion

The term "ambivalence" can be used for referring to many different facets within a multifaceted realm of phenomena. The concepts we proposed are conceptual tools that should help to pay attention to certain aspects in this realm of phenomena. Our conceptual distinctions help to focus on aspects of ambivalence that are really there. But our conceptual distinctions serve not only for better understanding the multifaceted real-world phenomena of ambivalence. They can also fit practical concerns in a variety of ways. Conceptual tools such as the distinction between local and global ambivalence and between mastered and unmastered ambivalence might support an understanding of successful interventions: a therapist might aim to transform cases of global ambivalence to cases of local ambivalence, and cases of unmastered ambivalence to cases of mastered ambivalence. The conceptual distinction between mental and situational ambivalence describes a therapist's concern to not only look at the mental attitudes of their clients, but also at the question how situational ambivalences might be attenuated by changing the objective features of situations. Other conceptual tools are helpful for avoiding misunderstandings in the ethics of ambivalence: It might be the case that all cases of strong and unmastered ambivalence are a painful threat to a personality, while being in a state of weak or mastered ambivalence can be a satisfying manifestation of one's rationality and resilience. Furthermore, other distinctions show the complexity of ambivalence, which is sometimes overlooked because the semantic fields used in certain disciplines do not leave enough conceptual space for capturing all the aspects of this complexity. For instance, not all cases of ambivalence are cases of option-related ambivalence, as some philosophers might think, and not all cases of ambivalence are cases of cognitive ambivalence, as some psychologists might tend to think. Not all cases of ambivalence are cases of first-order level ambivalence, as some psychologists might think, and not all cases of ambivalence are cases of second-order level ambivalence, as some philosophers think, and there are even asymmetrical cases which have not yet been appreciated at all. In other words, we hope that our conceptual tools will be helpful for bringing into view and articulating the complexity of ambivalence in a better way.[8]

Notes

1 By contrast, phenomenological authors such as Max Scheler (2014) see value attitudes as integral parts of motivational, cognitive and affective attitudes.
2 A more elegant solution would be to stick to our analysis of ambivalence as a binary relation between a subject S and an object X, and allow that object X can also be a set of options, for example {O1, O2, O3, O4, O5, O6, O7, O8, O9, O10}.
3 This case is not a perfect example, in the sense that is an example for both situation-related ambivalence and option-related ambivalence, where the situation-related ambivalence is grounded in the option-related ambivalence. However, there can also be cases of situation-related ambivalence that are nor option-related ambivalence, for instance meeting an old friend again after a long time without the possibility of speaking to her without social tensions.
4 A similar distinction between synchronic and diachronic ambivalence has also been used by authors such as Thomas Kwapil et al. (2022).
5 See René Baston's and Sanja Dembić's chapter "Philosophical Perspectives on Suicidal Ambivalence" in this book (Chapter 2) for a detailed discussion of this type of ambivalence.
6 For a fuller discussion, see Chapter 9.
7 For such an analysis, see also the Zuzanna Rucińska's, Lieke Asma's and Sabrina Coninx' chapter on situated suicidality in this book (Chapter 7).
8 We are grateful to everyone involved in the DFG-funded research network (BA 6721/3-1) on ambivalence in suicidal behavior for providing the stimulating intellectual context within which we wrote this chapter. In particular (and in addition), we would like to thank Lieke Asma, René Baston, Cato Benschop, Sabrina Coninx, Sanja Dembić, Zuzanna Rucińska, and Elisabeth Ventham for detailed written comments on an earlier version of this chapter.

References

Bleuler, E. (1911 / 2014). *Dementia praecox oder Gruppe der Schizophrenien* (Unchanged New Edition). Psychosozial-Verlag.

Brogaard, B., & Gatzia, D. E. (Eds.). (2021). *Routledge studies in contemporary philosophy. The philosophy and psychology of ambivalence: Being of two minds*. Routledge.

Coates, D. J. (2022). *In praise of ambivalence*. Oxford University Press.

Frankfurt, H. (1992). The faintest passion. *Proceedings and Addresses of the American Philosophical Association*, *66*(3), 5–16.

Grashoff, U. (Ed.). (2004). *"Ich möchte jetzt schließen": Briefe vor dem Freitod* (2nd ed.). Reclam.

Kwapil, T. R., Edmundson, M. S., Hernández, L. M., Kemp, K. C., Rbeiz, K. S., Clark, H. E., Bathery, A. J., Raulin, M. L., & Barrantes-Vidal, N. (2022). Schizotypal ambivalence is associated with schizophrenia-spectrum and borderline personality traits in young adults: Converging results from three interview studies. *Journal of Research in Personality*, *101*, 104312.

Maiese, M. (2016). Dissociative identity disorder and ambivalence. *Philosophical Explorations*, *19*(3), 223–237.

Otscheret, E. (1988). *Ambivalenz: Geschichte und Interpretation der menschlichen Zwiespältigkeit*. Asanger.

Raibley, J. R. (2021). Ambivalence, well-being, and prudential rationality. In B. Brogaard & D. E. Gatzia (Eds.), *The philosophy and psychology of ambivalence: Being of two minds* (pp. 269–293). Routledge.

Scheler, M. (2014). *Der Materialismus in der Ethik und die materiale Wertethik*. Meiner.

Shneidman, E. S. (1998). *The suicidal mind*. Oxford University Press.

Teismann, T., Siebert, A. M., & Forkmann, T. (2024). Suicidal ambivalence: A scoping review. *Suicide and Life-Threatening Behavior*, *54*, 802–813.

Part 2

Explaining Suicidal Ambivalence

4 Understanding Suicide, Acting for Reasons, and Ambivalence

Lieke Asma

4.1 Introduction

One of the central aims of suicide research is trying to understand why people decide to end their lives and to identify the persons particularly at risk of doing so. Despite extensive research into a large variety of potential risk factors, however, researchers have not been able to reliably predict which persons, under which circumstances, will display suicidal thoughts and behaviors (e.g., Franklin et al., 2017; Large et al., 2016). To complicate things even further, research shows that the wish to kill oneself can fluctuate strongly, even within hours (e.g., Bagge et al., 2014; Bryan et al., 2020; Kleiman et al., 2017), and persons considering suicide are often ambivalent, sometimes until right before or even during the act (e.g., Shneidman, 1998, see Introduction chapter of this book for discussion). These findings point to the exceedingly complex nature of suicide; it does not allow for simple explanations or solutions (see, e.g., Bryan, 2021).

Given this, one question that needs to be addressed is how to best move forward in understanding and preventing suicide. Should we continue exploring potential risk factors until we find something that can reliably predict suicide? Or might a different approach be more fruitful (see Baston, 2024)? This chapter is meant to support and explore such an alternative approach to understanding and preventing suicide, by paying attention to what is implied in defining suicide as intentional self-killing (e.g., Cholbi, 2011). Suicide is, by definition, not something that merely happens to a person; it is something they *do*. That suggests that a full understanding of the phenomenon is not just a matter of uncovering factors that may influence suicide, for example, biological factors, but also of understanding the *reasons* for which people decide to kill themselves (see, e.g., Anscombe, 1963; Davidson, 1963).[1]

Even though researchers have asked survivors of suicide attempts what their reasons were for trying to end their life, these studies typically do not make explicit what is distinctive about asking for reasons, how it is

DOI: 10.4324/9781003616221-7

different from uncovering mere causal influences. Indeed, the answers people give are typically treated as additional causes that explain why persons did what they did, that is, what 'pushed' them in the direction of suicide (see, e.g., Schnyder et al., 1999; Van Orden et al., 2015). As a result, asking survivors about their reasons seems to involve nothing over and above taking into account the agent's own perspective on the causal processes involved in their action, and does not explicitly consider that asking for reasons may involve something different, a distinct kind of understanding that is not (just) about causal explanation. Exploring the nature of acting for reasons is also important to better understand clinical practice: what are clinicians exactly involved in when they talk about reasons for and against suicide with their patients (see Britton, Bryan, & Valenstein, 2016)?

I will show that a deeper understanding of the nature of acting for reasons is of crucial importance to improve our understanding of suicide, and of what might be done to prevent persons from killing themselves. In order to make my points, some stage setting is required, which will be the goal of Section 4.2. I distinguish between explanatory, normative, and motivating reasons, and set out three ways in which acting for reasons is different from mere causal explanation. In Section 4.3, I connect these insights to the research on reasons for suicide, and argue why research into general risk factors may be generally unsuccessful in predicting suicide. Additionally, I will explain how fluctuations in suicidal ideation can be understood from the perspective of acting for reasons, and why it should not come as a surprise that persons are typically ambivalent about suicide. All in all, my analysis suggests that understanding suicide by identifying general risk factors is not the best approach. In Section 4.4, I move toward an alternative perspective on suicide prevention, in which understanding the reasons for suicide is not seen as independent from whether a person considers suicide or not. Differently put, my suggestion is that the process of coming to understand reasons for suicide, especially self-understanding of the person considering suicide, can itself contribute to preventing suicide. This insight is crucial, because there is reason to think that suicidal ideation hampers the process of self-understanding. As a result, ambivalent persons run the risk of becoming more suicidal rather than less. Section 4.5 concludes this chapter.

4.2 Beliefs, Facts, and Ends

In philosophy, a distinction is often made between three kinds of reasons: normative reasons, motivating reasons, and explanatory reasons (e.g., Alvarez, 2009; Alvarez & Way, 2024). Normative reasons are reasons that justify or speak in favor of an action, for example wearing a raincoat because it is raining, eating vegetables because they are healthy, or helping a child that is being bullied. A person may not, however, act for these reasons. The reasons a person actually acts for are referred to as motivating reasons, for example when I indeed wear my raincoat because it's raining, eat the healthy vegetables, or help the bullied child. Normative reasons are in some sense 'out there', and it is up to the person to recognize and respond to them.[2]

Traditionally, philosophers saw no problem in treating motivating reasons and explanatory reasons as one and the same. After all, motivating reasons also explain why agents do what they do. In recent years, however, philosophers have come to recognize that a distinction should be made between motivating and explanatory reasons as well. Sometimes an explanation of an action does not capture what motivated the agent to act as they did, that is, what they took to speak in favor of or justify the action. In the context of suicide, for example, research has shown that certain genetic factors are associated with suicidal behavior (e.g., Bondy, Buettner, & Zill, 2006),[3] but these are, exceptions aside, not a motivating reason for which the person decides to end their life. These genetic factors do not lead to suicide because the person took them to speak in favor of it. Also, if a person acts for an *apparent* reason, for example the false belief that nobody cares about them, it is important to distinguish between what *motivated* them to act – the alleged lack of care –, and what *explains* the action – the fact that the agent falsely believed that nobody cares (see Alvarez & Way, 2024, on Othello's killing of Desdemona). Sometimes, then, motivating and explanatory reasons come apart.

It is important to note that this talk of different kinds of reasons should not tempt the reader into thinking that they are distinct things or objects. These distinctions are supposed to capture the different questions that reasons can answer, roughly, in the context of suicide: (1) does the person have a good reason to end their life? (normative) (2) what motivated the person to end their life? (motivating), and (3) what explains this person ending their life? (explanatory). It is possible that the answer to all three questions refers to the same fact, for example, when a person is suffering from a painful and deadly illness.

This allows me to reframe the issue I addressed in the introduction. Research on reasons for suicide often treats the answers persons give as mere explanatory reasons. A further analysis of what it means for a person to be motivated by something instead of merely caused is missing. If we want to understand what motivated a person to end their life, however, we have to pay attention to what is implied in acting for a motivating reason. The philosophical literature offers roughly three proposals: (1) motivating reasons are psychological states like belief-desire pairs (e.g., Davidson, 1963), (2) they are facts about the world or ourselves (e.g., Alvarez, 2009;

Dancy, 2000), or (3) they are actions at a higher level of description (see, e.g., Anscombe, 1963; Thompson, 2008; Wiland, 2003).

According to the first view, which has long been the dominant view, wearing my raincoat for a motivating reason means that this action is the causal result of a desire to stay dry and a belief that by wearing my raincoat I will manage to do so. In recent decades, philosophers like Dancy (2000) and Alvarez (2009) have convincingly criticized this view, and argued that persons take the facts themselves, that is, what the beliefs are about, to speak in favor of the action: I take *the rain* to speak in favor of wearing a raincoat, and this fact motivates me to wear a raincoat. Of course, having the relevant beliefs and desires is crucial for acting as such, but these mental states are not the things the person takes to speak in favor of the action. When deciding what to do, we (ideally) deliberate about the facts, not about our beliefs (Dancy, 2000). These facts can also be facts about yourself: the fact that you experience suicidal ideation can be a motivating reason for talking to a close friend, for example.

There is reason to think, however, that the picture is not complete. After all, the fact that it is raining does not in itself speak in favor of or justify me wearing my raincoat. For that, we also need to consider my *end*: to stay dry. The rain motivates me to act in a certain way, only because there are certain things that I care about, that I find good or important (see, e.g., Wiland, 2003). This brings me to a third view: our ends, and our motivation to act, are reflected in the action at the highest level of description (see, e.g., Anscombe, 1963; Thompson, 2008). I do not act simply because it is raining, but in order to stay dry, and wearing my raincoat is a means to do so. Staying dry, my action at the highest level of description, justifies and explains the action at a lower level of description (see, e.g., Asma, 2022 for further discussion). When we act, we do one thing in order to do something else and, as a result, we do several things at the same time. In this approach, the motivating reason is not distinct from the action, but is internal to its means-end structure. Actions are not the causal outcome of or merely motivated by something that happened before. And even though we often cite the facts when we are asked for our reasons, for example, 'it is raining', this answer presupposes the existence of ends, that we as human beings often share and do not need mentioning anymore – for example, health, pleasure, comfort, or friendship. The ultimate end and ultimate motivator, in such a picture, is leading a good life (Frey, 2019).

My aim in discussing these views is not to argue for or against a specific understanding of motivating reasons, but to highlight three ways in which acting for reasons is different from mere causal influence.[4]

Firstly, actions are and are part of means-end structures, and understanding an action means seeing it as part of a larger structure. Motivating reasons thereby provide additional descriptions of the action (see, Anscombe, 1963, pp. 45-47): I am not just wearing a raincoat, I am also staying dry. I am doing both these things at the same time. In fact, understanding the action often goes beyond this structure and involves placing the action and the end in light of a person's life and the wider context (see, e.g., D'Oro, 2012, Tanney, 2009, Von Wright, 1971). I might be particularly motivated to stay dry because I have to give an important presentation that day, for example, or perhaps I enjoy wearing a raincoat because it reminds me of when I was young. Similarly, understanding why someone considers suicide because they lost their job (see Classen & Dunn, 2012) involves taking into account the wider context and their personal beliefs and values: do they live in a county with social security, are they the sole provider, to what extent is their self-worth connected to making money?

Secondly, acting for a reason does not involve blind causation. Reasons do not 'push' the person in a certain direction; what things *mean* for them plays a crucial role. First and foremost, in order to understand why an agent responds to the circumstances as they do, we should take into account their end. What ends are important for them, and how do the circumstances undermine their view of a good life? More generally, human beings can and do take a stance toward themselves and their experiences, actions, and circumstances (see, e.g., De Haan, 2020; Kloosterboer, 2022 for further discussion). For human beings, things aren't just as they are; we relate to them in a certain way and things have a certain meaning for us. That also implies that things can come to mean to something different by seeing it in a different light. Reflecting on reasons is not just a matter of discovery, but also of exploring and creating meaning. A person could take a different stance on getting wet for example, by experiencing it as refreshing or enjoying the feeling of rain on their skin, or, depending on the circumstances of course, coming to see losing your job as an opportunity to choose a different path. Understanding what something means for a person, then, is crucial for understanding why they act as they do.

Thirdly and finally, acting for reasons is not a purely internal affair: it involves a relationship between the person, their abilities, and the world. What I should do to arrive at work dryly and whether it is possible for me to do so, depends on the circumstances and my abilities. Similarly, keeping a job requires you to recognize and respond to circumstances in a good way: should you change jobs, study, or connect to the right people? That also means that you should act on the basis of things that are really the case. If I wrongly think that losing my job will imply that my partner will leave me or that nobody cares about whether I live or die, I could end up making a decision that is motivated by something that is not true.

Understanding what motivates a person to act, then, is not about uncovering causal influences, but about understanding how a person relates to certain facts, what they mean to them, in the context of their circumstances, ends, and beliefs.

4.3 Suicide and Acting for Reasons: Unpredictability, Fluctuations, and Ambivalence

In this section, I will apply these characteristics of acting for reasons to suicide by showing how the act of suicide is part of a means-end structure. After that, I connect the nature of acting for reasons to the three characteristics of suicide that I addressed in the introduction: its unpredictability, fluctuations in the person's wish to live and wish to die, and ambivalence.

The research on reasons for suicide suggests that ending one's life is often not an end in itself, but a means to a different end. Some of the most given answers were the wish to die (Schnyder et al., 1999; Van Orden et al., 2015; Williams, 1986), wanting to sleep and not wake up (Van Orden et al., 2015), or other ends for which suicide could be a means: getting relief from a terrible state of mind or from an unbearable situation, to end suffering, or to escape (Bancroft et al., 1979; Jobes & Mann, 1999; Kotila & Lönnqvist, 1989; Schnyder et al., 1999; Van Orden et al., 2015; Williams, 1986). Some persons also referred to interpersonal or communicative reasons, which could also be understood as further ends, for example to show desperate feelings or to make things easier for others (Schnyder et al., 1999; Williams, 1986).

Furthermore, persons cite facts about themselves or the world. Van Orden et al. (2015) found that older adults that tried to end their lives gave reasons like reduced functioning and autonomy, psychological problems like depression, and somatic problems and physical pain. The persons Shamsaei et al. (2020) interviewed refer to mental pain, for example living through grief, internal conflict, that the world is better without them, social challenges like lack of social connection and social support services, financial problems, and need for love and belonging, for example feeling understood and the need for empathy. Ali and Gibson (2019) found that people that felt suicidal reported feeling lonely and socially disconnected, experiencing stigma, failing to meet expectations, being helpless, feeling worthless, and experiencing mental ill-health. Other examples are feeling having failed in life, feeling lonely and unwanted, or being angry at someone (Birtchnell & Alarcon, 1971).

The answers given in these studies provide a picture of the means-end structure of suicide. The person has a certain end – to die, to end their suffering, or to escape – and takes suicide as means to do so. Furthermore, the persons cite facts that explain why they want to die, end their suffering, or want to escape. Indeed, lack of social connection, financial problems, mental ill-health, and failing to meet expectations are the opposite of what people typically take a good life to amount to. Some interesting issues emerge from this that are worth pointing out. First, these answers only show a small part of the full picture, because it does not consider the wider background within which this means-end structure should be understood (see also De Haan, 2020, p. 241). Second, it is important to note that the end – the action at the highest level of description – is no longer a good life, but rather to *end* something, often because the person's situation and experiences have become too much to bear. That is what the mentioned facts typically refer to; reasons why the person is suffering and considers ending things by means of suicide. Suicide, then, often seems to be a response to a difficult situation and knowing of no other means to make life worth living, or perhaps just livable, again. Third, based on the insight that actions allow for several descriptions, we could argue that typically, from the perspective of the acting person, suicide is not just suicide, but ending an unbearable situation at the same time, for example. It is worthwhile to reflect on why we tend to use the description 'suicide' for all these cases, and whether this is the most suitable label from the perspective of the person.

Fourth, the research shows that reasons for suicide are personal: the means-end structures share that suicide shows up as part of it, but other than that, persons have their own ends and mention their individual circumstances – this would become even clearer if we would take the wider context of each person into account. Moreover, as the research (e.g., Franklin et al., 2017; Nielssen, Wallace, & Large, 2017) shows, most people in similar circumstances end up *not* seriously considering suicide or ending their lives. Many people live their life while experiencing mental ill-health, financial problems, or loneliness, perhaps leading a life they find worthwhile, suffering but having found a way to live with this, or having considered suicide but not gone through with it, for example because they are not capable of ending their lives (e.g., Van Orden et al., 2010). This probably, at least partly, has to with the wider context I pointed to earlier: taking financial problems to be a reason for suicide cannot be understood independently from a person's conceptions of a good life, their beliefs, values, but also whether they might become homeless because of it or their partner might leave them. We should not, however, simply reduce a person's relationship to (potential) reasons to these factors. First and foremost, we need to recognize that the person's relates to their circumstances, ends, feelings, and beliefs in a certain way, and that this should take a central place in understanding why persons act as they do. Financial problems do not mean the same for everyone, and we cannot assume that we can completely distill this meaning from the wider context.

We are now in a position to reflect on the three characteristics of suicide I pointed out in the introduction, starting with the unpredictability. If we look at the answers the persons in these different studies give, it becomes clear that in fact the only aspect these persons more or less share is their relationship to suicide: they experience suicidal ideation, consider suicide, or tried to end their lives. Given this, it should come as no surprise that research in which findings are generalized over large groups of people will not find general risk factors. Persons do not all suffer in the same way and for the same reasons, and have their own story of why they might end their lives. Simply put, we have good reason to think that suicide is too personal and context-dependent to make sense of by means of generalizations.

What is more, acting for reasons (or considering something for reasons) necessarily involves the agent relating to the facts and ends in a certain way. If a person considers suicide for a certain reason, they *take* these circumstances or beliefs to be a reason for suicide – again, given but not reduced to their circumstances, ends, and beliefs. In order to understand why a person considers suicide, then, involves taking into account how they relate to these factors, what being lonely or ill-health means to them. Indeed, the insight that many people in similar circumstances do not seriously consider suicide (see Nielssen et al., 2017) suggests that this relationship is of crucial importance. For some people diminished autonomy is the worst thing that could happen, while others find a way to live with these circumstances. Again, not being able to predict suicide on the basis of general risk factors should come as no surprise.

Furthermore, even though I think, like Anscombe (1963) and Davidson (1963) for example, that persons have first-person authority over what they do and why, persons could have given reasons that were in fact not (their) motivating reasons. Most notably, they could consider suicide for an apparent reason, for example the false belief that nobody cares about them. Or they could give a reason that they did not actually act for, but that they cite to make sense of what they did, for themselves or for others (see, e.g., Jefferson, 2020). This could involve an explanatory reason – after analyzing the causal structures in their lives, they conclude that it must have been their mental ill-health – or a normative reason – what *would be* a good reason to end my life? Given the fact that persons sometimes cannot make sense of why they tried to take their own lives (e.g., Hjelmeland et al., 1998; Kotila & Lönnqvist, 1989; Van Orden et al., 2015), this possibility should seriously be considered. That means that persons giving some fact as their reason may relate to this in a variety of ways and, accordingly, relate to suicide as an answer or possibility in a different way as well. Does the person experience themselves to be 'pushed' to act as they did, or did they rather take it to justify their action?

Finally, acting for reasons involves choice. When a person ends up acting in a certain way and for certain reasons, they take these ends and facts to speak in favor of this action. In such a picture, suicide is not a causal outcome of a variety of factors, but a way in which a person that is suffering expresses themselves and responds to their suffering, in this context and at this time in their lives. Afterwards we can say that financial problems or unbearable suffering was the reason, but that is because the person, in this (social) context and in relation to their personal characteristics, treated these factors as such. In this picture, we partly constitute ourselves into the person we are *in action*, in responding to the situation in a certain way. This approach of acting for reasons rejects a causal-explanatory picture, the assumption that there *must be* a decisive explanation, and accordingly is in line with the findings by Franklin et al. (2017). We cannot easily predict suicide, because it involves genuine decision-making, not just psychological states pushing the person in a certain direction.

The importance of meaning seems relevant for the second characteristic as well: fluctuations. Research shows that suicidal ideation can vary dramatically, even within hours (e.g., Kleiman et al., 2017). How is this possible? Crucially, Kleiman et al.'s (2017) study shows that common risk factors, like hopelessness, burdensomeness, and loneliness, correlate with suicidal ideation, but are limited in predicting short-term change in suicidal ideation (see also Rath et al., 2021). How can this be explained? The nature of acting for reasons offers an interesting possibility, namely that the person's stance toward their circumstances, feelings, thoughts, and life in general plays an important role. Sometimes loneliness can be acceptable, while in other circumstances it seems the most terrible situation to be in. Sometimes physical problems do not seem like a major obstacle, while the next day you may experience yourself as a terrible burden. Indeed, as the findings suggest, perhaps hopelessness and burdensomeness reflect a person's stance to their situation as well, and are not best seen as causes of suicidal ideation. Changes in how you relate to the situation you are in and how you feel can depend on mood or other circumstances, but sometimes seem to change without any clear explanation. We suddenly see our life in a different light or experience a loss of meaning. This suggests that suicidal ideation is not (just) the result of risk factors being there or not, but of fluctuations in a person's stance toward these circumstances and their experiences. Indeed, in a recent study by Usipuik (2024) a person states:

> That's I guess how I think about suicide thoughts – that they just come and go. They come and then they go and you don't have to attach big meaning to them. They're maybe a signal that I need something, like, I need support or connection or conversation.
>
> (p. 72)

Similarly, Webb (2010) emphasizes the importance of creating space for suicidal feelings to be experienced in a different way. This suggests that how we relate to our experiences and circumstances is of crucial importance to understand the role they play in our lives, and that we should consider how our stance toward these things can fluctuate.[5]

This brings me to the third characteristic: ambivalence. Research shows that persons can remain, right before or even during the act, ambivalent about suicide (e.g., Shneidman, 1998). When we understand the act of suicide as part of a means-end structure, and as a means to a certain end, it is not surprising that persons are typically ambivalent about suicide, even up until the very end. Suicide is often a means to end a bad situation the person is in, by taking a highly consequential and potentially painful action. Often, the person does not want to die per se, but sees suicide as a, and perhaps the only, way out. As long as there is a flicker of hope that circumstances will change or they would be able to cope with them – which, as the research on fluctuations show, may change constantly – they will have doubts about whether to go through with it. It is perfectly rational to be ambivalent about what to do in such a situation; a decision with such implications *should* involve doubt and second thoughts (see Coates, 2017). This also suggests that persons may often not be ambivalent about suicide itself, but about whether suicide is the right (or only) response to end the situation they are in (Chapter 3).

To sum up, taking seriously that suicide is an action that persons typically have reasons for and that understanding this action involves considering the person's stance on these reasons and their life in general, it is not surprising: (1) that suicide is hard to predict by means of general risk factors, (2) that persons experience substantial fluctuations in their wish to die and wish to live, and (3) that persons are typically ambivalent about what to do.

4.4 Suicide and the Practice of Understanding

In order to understand suicide, it does not suffice to uncover facts about suicidal persons in general, but it is also insufficient to investigate the person and their circumstances from a neutral perspective. When persons act for reasons, they respond to facts in the world (and about themselves), but whether they take these facts speak in favor of an action crucially depends on the wider context and the person's stance: why does this person at this moment take this to speak in favor of the action? This is not independent from the person's (other) ends, (other) circumstances, and beliefs, but we should also be careful to simply reduce this stance to these factors. Accordingly, identifying potential risk factors out of context and without paying attention to a person's stance toward them will only provide limited understanding of why this person considered suicide or ended their life. We need to consider the perspective of the person to understand how they make sense of their situation (see Webb, 2010). This implies that preventing suicide is not identical to identifying and eliminating potential risk factors; it can be as simple as that, but often things are much more complex. We need to understand what certain experiences and circumstances mean for the person, in the larger context of their life.

But what does this mean for suicide prevention? Should the aim of understanding and taking the perspective of the person seriously still be to identify reliable predictors of suicide? Or should we adopt a different strategy to suicide prevention? In this section, I will propose that attempting to understand why a person considers suicide may itself play an important role in preventing suicide. Differently put: the practice of understanding why a person considers suicide, most notably the person's self-understanding, may not be independent from whether a person considers suicide. This insight is of crucial importance, because there is reason to think that suicidal ideation hampers the process of self-understanding, because of which ambivalent persons run the risk of becoming more suicidal rather than less.

As I discussed in previous sections, understanding an action and understanding the reasons does not involve finding out what 'pushes' persons in a certain direction, but involves placing the action and (potential) reasons in their larger context and understanding what the action, reasons, and context mean for a person, and why they have the meaning they do. Because of this, understanding reasons for action is not simply a matter of discovery, but of interpretation and sense-making as well. It is about seeing your experiences and your circumstances in a certain light. In this context, Naomi Scheman (1993) criticizes the idea that psychological understanding is a matter of uncovering leaves that were thrust to the bottom and covered with silt. Rather, in trying to understand yourself, the challenge is to put "a name to a mass of rather disparate stuff" and "to note a meaningful pattern" (1993, p. 23). These meanings cannot just be 'read off', and how to interpret your experiences has a normative dimension as well. For example, by placing financial problems in a larger context and considering what a just society would look like, a person can come to see it as something not to be ashamed of, but the result of problematic structures in society. Or by understanding your loneliness as resulting from living far away from family and friends, you may reconsider some of your life's choices and reflect on what is important to you. Is your career worth feeling lonely? Can you live with this or see this as part of the life you've chosen? Moreover, do you feel shame of having made this choice earlier, or do you understand it as part of the process of finding out what matters to you? Similarly, what does having suicidal thoughts mean? Does it mean you are going crazy, or does it mean you need to talk to a friend (see Usipuik, 2024)? Understanding your experiences can make it so that they appear in a different light, because of which several meanings and also several responses to these experiences can be explored and evaluated. To put this in terms of reasons: in the process of coming to understand oneself, experiences and circumstances that were treated as a potential normative reason for suicide by a person in a certain context can come to mean something different, if the person is able to change their stance toward them and can come to recognize other ways of coping with them.

This suggests that self-understanding itself plays a role in whether a person considers suicide. It is of crucial importance for a person to be able to see their situation in a different light and to explore what could be done to change things. Of course, in this process of self-understanding, a person could come to the conclusion that suicide indeed makes a lot of sense. There is reason to think, however, that often this is not the case.[6] Research suggests that talking about suicide reduces instead of increases suicidal ideation (Dazzi et al., 2014), and in clinical practice talking is taken to be an important means to prevent suicide (e.g., 113 zelfmoordpreventie, n.d.; Britton et al., 2016; GGZ nieuws, 2019, Meerdinkveldboom, Rood, & Kerkhof, 2016).[7] Clinicians have proposed that talking about suicide can take the pressure off and make bad circumstances seem less overwhelming (e.g., 113 zelfmoordpreventie, n.d.; GGZ nieuws, 2019). Even though more attention should be paid to how this exactly functions, especially from the perspective of the person considering suicide (cf. Webb, 2010), this suggests that activating the person to engage in the process of self-understanding and to explore alternative meanings may be worthwhile in itself (cf. Miller & Rollnick, 2012).[8]

If self-understanding could itself diminish suicide, we should pay attention to the conditions that facilitate or undermine it. This brings me back to suicidal ambivalence. Research shows that persons considering suicide are often ambivalent about whether to kill themselves. For these persons, it seems, things could go in either direction. If, however, suicidal ideation in itself makes it more difficult to engage in the practice of self-understanding, we have reason to think that considering suicide may lead to a vicious circle in which the person is more likely to seriously consider ending their life. In the remainder of this section, I discuss two reasons for why this indeed may be how things tend to work.

First of all, research suggests that persons considering suicide are often not in a state in which they can take a stance on their experiences and what they mean in the larger context of their lives. Suicidal persons and clinicians tend to describe this as being in a tunnel, bubble, or a trap (see, e.g., 113 zelfmoordpreventie, n.d.; GGZ nieuws, 2019; Owens, Derges, & Abraham, 2019; Vatne & Nåden, 2012).[9] Instead of being able to take the wider context into account and reflecting on the meaning of their suicidal ideation, persons in the grip of suicidal ideation can experience a strong tension in which the thought of killing themselves seems to completely fill their minds (see, e.g., Michel, 2023). Related to this, *demoralization* has been associated with suicidal ideation (e.g., Constanza et al., 2022, but see De Figuereido, 1993). Even though I cannot explore this phenomenon in detail in this chapter, demoralization is described as disorder or confusion (Frank & Frank, 1991, p. 35), a feeling of incompetency and uncertainty about the right direction of action (De Figuereido, 1993), and an experience of loss of meaning (e.g., Clarke & Kissane, 2002). The state of demoralization reflects a person's inability to make sense of their experiences, which has the tendency to amplify the problematic situation the person is already in.

It is important to address here that a substantial number of persons seem to (attempt to) end their lives without knowing why they are doing it, or even what they are doing (e.g., Hjelmeland et al., 1998; Kotila & Lönnqvist, 1989; Van Orden et al., 2015). These persons report being in the grips of anxiety and panic or having difficulty communicating their reasons (e.g., Van Orden et al., 2015, p. 541).[10] What is more, Kotila & Lönnqvist (1989) found that "suicide attempters who are able to point out some definitive difficulties that create a dead-end life situation seem to have a smaller risk of subsequent suicide or violent death than those whose reasons for attempting suicide remain unclear" (p. 457). This supports the view that a breakdown of the practice of self-understanding, for example because of the anxiety, panic, or demoralization suicidal ideation may trigger, may pose a particular risk. As long as persons keep reflecting on their reasons and try to make sense of their experiences, alternative understandings of experiences and circumstances are possible.

This brings me to the second reason why suicidal ideation may make it so that persons are more likely to seriously consider suicide instead of moving in the other direction. In her chapter, Scheman (1993) adds that "our vocabulary of the emotions,[11] are given socially: the patterns to be found are various but not infinite and not wholly in our individual power to change" (p. 22). In other words, our practice of understanding our actions, feelings, thoughts, and circumstances depends on our social context; what ways of making sense of bad circumstances and suicidal ideation are available and acceptable? But also: is the widely shared norm that financial problems mean that you have failed as an individual, and how do people around you perceive your place in society when you suffer from mental or physical illnesses?

In other words, social factors like stigma may make it hard for ambivalent persons to explore how to relate to their experiences and circumstances, and the existing norms may make it so that the meanings that are available are harmful. As a result, persons that consider suicide may have a hard time engaging in the practice of self-understanding. This suggestion is in line with reasons for feeling suicidal that have often been mentioned in the literature: stigma, feeling disconnected, misunderstood, and a lack of social support (e.g., Ali & Gibson, 2019; Shamsaei et al., 2020; Van Orden et al., 2015, see also Krychiw & Ward-Cieselski, 2019, for discussion). Of course, in and of itself social bonds are important for leading a good life. But social bonds also seem to be important for engaging in the practice of self-understanding, especially in difficult times and when the person feels trapped or in a bubble. Others can play an important role in offering space to explore the meaning of your feelings and thoughts and to reflect on life and the ends you tend to pursue from different perspectives (see, e.g., Teismann, Siebert, & Forkmann, 2024). Moreover, others can help reflect on whether certain beliefs point to facts or mere apparent reasons.

This points to another difficulty, which is that understanding a person who considers suicide may not be easy for a person who does not. Research shows that persons that tried to end their lives tend to give different answers than nurses and doctors, for example (e.g., Krychiw & Ward-Cieselski, 2019; Schnyder et al., 1999). Furthermore, the seriousness of the attempt is often underestimated and signs are not taken seriously (see Krychiw & Ward-Cieselski, 2019 for discussion). There could be a variety of explanations for why this happens.[12] From the perspective of acting for reasons, a potential explanation is that persons that seriously consider suicide relate to their circumstances and ends in a way that is difficult to understand for a person that is not considering suicide. More concretely, the answers nurses and doctors gave in Schnyder et al.'s (1999) study may reflect, to some extent, their own perspective on potential reasons for suicide, that is, what *they* would take to speak in favor of suicide, given the circumstances. And since they are probably not suicidal, it is likely that it is hard for them to understand the patient's motivation. Wishing to die or suffering badly from circumstances that others seem to be able to live with may be harder to understand than desperately trying to communicate your suffering to others, for example. This may lead to a further disconnect between the person considering suicide and important others.

In other words, thinking about suicide often involves a stance on circumstances and life in general that may be difficult to understand for others, precisely because it is not simply the circumstances that lead to suicidality. Instead of receiving support or having the feeling that your experiences make sense, which can often be achieved by talking to others about your struggles, the person considering suicide may not find this recognition in others. The experiences, thoughts, and feelings of the suicidal person *are* hard to understand for persons who do not consider suicide. What is more, persons may be motivated to not understand the suicidal person. After all, it can be scary to understand why a person considers suicide, and extremely hard to find out that someone you care about has these kinds of thoughts and feelings.

Given the role others tend to play in our practice of self-understanding, this suggests that experiences like thwarted belongingness and perceived burdensomeness, which are taken to be the central risk factors according to the Interpersonal Theory of Suicide (Van Orden et al., 2010), may not (just) be independent causes of (considering) suicide, but could be seen as part of how suicidal ideation undermines the practice of self-understanding and meaning-making. Suicidal ideation can be the starting point of a vicious circle, toward diminished self-understanding and enhanced social isolation, because of a growing mismatch between your (normative) outlook on life and what people close to you can understand or are willing to engage with. This approach can also explain the interesting relationship that seems to exist between stigma and suicide. In many cases, reducing stigma makes it so that persons come to act in a way that was stigmatized before, for example to remain single or child free. In case of suicide, however, reducing stigma seems to *reduce* suicide. A potential explanation for this is that reducing stigma facilitates the practice of self-understanding, which in turn diminishes the chance that the person will in fact end their life.[13]

To sum up, a variety of factors may undermine self-understanding once a person starts seriously considering suicide, which in turn may make it so that suicide becomes more likely for the person who is ambivalent about what to do, because the person is not in a position to explore alternative meanings by seeing their experiences and circumstances in a different light. Relatedly, the important role others play in self-understanding explains how persons considering suicide may end up in a vicious circle. Persons that consider suicide but are still ambivalent, then, may be more likely to end up in a worse situation than a better one.

4.5 Conclusion, Implications, and Further Research

In this chapter, I aimed to show that connecting a deeper understanding of acting for reasons to research on reasons for suicide leads to interesting insights. Acting for reasons is not the same as being causally influenced by certain factors, but involves seeing the action in a certain light by taking into account the person's ends and stance on things, and considering the wider context. In order to understand why the person considers suicide, then, their perspective cannot be ignored. I also argued that the unpredictability of suicide, fluctuations in wish to die and wish to live, and ambivalence are not surprising when we take the nature of acting for reasons into account. I concluded that predicting suicide by identifying general risk factors may not be the best approach, and proposed that understanding the reasons for suicide, most notably the person's self-understanding, may itself play a role in preventing suicide. If that is indeed the case, it suggests that ambivalent persons are at risk of becoming more suicidal rather than less.

Even though this proposal needs to be investigated and developed in more detail, it points to some implications for suicide prevention and to suggestions for further research. First, other persons, also outside of clinical practice, can play an important role in suicide prevention by facilitating the process of self-understanding. One thing to note is that many researchers have emphasized the importance of social connections, but that it has not been seriously considered how difficult it is for loved ones to deal with these talks, and that it is not strange at all that they experience this as a burden. Educating loved ones on how to deal with this, but perhaps also the availability of persons to talk to that are not personally invested seems to be of crucial importance. Second, it emphasizes, in line with Webb (2010), that in order to understand suicide, we have to take the perspective of the suicidal person seriously. We should reject the view that we can come to understand the suicidal person by investigating potential risk factors independent from the person's stance on things. Third, more attention should be paid to what is involved in taking a stance and how circumstances and experiences come to mean something for the person, and how these meanings can change in a positive direction. Indeed, Motivational Interviewing (Miller & Rollnick, 2012) could be an important means to preventing suicide (see, e.g., Britton et al., 2016), but the mechanisms behind it are still a topic of discussion (e.g., Miller & Rose, 2009). Also here, taking into account the nature of acting for reasons is important.[14]

Notes

1 I do not mean to suggest that all intentional actions, for example, suicide, are done for reasons, only that this sense of the question 'Why?' has application (Anscombe, 1963). When someone acts intentionally, asking for reasons is suitable, even though the answer could be 'no reason'.

2 One important topic of discussion is whether reasons are agent-relative or agent-neutral (see Ridge, 2022 for discussion). I cannot go into this discussion in detail, but I do want to emphasize that, at least in the context of suicide, my view is that normative reasons for living and dying are out there, but for a certain person seeing it in a certain light. I say more about this in Section 4.4 of this chapter.

3 As these scholars point out, in line with the findings of Franklin et al. (2017), even if certain genetic factors are associated with suicide, suicidal behavior is a complex phenomenon resulting from many interacting factors and cannot

simply be predicted based on a genetic predisposition. Thanks to René Baston for addressing this issue.

4 Because of which I will use 'reasons' for facts, ends, and actions at a higher level of description.

5 This, and also my previous point about choice, emphasizes the importance of means restriction to prevent suicide (e.g., Daigle, 2005). Means restriction may not just be something that 'blocks' the agent from the possibility of suicide, but may make it so that the person ends up making a different decision altogether (see Chapter 7). Moreover, meaning probably plays an important role here as well: jumping in front of a train can have a different meaning for a person in comparison to taking pills, for example, because of which they consider one method but not the other.

6 As I pointed out previously, there is good reason to think that there is not one kind of suicidal person.

7 I am grateful to Monique Aveskamp for discussing suicidal ideation in clinical practice with me.

8 This is definitely not to say that people can simply change their minds and can therefore be blamed for their suicidal ideation, or that we shouldn't do our best to improve the circumstances suffering persons are in. My aim is only to explore the important role of self-understanding in suicide prevention.

9 Again, thanks to Monique Aveskamp.

10 This points to the question of whether all examples of suicide even count as *intentional* self-killing, which I cannot explore further in this chapter, unfortunately.

11 Her focus is on emotions, but the same applies to actions, thoughts, and circumstances – for example, what it means to have financial problems.

12 Krywich and Ward-Cieselski (2019) use these findings to explain why suicide is taken to be unpredictable: the problem seems to lie in communicative issues, for example, misinterpretation, invalidation, or lack of communication due to stigmatizing reactions (p. 2). One important factor, they maintain, may be actor-observer bias. According to this bias, actors tend to cite external facts to explain why they do what they do, while observers tend to cite internal characteristics of the agent. Different from Franklin et al. (2017), however, this explanation addresses interpersonal unpredictability.

13 This can be contrasted with Miller and Rollnick's (e.g., 2012) explanation of why Motivational Interviewing works, a method that has also been used to prevent suicide (Britton et al., 2016). They propose to explain it in terms of self-regulation theory: when behavior gets outside the normal or expected range, self-regulation kicks in. Motivational Interviewing "triggers self-regulation by enhancing awareness of current behavior and judgment about its acceptability relative to important personal values" (Miller & Rollnick, 2012, p. 95). Again, this would suggest that when the stigma is diminished, *more* people would end their lives.

14 I would like to thank Monique Aveskamp, Cato Benschop, René Baston, Daphne Brandenburg, Michael Cholbi, Sabrina Coninx, Sanja Dembić, Thomas Forkmann, Friedrich Hausen, Naomi Kloosterboer, Tobias Teismann,

Martin Weichold, Zuzanna Rucińska, and Elizabeth Ventham for their helpful comments on earlier versions of this chapter and for the insightful discussions.

References

113 zelfmoordpreventie (n.d.) *Durf te praten*. Retrieved February 27, 2025, from www.113.nl/durftepraten

Ali, A., & Gibson, K. (2019). Young people's reasons for feeling suicidal. *Crisis: The Journal of Crisis Intervention and Suicide Prevention, 40*(6), 1–7. https://doi.org/10.1027/0227-5910/a000580

Alvarez, M. (2009). How many kinds of reasons? *Philosophical Explorations, 12*(2), 181–193. https://doi.org/10.1080/13869790902838514

Alvarez, M., & Way, J. (2024, August 22). *Reasons for action: Justification, motivation, explanation*. Stanford Encyclopedia of Philosophy. https://plato.stanford.edu/entries/reasons-just-vs-expl/

Anscombe, G. E. M. (1963). *Intention* (second edition). Blackwell.

Asma, L. J. F. (2022). Habitual virtuous action and acting for reasons. *Philosophical Psychology, 35*(7), 1036–1056. https://doi.org/10.1080/09515089.2022.2045008

Bagge, C. L., Littlefield, A. K., Conner, K. R., Schumacher, J. A., & Lee, H. J. (2014). Near-term predictors of the intensity of suicidal ideation: An examination of the 24h prior to a recent suicide attempt. *Journal of Affective Disorders, 165*, 53–58. https://doi.org/10.1016/j.jad.2014.04.010

Bancroft, J., Hawton, K., Simkin, S., Kingston, B., Cumming, C., & Whitwell, D. (1979). The reasons people give for taking overdoses: A further inquiry. *British Journal of Medical Psychology, 52*(4), 353–365. https://doi.org/10.1111/j.2044-8341.1979.tb02536.x

Baston, R. (2024). Beyond prediction: A new paradigm for understanding suicide risk. *Synthese, 204*(1), 35. https://doi.org/10.1007/s11229-024-04689-7

Birtchnell, J., & Alarcon, J. (1971). The motivation and emotional state of 91 cases of attempted suicide. *British Journal of Medical Psychology, 44*(1), 45–52. https://doi.org/10.1111/j.2044-8341.1971.tb02145.x

Bondy, B., Buettner, A., & Zill, P. (2006). Genetics of suicide. *Molecular Psychiatry, 11*(4), 336–351. https://doi.org/10.1038/sj.mp.4001803

Britton, P. C., Bryan, C. J., & Valenstein, M. (2016). Motivational interviewing for means restriction counseling with patients at risk for suicide. *Cognitive and Behavioral Practice, 23*(1), 51–61. https://doi.org/10.1016/j.cbpra.2014.09.004

Bryan, C. J. (2021). *Rethinking suicide: Why prevention fails, and how we can do better*. Oxford University Press. https://doi.org/10.1093/med-psych/9780190050634.001.0001

Bryan, C. J., Butner, J. E., May, A. M., Rugo, K. F., Harris, J. A., Oakey, D. N., Rozek, D. C., & Bryan, A. O. (2020). Nonlinear change processes and the emergence of suicidal behavior: A conceptual model based on the fluid vulnerability theory of suicide. *New Ideas in Psychology, 57*, 100758. https://doi.org/10.1016/j.newideapsych.2019.100758

Cholbi, M. (2011). *Suicide: The philosophical dimensions*. Broadview Press Ltd.

Clarke, D. M., & Kissane, D. W. (2002). Demoralization: Its phenomenology and importance. *Australian & New Zealand Journal of Psychiatry, 36*(6), 733–742. https://doi.org/10.1046/j.1440-1614.2002.01086.x

Classen, T. J., & Dunn, R. A. (2012). The effect of job loss and unemployment duration on suicide risk in the United States: A new look using mass-layoffs and unemployment duration. *Health Economics, 21*(3), 338–350. https://doi.org/10.1002/hec.1719

Coates, D. J. (2017). A wholehearted defense of ambivalence. *The Journal of Ethics, 21*, 419–444. https://doi.org/10.1007/s10892-017-9257-x

Costanza, A., Vasileios, C., Ambrosetti, J., Shah, S., Amerio, A., Aguglia, A., Serafini, G., Piguet, V., Luthy, C., Cedraschi, C., Bondolfi, G., & Berardelli, I. (2022). Demoralization in suicide: A systematic review. *Journal of Psychosomatic Research, 157*, 110788. https://doi.org/10.1016/j.jpsychores.2022.110788

Daigle, M. S. (2005). Suicide prevention through means restriction: Assessing the risk of substitution: A critical review and synthesis. *Accident Analysis & Prevention, 37*(4), 625–632. https://doi.org/10.1016/j.aap.2005.03.004

Dancy, J. (2000). *Practical reality*. Oxford University Press. https://doi.org/10.1093/0199253056.001.0001

Davidson, D. (1963). Actions, reasons and causes. *The Journal of Philosophy, 60*(23), 685–700. https://doi.org/10.2307/2023177

Dazzi, T., Gribble, R., Wessely, S., & Fear, N. T. (2014). Does asking about suicide and related behaviours induce suicidal ideation? What is the evidence?. *Psychological Medicine, 44*(16), 3361–3363. https://doi.org/10.1017/S0033291714001299

De Figueiredo, J. M. (1993). Depression and demoralization: Phenomenologic differences and research perspectives. *Comprehensive Psychiatry, 34*(5), 308–311. https://doi.org/10.1016/0010-440X(93)90016-W

De Haan, S. (2020). *Enactive psychiatry*. Cambridge University Press. https://doi.org/10.1017/9781108685214

D'Oro, G. (2012). Reasons and causes: The philosophical battle and the meta-philosophical war. *Australasian Journal of Philosophy, 90*(2), 207–221. https://doi.org/10.1080/00048402.2011.583930

Frank, J. D., & Frank, J. B. (1991). *Persuasion and healing. A comparative study of Psychotherapy* (Third edition). The John Hopkins University Press.

Franklin, J. C., Ribeiro, J. D., Fox, K. R., Bentley, K. H., Kleiman, E. M., Huang, X., Musacchio, K. M., Jaroszewski, A. C., Chang, B. P., & Nock, M. K. (2017). Risk factors for suicidal thoughts and behaviors: A meta-analysis of 50 years of research. *Psychological Bulletin*, 143(2), 187–232. https://doi.org/10.1037/bul0000084

Frey, J. A. (2019). Anscombe on practical knowledge and the good. *Ergo, an Open Access Journal of Philosophy, 6*(39), 1121–1151. https://doi.org/10.3998/ergo.12405314.0006.039

GGZ nieuws (2019, September 12). *Dit kun je doen als je vermoedt dat iemand zelfmoord overweegt*. Retrieved February 27, 2025, from www.ggznieuws.nl/dit-kun-je-doen-als-je-vermoedt-dat-iemand-zelfmoord-overweegt/

Hjelmeland, H., Stiles, T. C., Bille-Brahe, U., Ostamo, A., Renberg, E. S., & Wasserman, D. (1998). Parasuicide: The value of suicidal intent and various motives as predictors of future suicidal behaviour. *Archives of Suicide Research, 4*(3), 209–225. https://doi.org/10.1080/13811119808258297

Jefferson, A. (2020). Confabulation, rationalisation and morality. *Topoi, 39*(1), 219–227. https://doi.org/10.1007/s11245-018-9608-7

Jobes, D. A., & Mann, R. E. (1999). Reasons for living versus reasons for dying: Examining the internal debate of suicide. *Suicide and Life-Threatening Behavior, 29*(2), 97–104. https://doi.org/10.1111/j.1943-278X.1999.tb01048.x

Kleiman, E. M., Turner, B. J., Fedor, S., Beale, E. E., Huffman, J. C., & Nock, M. K. (2017). Examination of real-time fluctuations in suicidal ideation and its risk factors: Results from two ecological momentary assessment studies. *Journal of Abnormal Psychology, 126*(6), 726–738. https://doi.org/10.1037/abn0000273

Kloosterboer, N. (2022). Substantial self-knowledge and the necessity of avowal. *The Journal of Value Inquiry, 58,* 629–649. https://doi.org/10.1007/s10790-022-09916-3

Kotila, L., & Lönnqvist, J. (1989). Suicide and violent death among adolescent suicide attempters. *Acta Psychiatrica Scandinavica, 79*(5), 453–459. https://doi.org/10.1111/j.1600-0447.1989.tb10287.x

Krychiw, J. K., & Ward-Ciesielski, E. F. (2019). Factors related to suicide's unpredictability: A qualitative study of adults with lived experience of suicide attempts. *International Journal of Qualitative Studies on Health and Well-Being, 14*(1), 1650585. https://doi.org/10.1080/17482631.2019.1650585

Large, M., Kaneson, M., Myles, N., Myles, H., Gunaratne, P., & Ryan, C. (2016). Meta-analysis of longitudinal cohort studies of suicide risk assessment among psychiatric patients: Heterogeneity in results and lack of improvement over time. *PLOS ONE, 11*(6), e0156322. https://doi.org/10.1371/journal.pone.0156322

Meerdinkveldboom, J., Rood, I., & Kerkhof, A. (2016). *Handboek suicidaal gedrag bij jongeren. Individuele en gezinsbehandeling.* Boom uitgevers Amsterdam.

Michel, K. (2023). *The suicidal person.* Columbia University Press.

Miller, W. R., & Rollnick, S. (2012). *Motivational interviewing: Helping people change.* Guilford Press.

Miller, W. R., & Rose, G. S. (2009). Toward a theory of motivational interviewing. *American Psychologist, 64*(6), 527–537. https://doi.org/10.1037/a0016830

Nielssen, O., Wallace, D., & Large, M. (2017). Pokorny's complaint: The insoluble problem of the overwhelming number of false positives generated by suicide risk assessment. *BJPsych Bulletin, 41*(1), 18–20. https://doi.org/10.1192/pb.bp.115.053017

Owens, C., Derges, J., & Abraham, C. (2019). Intervening to prevent a suicide in a public place: A qualitative study of effective interventions by lay people. *BMJ Open, 9*(11), e032319. https://doi.org/10.1136/bmjopen-2019-032319

Rath, D., Teismann, T., Hoeller, I., Glaesmer, H., Paashaus, L., Schönfelder, A., Juckel, G., & Forkmann, T. (2021). Predicting suicidal ideation in a longitudinal high-risk sample: Multilevel analyses and 12-month trajectories. *Journal of Clinical Psychology, 77*(10), 2353–2369. https://doi.org/10.1002/jclp.23159

Ridge, M. (2022, December 23). *Reasons for action: Agent-neutral vs. agent-relative. Stanford Encyclopedia of Philosophy.* https://plato.stanford.edu/entries/reasons-agent/

Scheman, N. (1993). Anger and the politics of naming. In N. Scheman (Ed.), *Engenderings: Constructions of knowledge, authority, and privilege* (pp. 22–35). Routledge.

Schnyder, U., Valach, L., Bichsel, K., & Michel, K. (1999). Attempted suicide: Do we understand the patients' reasons?. *General Hospital Psychiatry, 21*(1), 62–69. https://doi.org/10.1016/S0163-8343(98)00064-4

Shamsaei, F., Yaghmaei, S., & Haghighi, M. (2020). Exploring the lived experiences of the suicide attempt survivors: A phenomenological approach. *International Journal of Qualitative Studies on Health and Well-Being, 15*(1), 1745478. https://doi.org/10.1080/17482631.2020.1745478

Shneidman, E. S. (1998). *The suicidal mind.* Oxford University Press.

Tanney, J. (2009). Reasons as non-causal, context-placing explanations. In C. Sandis (Ed.), *New essays on the explanation of action* (pp. 94–111). Palgrave Macmillan.

Teismann, T., Siebert, A. M., & Forkmann, T. (2024). Suicidal ambivalence: A scoping review. *Suicide and Life-threatening Behavior, 54*(5), 802–813. https://doi.org/10.1111/sltb.13092

Thompson, M. (2008). *Life and action. Elementary structures of practice and practical thought.* Harvard University Press.

Usipuik, M. R. (2024). *"It definitely saved my life, just telling people": Experiences of northern individuals seeking support for suicidal ideation* [Doctoral dissertation, University of Northern British Columbia].

Van Orden, K. A., Wiktorsson, S., Duberstein, P., Berg, A. I., Fässberg, M. M., & Waern, M. (2015). Reasons for attempted suicide in later life. *The American Journal of Geriatric Psychiatry, 23*(5), 536–544. https://doi.org/10.1016/j.jagp.2014.07.003

Van Orden, K. A., Witte, T. K., Cukrowicz, K. C., Braithwaite, S. R., Selby, E. A., & Joiner Jr, T. E. (2010). The interpersonal theory of suicide. *Psychological Review, 117*(2), 575–600. https://doi.org/10.1037/a0018697

Vatne, M., & Nåden, D. (2012). Finally, it became too much–experiences and reflections in the aftermath of attempted suicide. *Scandinavian Journal of Caring Sciences, 26*(2), 304–312. https://doi.org/10.1111/j.1471-6712.2011.00934.x

Von Wright, G. H. (1971). *Explanation and understanding.* Routledge and Kegan Paul.

Webb, D. (2010). Thinking about suicide: Contemplating and comprehending the urge to die. *Psychotherapy in Australia, 16*(4), 28–33.

Wiland, E. (2003). Theories of practical reason. *Metaphilosophy, 33*(4), 450–467. https://doi.org/10.1111/1467-9973.00239

Williams, J. M. G. (1986). Differences in reasons for taking overdoses in high and low hopelessness groups. *British Journal of Medical Psychology, 59*(3), 269–277. https://doi.org/10.1111/j.2044-8341.1986.tb02693.x

5 The Ambivalence Model of Suicidality

Tobias Teismann, Peter C. Britton, and Thomas Forkmann

5.1 Introduction

The Ambivalence Model of Suicidality (ABS-Model; Teismann, Britton & Forkmann, 2024a; Teismann & Forkmann, 2024) is a clinical working model that aims to provide a framework for risk assessment, case conceptualization and treatment planning in crisis intervention and psychotherapy of suicidal individuals. At the core of the model stands the observation that ambivalence toward suicide/death accompanies the entire suicidal process of many affected individuals (Teismann et al., 2024a), is central to understanding an individual suicidal crisis and offers a therapeutic starting point in all phases of the suicidal process (Britton et al., 2011; Omer & Elitzur, 2003). By exploring the "internal suicide debate" (Harris et al., 2010), individually significant risk and protective factors both come into view. In this sense, a focus on suicidal ambivalence may not only serve to motivate those affected to take a first step back from acting on a suicide wish (Britton et al., 2008, 2011, 2016, 2020), but also inform case conceptualization and treatment planning.

The ABS-Model divides the suicidal process into three phases: the uncertainty phase, the transition phase and the action phase (see Figure 5.1).

In the following text, the suicidal process is described in relation to the three phases, and later on phase-specific information on (therapeutic) interventions are provided.

5.2 Uncertainty Phase

The possibility of suicide usually comes into focus when individuals are exposed to significant (e.g., separation, death, unemployment, financial loss, trauma) and/or multiple long lasting stressors (e.g., physical illness, bullying, maltreatment; Liu & Miller, 2014) and/or suffer from vulnerabilities such as a mental disorder (Favril et al, 2022). Given the significance of a suicide decision and the difficulty of enacting suicidal behavior, it is to

DOI: 10.4324/9781003616221-8

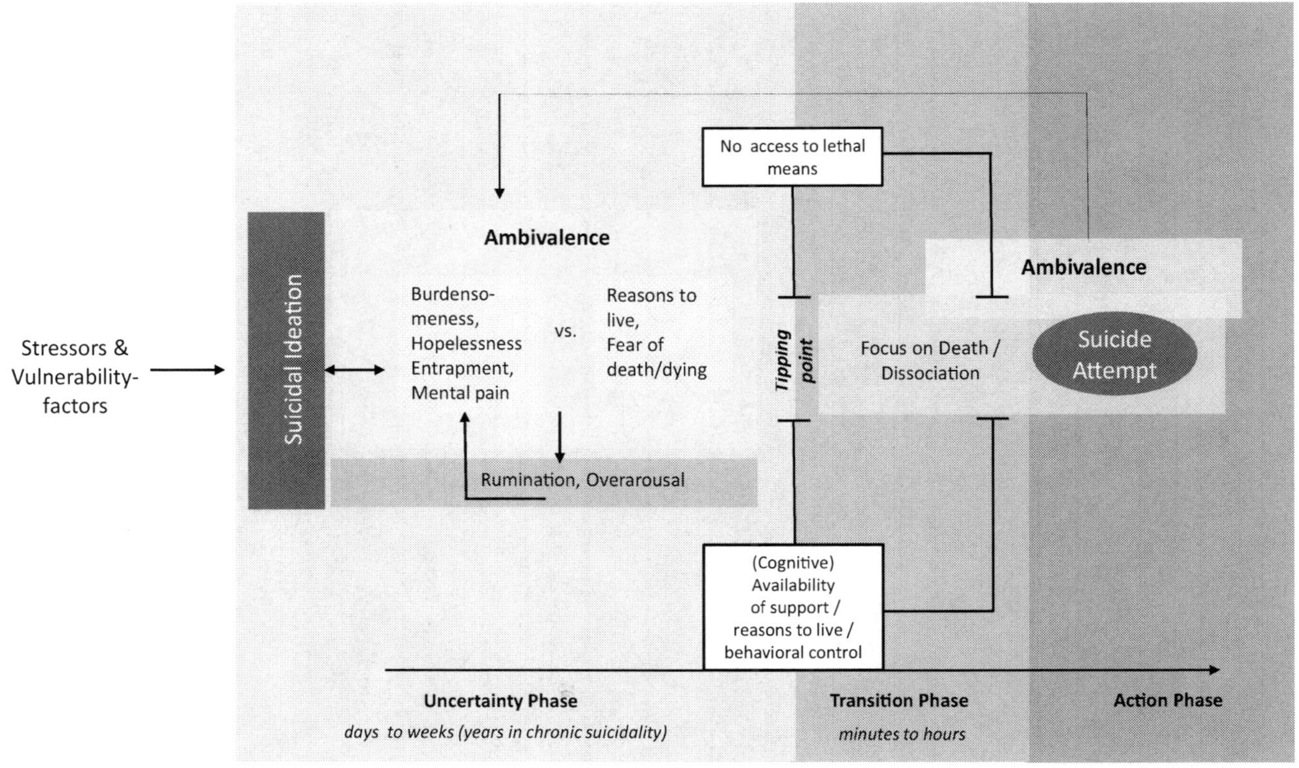

Figure 5.1 Ambivalence model of suicidality (ABS-Model).

be expected that suicidal ideation will be accompanied by the experience of ambivalence (cf. Buttlar et al., 2024).

In general, "ambivalence" can be taken to refer to the simultaneous existence of positive and negative (implicit or explicit) evaluations regarding a given person, experience or other (sets of) objects (cf. Connor & Sparks, 2002). The term "suicidal ambivalence" refers to the fact that wishes/reasons to die (e.g., "I can't bear the pain any longer") are experienced simultaneously with wishes/reasons to live (e.g., "I have to take care for my grandfather") or to not die (e.g., "I'm afraid of the pain involved in killing oneself"). Ambivalence can vary greatly in intensity and some individuals may openly acknowledge it, whereas others may not explicitly express ambivalence, but reveal it implicitly, for example, through the usage of words such as "maybe", "not now" and "possibly" when talking about suicidal intentions (van Wyk & Gibson, 2022).

Explicit suicidal ambivalence usually comprises the following components:

- **Reasons for dying (RFD)**: RFD are heterogeneous and might be associated with physical health issues, relationship problems, the desire to escape, loneliness, a negative self-perception, hopelessness and financial difficulties (Madsen & Harris, 2021). Moreover, individual RFD can cover all the perceptions that have been identified as central risk factors in different suicide theories: *I am a burden and others would be better off if I were dead* (perceived burdensomeness; Joiner, 2005). *I don't really belong anywhere/I am not important to anyone* (thwarted belongingness; Joiner, 2005). *My situation will never change, it is hopeless* (hopelessness; Wenzel & Beck, 2008). *I am trapped in a hopeless situation* (entrapment; O'Connor & Kirtley, 2018). *I just can't take the thoughts/memories anymore;* (unbearability; Wenzel & Beck, 2008). *The feelings are so bad; it's like physical pain, I can't stand them any more* (mental pain/psychache; Klonsky & May, 2015).
- **Reasons to live (RFL)**: RFL include themes such as family/friends (*I don't want my husband to think I didn't love him*), future plans (*There are still things on my bucket list*), enjoyable things (*I could never go swimming again if I were dead*), self-image (*I don't want anyone to think I was a coward*) and religion (*My religion forbids suicide*; Jobes & Mann, 1999; Linehan et al., 1983).
- **Reasons not to die (RND)**: RND complement RFL and include aspects such as fear of the pain involved in dying, fear of death (Joiner, 2005; Linehan et al., 1983) and/or fear of emerging disabled from a suicide attempt (*I would so like to be dead, but I don't dare*).

RFD, RFL and RND are cognitive representations that are presumed to underlie the wish to die/wish to live and result in felt suicidal ambivalence. The strength of felt suicidal ambivalence can vary to a great deal (Brown et al., 2005) and seems to show considerable fluctuations over time (Ernst et al., 2024; Fartacek et al., 2024). In that way, suicidal ambivalence adds to the unpredictability of suicidal behavior (Teismann et al., 2022). Furthermore, ambivalence has been shown to cause discomfort, anxiety and tension – particularly in situations when both the positive and negative components of the attitude are simultaneously accessible and when a choice needs to be made (van Harreveld et al., 2009a,b). It is therefore to be expected that suicidal ambivalence is experienced as an exhausting and stressful state (*I just can't stand this back and forth in my head anymore*; Bergmans et al., 2017), that can contribute to rumination, overarousal and emotional turmoil in suicidal individuals. In consequence, persistent suicidal ambivalence possibly contributes to the maintenance of suicidal ideation. It is therefore important to support suicidal individuals in resolving suicidal ambivalence and/or to step out of a constant engagement with suicidal ambivalence. The uncertainty phase can last minutes, days, weeks or – in the case of chronic suicidal ideation – even years (cf. Xu et al., 2024).

5.3 Transition Phase

The decision to die by suicide marks the progression from the uncertainty phase to the transition phase. The transition phase, therefore, describes suicidal individuals in a state of imminent suicide risk. Whether and when suicidal individuals enter the transition phase cannot be predicted (e.g., Franklin et al., 2017; Hawton et al., 2022; Woodford et al., 2019)[1]; some authors speak of a "mental accident" in which behavioral control over suicidal impulses (suddenly) fails (Ajdacic et al., 2019), others speak of coincidence (Soper et al, 2022) and within dynamic systems approaches (de Beurs et al., 2021) the term tipping points is used to characterize the sudden shift into a state of imminent suicidality. Suddenly – and possibly depending on situational cues – death-affirming motives gain the upper hand and carry the decision or impulse to die by suicide. From qualitative studies, it is known that ambivalence does not have to be resolved in order to enter the transition phase such that reasons for dying or the wish to die outweighs reasons for living or wish to live; rather, for some individuals, ambivalence seems to be pushed aside at these moments (Galasiński & Ziółkowska, 2024). Though different modern suicide theories (Joiner, 2005; Klonsky & May, 2015; O`Connor & Kirtley, 2018) posit that the transition from suicidal ideation to suicidal behavior is driven by factor such as fearlessness of death and dying, pain tolerance, suicide plans, exposure to suicide, there is insufficient evidence that these factors are of causal importance to enter the transition phase (e.g., Chu et al., 2017; Huang et al., 2020; Risch et al., 2024).

From an empirical standpoint two factors might be most relevant to entering the transition/action phase:

- **Availability of lethal means**: Access to lethal means appears to be central risk factor for suicidal behavior (e.g., Dempsey et al., 2019; Rogers et al., 2022) and a lack of (immediate) availability of lethal means may protect against entering the transition phase as identifying and obtaining lethal means when they are not available requires active problem solving and planning (cf. Nevarez-Flores et al., 2024).
- **Availability of (professional/private) support, reasons to live and skills**: Social and professional support, an explicit and easily retrievable knowledge of personal RFL and the availability of (behavioral and cognitive) coping skills in dealing with significant emotional crises seem to protect against showing a progression from the uncertainty phase to the transition phase (Kuehn et al., 2020).

Entering the transition phase seems to be accompanied by a change in the mental state of suicidal individuals: Michel (2023) highlights the importance of a dissociative state of mind in the immediate run-up to a suicidal act – in line with this the suicidal person may appear "zombie-like" to outsiders (Owens et al, 2019). Suicidal individuals in the transition phase describe an all-embracing "focus on death" (Joiner, 2024; Wenzel & Beck, 2008).

In general, the transition phase seems to be rather brief: When asked about the time that passed between the decision to die by suicide and the suicidal act, up to 48% of suicide attempters reported a period of less than 10 minutes (Paashaus et al, 2021; Simon et al, 2001; see also Millner et al, 2017; Xu et al., 2024). This points to the considerable dynamic of a suicidal crisis.

A non-violent exit from the transition phase is nevertheless possible; however, it often depends on chance factors: the phone rings, the cats scratch at the door, one is approached by a by-stander; or, to put it differently, something happens that "bursts the bubble" (Owens et al., 2019) the suicidal individual is captured in. Unavailability of lethal means or a sudden reminder of important social partners may also help to live through the transition phase: In such cases suicidal ambivalence might kick in again and a suicide attempt is aborted before the act of killing has been initiated.

5.4 Action Phase

The enactment of suicidal behavior marks the progression from the transition phase to the action phase. The action phase and the transition phase are closely interwoven and it can be assumed that the psychological state of suicidal individuals does not differ between the two phases. However, it should be emphasized that ambivalent experiences can also be reactivated after the initiation of a suicidal act: For example, the experience of pain during the suicidal act or the emergence of anxiety after taking medication can call into question the decision to die by suicide and put those affected in a state of ambivalence again. It should be emphasized that the ambivalence experienced at this point in the suicidal process may focus on different questions than during the uncertainty phase. For example, for methods that take time such as overdose, cutting or hanging individuals may ask "Should I call an ambulance?" or "Should I carry on despite the pain?" However, the underlying ambivalence for and against dying is essentially the same as the ambivalence experienced during the uncertainty phase: "Should I kill myself?" or "Should I keep on living?"

In this sense, 50% of suicide attempters reported in one study that they were still ambivalent during the suicide attempt (Kovacs & Beck, 1977). And even in the aftermath of a suicide attempt, 36% to 43% of suicide attempters report that they feel ambivalent about having survived (Bhaskara et al., 2014; Henriques et al., 2005); as such some, but not all individuals will re-enter the uncertainty phase after a suicide attempt. Taken together, this underlines the idea that cognitive and affective ambivalence accompanies the whole suicidal process.

5.5 Clinical Implications of the ABS-Model

In the event that suicidal individuals disclose suicidal ideation and behavior in a clinical context, the ABS-Model provides a framework for exploring the nature and individual functioning of suicidality (Teismann, Britton, & Forkmann, 2024a; Teismann & Forkmann, 2024). When dealing with suicidal patients in the uncertainty phase, the following steps should be taken:

1. Explore the nature and intensity of suicidal ideation, suicide plans, suicide intent, (lifetime) and suicidal behavior.
2. Obtain a picture of existing vulnerabilities and current stressors.
3. Focus on symptoms of overexcitement and rumination.
4. Explore the individual nature of suicidal ambivalence.

In the following, only the last point is discussed further; interested readers are referred to the relevant literature regarding the other aspects (e.g., Freedenthal, 2017; Teismann & Friedrich, 2022). With regard to the exploration of suicidal ambivalence, the literature on Motivational Interviewing with suicidal individuals provides detailed instructions (Britton et al., 2008, 2011, 2016, 2020a; Koban & Teismann, 2017). In a first step, patients are invited to reflect on the personally relevant

RFD (*What exactly makes you say that it is better for you to die?*), providing opportunity for development of therapeutic empathy and identifying targets for intervention. In a second step, RFL and RND become explored (*Is there a part of you – perhaps a very small one – that is not yet convinced about dying? Are there still obstacles on the way to suicide?*). RFL are explored in greater depth through active listening (*You are worried about your mother*), inquiries about specific examples (*Tell me a positive story that connects you with your mother*) or with a request for further clarification (*What exactly do you think will happen to your mother if you take your own life?*). In this way, suicidal individuals should be brought into (emotional) contact with reasons that conflict with the intention to die; they should experience the ways in which suicide conflicts with personally relevant goals and values. Finally, the motives against and for life are summarized before asking what changes and adjustments would be needed to make life worth living again (Britton et al., 2011). The aim of this approach is that suicidal ideators step back from immediate implementation intentions and become motivated to stay alive (for the time being) and seek further (therapeutic) help.

Together the precise exploration of ambivalent attitudes not only serves to motivate patients, but also forms the backbone of an individual case conceptualization and further treatment planning:

- **Individually significant RFD** – just like modifiable vulnerabilities and stressors – define the focus of therapy: If an individually significant RFD is, for example, feeling as a burden to others, therapy could focus on this belief and make use of cognitive therapy strategies to modify it. If an individually significant RFD is the perception that one does not belong, therapy might focus on social anxiety to overcome solitude and loneliness. If an individually significant RFD is the impression of being trapped in a hopeless situation, therapy might focus on problem-solving training to overcome entrapment (cf. Teismann & Friedrich, 2022).
- **Individually significant RFL** represent strengths and resources of suicidal individuals, that offer additional helpful hints on how to design the therapeutic process (including the therapeutic alliance), information, for example, on whom to invite to therapy (e.g., spouses, parents), increase self-efficacy and foster hope.

With the aim to prevent suicidal individuals from entering the transition phase suicidal individuals have to become prepared for dealing with strong suicidal impulses and urges: Means restriction counselling (Britton et al., 2016), safety planning or crisis response planning (Bryan & Rudd, 2018; Stanley & Brown, 2012), hope box interventions (Bryan & Rudd, 2018) and (cognitive and behavioral) skills training (Bryan & Rudd, 2018;

Linehan, 1993) are suitable interventions, that support suicidal individuals to establish behavioral control in dealing with suicidal impulses and possibly prevent them from entering the transition and action phases.

Finally, it should be noted that the interventions in dealing with immediate suicidality, that is, for people who are encountered in the transition phase, are not fundamentally different from strategies used in less acute crisis intervention situations. Still, the starting point is naturally different: the person must first step back from the edge of a tower block, put down a gun, untie a rope; that means a cautious approach and an offer of conversation based on understanding and respect is required. As the conversation progresses, a gentle focus on suicidal ambivalence (Omer & Elitzur, 2003), with particular emphasis on why the individual might want to continue living or not engage in suicidal behavior, may then become possible.

In general, the whole ABS-Model might also be used for psychoeducational purposes to inform suicidal individuals about our understanding of a suicidal crisis and to delineate the interventions used in crisis management and therapy.

5.6 Discussion

Suicidal ambivalence is a central characteristic of individuals in a suicidal crisis (Teismann, Siebert & Forkmann, 2024b), it can be addressed by clinicians at any stage of the suicidal process and used as a starting point for therapeutic interventions. By emphasizing the significance of ambivalence, the ABS-Model presented here attempts to provide a framework for understanding and treating suicidal individuals.

The ABS-Model shows similarities and differences with other contemporary suicide theories, such as the Interpersonal Theory of Suicidal Behavior (ITS; Joiner, 2005), the Integrative Motivational-Volitional (IMV) model of suicidal behavior (O'Connor & Kirtley, 2018) and the 3-Steps Theory (3-ST; Klonsky & May, 2015). The ABS-Model is – just like all the models mentioned – couched within an ideation-to-action framework (Díaz-Oliván et al., 2021) in that it clearly distinguishes suicidal ideation and its risk factors from suicidal behaviors and their (distinct) risk factors. In addition, the ABS-Model attaches particular importance to certain perceptions – such as perceived burdensomeness, thwarted belongingness, hopelessness, entrapment – which are understood as central drivers for suicidal ideation in other suicide theories (Joiner, 2005; O`Connor & Kirtley, 2018, Klonsky & May, 2015). Furthermore the ABS-Model, just like the other models, stresses the importance of availability of lethal means as an important risk factor for the transition from suicidal ideation to suicidal behavior. Finally, the ABS-Model implies – like the IMV model (O'Connor & Kirtley, 2018) –, a differentiation between a motivational and a volitional phase in the suicidal process. However, in contrast to the aforementioned models, the ABS-Model highlights the role of suicidal ambivalence and in this way explicitly takes into account not only suicidal drivers but also the importance of resources and protective factors for understanding suicidal crises (cf. Cheavens et al., 2015). With regard to the so-called suicide drivers (Jobes, 2023), the ABS-Model does not highlight specific perceptions (e.g., perceived burdensomeness, entrapment), allowing suicidal individuals to share their subjective understanding of which factors ("reasons for dying") they experience as particularly stressful and important (cf. Bryan & Rudd, 2018). The model furthermore explicitly emphasizes the unpredictability of suicidal behavior and attempts to describe the entire suicidal process. Most important and unlike the classic ideation-to-action models, the ABS-Model has been explicitly designed as a model of understanding and orientation for the treatment of suicidal patients, in particular, by providing guidance regarding how to attend to both sides of an individual's ambivalence as an individual progresses from uncertainty about engaging in suicidal behavior to action.

Yet, it has to be noted that despite the widespread consensus that ambivalence is a core characteristic of suicidal individuals (Evans & Farberow, 1988; Shneidman, 1996), there is comparatively little high-quality empirical research on suicidal ambivalence (Teismann et al., 2024b). In view of this, various model descriptions of the ABS-Model must be regarded as provisional.

With regard to clinical implications timing, for example, could be critical as it could generally be more beneficial to attend to the positive or negative side of ambivalence at different phases (i.e., uncertainty, transitional, action), or individual differences could impact the protective potential of addressing the positive or negative side of ambivalence (i.e., among people with or without reasons for living such as family or careers; Britton et al., 2020b). Further, most clinical interventions being studied today address ambivalence in some way, but a comprehensive description of similarities and differences across these interventions, as well as potential implication of the promoted strategies is beyond the scope of this chapter. However, none of this changes the fact that the model parameters can already be used as an orientation framework for the treatment of suicidal patients.

Note

1 The decision to die by suicide does not only depend on explicit decision-making factors, but also on immediate situational circumstances, opportunities and sensitivities of which a person may be unaware or only slightly aware (e.g.,

menstrual cycle or temperature changes; Lehmann et al., 2022, Tauseef et al., 2024). In consequence, suicidal individuals themselves can be surprised by the dynamics of suicidal crises.

References

Ajdacic-Gross, V., Hepp, U., Seifritz, E., & Bopp M. (2019). Rethinking suicides as mental accidents. *Journal of Affective Disorders, 252,* 141–151.

Bergmans, Y., Gordon, E., & Eynan, R. (2017). Surviving moment to moment: The experience of living in a state of ambivalence for those with recurrent suicide attempts. *Psychology and Psychotherapy, 90*, 633–648.

Bhaskara, J., Wang, Y., Roos, L., Sareen, J., Skakum, K., & Bolton, J. M. (2014). Method of suicide attempt and reactions to survival as predictors of repeat suicide attempts: A longitudinal analysis. *Journal of Clinical Psychiatry, 75*, e802–e808.

Britton, P. C., Bryan, C. J., & Valenstein, M. (2016). Motivational interviewing for means restriction counseling with patients at risk for suicide. *Cognitive and Behavioral Practice, 23*, 51–61.

Britton, P. C., Conner, K. R., Chapman, B. P., & Maisto, S. A. (2020a). Motivational interviewing to address suicide ideation: A randomized controlled trial I veterans. *Suicide and Life-Threatening Behavior, 50*, 233–248.

Britton, P. C., Conner, K. R., & Maisto, S. A. (2020b). The living ladder: Introduction and validity over 6-month follow-up of a one-item measure of readiness to continue living in suicidal patients. *Suicide and Life-Threatening Behavior, 50*, 1025–1040.

Britton, P. C., Patrick, H., Wenzel, A., & Williams, G. (2011). Integrating motivational interviewing and self-determination theory with cognitive behavioral therapy to prevent suicide. *Cognitive and Behavioral Practice, 18*, 16–27.

Britton, P. C., Williams, G. C., & Conner, K. R. (2008). Self-determination theory, motivational interviewing, and the treatment of clients with acute suicidal ideation. *Journal of Clinical Psychology, 64*, 52–66.

Brown, G. K., Steer, R. A., Henriques, G. R., & Beck, A. T. (2005). The internal struggle between the wish to die and the wish to live: A risk factor for suicide. *American Journal of Psychiatry, 162*(10), 1977–1979.

Bryan, C. J., & Rudd, M. D. (2018). *Brief cognitive behavioral therapy for suicide prevention*. New York: Guilford.

Buttlar, B., Pauer, S., & van Harreveld, F. (2024). The model of ambivalent choice and dissonant commitment: An integration of dissonance and ambivalence frameworks. *European Review of Social Psychology, 36*(1), 195–237. https://doi.org/10.1080/10463283.2024.2373547

Cheavens, J., Cukrowicz, K., Hansen, R. & Mitchell, S. (2015). Incorporating resilience factors into the Interpersonal Theory of Suicide: The role of hope and self-forgiveness in an older adult sample. *Journal of Clinical Psychology. 72*. https://doi.org/10.1002/jclp.22230

Chu, C., Buchman-Schmitt, J. M., Stanley, I. C. H., Hom, M. A., Tucker, R. P., Hagan, C. R., Rogers, M. L., Podlogar, M. C., Chiurliza, B., Ringer, F. B., Michaels, M. S., Patros, C. H. G., & Joiner, T. E. (2017). The interpersonal theory of suicide. A systematic review and meta-analysis of a decade of cross-national research. *Psychological Bulletin, 143*, 1313–1345.

Conner, M., & Sparks, P. (2002). Ambivalence and attitudes. *European Review of Social Psychology, 12*, 37–70. https://doi.org/10.1080/14792772143000012

de Beurs, D., Bockting, C., Kerkhof, A., Scheepers, F., O'Connor, R., Penninx, B., & van de Leemput, I. (2021). A network perspective on suicidal behavior: Understanding suicidality as a complex system. *Suicide & Life-Threatening Behavior, 51*(1), 115–126. https://doi.org/10.1111/sltb.12676

Dempsey, C. L., Benedek, D. M., Zuromski, K. L., Riggs-Donovan, C., Ng, T. H. H., Nock, M. K., Kessler, R. C., & Ursano, R. J. (2019). Association of firearm ownership, use, accessibility, and storage practices with suicide risk among US army soldiers. *JAMA Net Open, 2*, e195383.

Díaz-Oliván, I., Porras-Segovia, A., Barrigon, M., Jiménez-Muñoz, L., & Baca-Garcia, E. (2021). Theoretical models of suicidal behavior: A systematic review and narrative synthesis. *European Journal of Psychiatry, 35*, 181–192.

Ernst, M., Gemke, T. J., Olivi, L. J., & O'Connor, R. C. (2024). Ambulatory assessment of suicidal ambivalence: The temporal variability of the wish to live and the wish to die and their relevance in the concurrent and prospective prediction of suicidal desire. *Suicide & Life-Threatening Behavior, 54*, 831–843. https://doi.org/10.1111/sltb.13120

Evans, G., & Farberow, N. L. (1988). *The encyclopedia* of *suicide*. New York: Facts on File.

Fartacek, C., Fartacek, R., Schiepek, G. K., Sturm, J., Aichhorn, W., & Plöderl, M. (2024). Dynamic association between suicidal ambivalence and suicide risk among individuals with a history of suicide attempts. *Suicide & Life-Threatening Behavior, 54*, 860–868. https://doi.org/10.1111/sltb.13096

Favril, L., Yu, R., Uyar, A., Sharpe, M., & Fazel, S. (2022). Risk factors for suicide in adults: Systematic review and meta-analysis of psychological autopsy studies. *Evidence Based Mental Health, 25*, 148–155.

Franklin, J. C., Ribeiro, J. D., Fox, K. R., Bentley, K. H., Kleiman, E. M., Huang, X., Musacchio, K. M., Jaroszewski, A. C., Chang, B. P., & Nock, M. K. (2017). Risk factors for suicidal thoughts and behaviors: A meta-analysis of 50 years of research. *Psychological Bulletin, 143*, 187–232.

Freedenthal, S. (2017). *Helping the suicidal person*. Milton Park: Routledge.

Galasiński, D., & Ziółkowska, J. (2024). The end of ambivalence. A narrative perspective on ambivalence in the suicidal process. *Suicide & Life-Threatening Behavior, 54*(5), 888–899. https://doi.org/10.1111/sltb.13101

Harris, K. M., McLean, J. P., Sheffield, J., & Jobes, D. (2010). The internal suicide debate hypothesis: Exploring the life versus death struggle. *Suicide and Life-Threatening Behavior, 40*, 181–192.

Hawton, K., Lascelles, K., Pitman, A., Gilbert, S., & Silverman, M. (2022). Assessment of suicide risk in mental health practice: Shifting from prediction to therapeutic assessment, formulation, and risk management. *Lancet Psychiatry, 9*, 922–928.

Henriques, G., Wenzel, A., Brown, G. K., & Beck, A. T. (2005). Suicide Attempters´reaction to survival as a risk factor for eventual suicide. *American Journal of Psychiatry, 162*, 2180–2182.

Huang, X., Ribeiro, J. D., & Franklin, J. C. (2020). The differences between suicide ideators and suicide attempters: Simple, complicated, or complex? *Journal of Consulting and Clinical Psychology, 88*, 554–569.

Jobes, D. A. (2023). *Managing suicidal risk: A collaborative approach.* New York: Guilford Press.

Jobes, D. A., & Mann, R. E. (1999). Reasons for living versus reasons for dying: Examining the internal debate of suicide. *Suicide & Life-Threatening Behavior*, *29*(2), 97–104.

Joiner, T. E. (2024). *The varieties of suicidal experience.* New York: New York University Press.

Joiner, T. E. (2005). *Why people die by suicide.* Cambridge: Harvard University Press.

Klonsky, E. D., & May, A. M. (2015). The three-step theory (3ST): A new theory of suicide rooted in the "ideation-to-action" framework. *International Journal of Cognitive Therapy, 8,* 114–129.

Koban, C., & Teismann, T. (2017). Psychotherapy with suicidal patients: Understanding and improving the motivational starting point. *Psychotherapie Aktuell, 9*, 24–31.

Kovacs, M., & Beck, A. T. (1977). The wish to die and the wish to live in attempted suicides. *Journal of Clinical Psychology*, *33*, 361–365.

Kuehn, K. S., King, K. M., Linehan, M. M., & Harned, M. S. (2020). Modeling the suicidal behavior cycle: Understanding repeated suicide attempts among individuals with borderline personality disorder and a history of attempting suicide. *Journal of Consulting and Clinical Psychology, 88*, 570–581.

Lehmann, F., Alary, P. E., Rey, G., & Slama, R. (2022). Association of daily temperature with suicide mortality: A comparison with other causes of death and characterization of possible attenuation across 5 decades. *American Journal of Epidemiology*, *191*(12), 2037–2050. https://doi.org/10.1093/aje/kwac150

Linehan, M. M. (1993). *Cognitive-behavioral treatment of Borderline Personality Disorder*. New York: Guilford Press.

Linehan, M. M., Goodstein, J. L., Nielsen, S. L., & Chiles, J. A. (1983). Reasons for staying alive when you are thinking of killing yourself: The reasons for living inventory. *Journal of Consulting and Clinical Psychology*, *51*, 276–286.

Madsen, J., & Harris, K. M. (2021). Negative self-appraisal: Personal reasons for dying as indicators of suicidality. *PloS One*, *16*(2), e0246341. https://doi.org/10.1371/journal.pone.0246341

Michel, K. (2023). *The suicidal person*. New York: Columbia University Press.

Millner, A. J., Lee, M. D., & Nock, M. K. (2017). Describing and measuring the pathway to suicide attempts: A preliminary study. *Suicide and Life-Threatening Behavior*, 47, 353–369.

Nevarez-Flores, A. G., Pandey, V., Angelucci, A. P., Neil, A. L., McDermott, B., & Castle, D. (2025). Means restriction for suicide prevention: An umbrella review. *Acta Psychiatrica Scandinavica*, *151*(6), 653–667. https://doi.org/10.1111/acps.13783

O'Connor, R. C., & Kirtley, O. (2018). The integrated motivational-volitional model of suicidal behaviour. *Philosophical Transactions of the Royal Society of London. Series B, Biological sciences*, *373*, 20170268.

Omer, H., & Elitzur, A. (2003). How to talk to the "person on the roof?" *PiD, 4*, 354–359.

Owens, C., Derges, J., & Abraham, C. (2019). Intervening to prevent a suicide in a public place: A qualitative study of effective interventions by lay people. *BMJ Open, 9*: e032319.

Paashaus, L., Forkmann, T., Glaesmer, H., Juckel, G., Rath, D., Schönfelder, A., & Teismann, T. (2021). From decision to action: Suicidal history and time between decision to die and actual suicide attempt. *Clinical Psychology and Psychotherapy, 28*, 1427–1434.

Risch, N., Alacreu-Crespo, A., Khan, S., Caceda, R., Teismann, T., Rogers, M., Courtet, P., & Olié, E. (2024). Pain tolerance and threshold in suicide attempters: A systematic review and meta-analysis. *Psychiatry Research, 331*, 113618.

Rogers, M. L., Gai, A. R., & Joiner, T. E. (2022). Fluctuations in and associations between physical and psychological distance to suicide methods, fearlessness about death, and suicidal intent. *Journal of Psychopathology and Clinical Science, 131*, 868–880.

Shneidman, E. S. (1996). *The suicidal mind.* Oxford: Oxford University Press.

Simon, T., Swann, A., Powell, K., Potter, L., Kresnow, M., & O'Carroll, P. (2001). Characteristics of impulsive suicide attempts and attempters. *Suicide and Life-Threatening Behavior, 32*, 49–59.

Soper, C. A., Malo Ocejo, P., & Large, M. (2022). On the randomness of suicide: An evolutionary, clinical call to transcend suicide risk assessment. In R. Abed R & P. St John-Smith (Eds.), *Evolutionary psychiatry: Evolutionary perspectives on mental health* (pp. 134–152). Cambridge, UK: Cambridge University Press.

Stanley, B., & Brown, G. K. (2012). Safety planning intervention: A brief intervention to mitigate suicide risk. *Cognitive and Behavioral Practice, 19*, 256–264.

Tauseef, H. A., Coppersmith, D. D. L., Reid-Russell, A. J., Nagpal, A., Ross, J., Nock, M. K., & Eisenlohr-Moul, T. (2024). A call to integrate menstrual cycle influences into just-in-time adaptive interventions for suicide prevention. *Frontiers in Psychiatry, 15*, 1434499. https://doi.org/10.3389/fpsyt.2024.1434499

Teismann, T., Britton, P. C., & Forkmann, T. (2024a). Ambivasslence model of suicidality [ABS-model]: An orientation model for the treatment of suicidal individuals. *Frontiers in Psychiatry, 15*, 1449565.

Teismann, T., & Forkmann, T. (2024). Ambivalenzmodell der Suizidalität (ABS-Modell): Ein Verstehens- und Orientierungsmodell für die Behandlung suizidaler Personen. *Verhaltenstherapie, 34*, 85–92.

Teismann, T., & Friedrich, S. (2022). *Therapie-Tools: Suizidalität und Krisenintervention.* Weinheim: Beltz.

Teismann, T., Hilbert, K., & Forkmann, T. (2022). Prädiktion suizidalen Verhaltens: Von der klinischen Urteilsbildung zur künstlichen Intelligenz. *Nervenheilkunde*, 41, 253–257.

Teismann, T., Siebert, A., & Forkmann, T. (2024b). Suicidal ambivalence: A scoping review. *Suicide and Life-Threatening Behavior, 54*, 802–813.

van Harreveld, F., Rutjens, B. T., Rotteveel, M., Nordgren, L. F., & van der Pligt, J. (2009a). Ambivalence and decisional conflict as a cause of psychological discomfort: Feeling tense before jumping off the fence. *Journal of Experimental Social Psychology, 45*(1), 167–173. https://doi.org/10.1016/j.jesp.2008.08.015

van Harreveld, F., van der Pligt, J., & de Liver, Y. N. (2009b). The agony of ambivalence and ways to resolve it: Introducing the MAID model. *Personality and Social Psychology Review*, *13*(1), 45–61. https://doi.org/10.1177/1088868308324518

Van Wyk, J., & Gibson, K. (2022). An analysis of young clients communications about their suicidality on a text message helpline: "I`m scared of what I might do to myself". *Frontiers in Psychiatry, 13*, 925830.

Wenzel, A., & Beck, A. T. (2008). A cognitive model of suicidal behavior: Theory and treatment. *Applied Preventive Psychology, 12*, 189–201.

Woodford, R., Spittal, M. J., Milner, A., McGill, K., Kapur, N., Pirkis, J., Mitchell, A., & Carter G. (2019). Accuracy of clinician predictions of future self-harm: A systematic review and meta-analysis of predictive studies. *Suicide and Life-Threatening Behavior*, 49, 23–40.

Xu, I., Millner, A. J., Fortgang, R. G., & Nock, M. K. (2024). Suicide decision-making: Differences in proximal considerations between individuals who aborted and attempted suicide. *Suicide & Life-Threatening Behavior*, *54*, 814–830. https://doi.org/10.1111/sltb.13127

6 Competing Motives and Forces

A Complex Systems View of Suicidal Ambivalence

Craig J. Bryan and Melanie Bozzay

6.1 Introduction

Although significant advances have been made in our understanding of suicide risk in recent decades, efforts to prevent suicide remain hampered by our general inability to reliably determine *who* will try to end their life and *when*. During the past few decades, researchers have addressed this issue by developing new theories and models of suicide that seek to describe the causal processes that lead to suicidal thoughts and behaviors (Klonsky & May, 2015; O'Connor & Kirtley, 2018; Van Orden et al., 2010). Although each theory emphasizes different variables and processes, all are based to some degree on the concept of emergence—the process by which something comes into being (Goldstein, 1999). Emergent phenomena are not caused by any single event or cause; rather, they come into being because of complex interactions among multiple variables and components. Owing to this complexity, the behavior of emergent phenomena typically cannot be explained by the behavior of its constituent components. Said another way, the whole is greater than the sum of its parts. For this reason, suicide cannot be readily explained or predicted by its many risk factors and presumed causes (e.g., depression, hopelessness, suicidal thinking), even when using complicated algorithms developed using sophisticated methods like machine learning and artificial intelligence (Fazel & O'Reilly, 2020; Schafer et al., 2021).

Our inability to reliably predict suicide does not mean we cannot recognize when someone may be trying to end their life, however. Rather, this current situation implicates the need to approach the problem from a different perspective. In this chapter, we outline one such perspective that uses suicidal ambivalence—the intrapsychic struggle between the wish to live and the wish to die—as a complex dynamic process that is directly related to the emergence of suicidal behavior. We first provide an overview of emergence and several of its core principles, next discuss how suicidal ambivalence can be understood from an emergence framework, and

DOI: 10.4324/9781003616221-9

conclude with an illustrative example showing how this approach can help us understand the process by which people transition from a state in which they are not trying to die by suicide to a state in which they are.

6.2 Core Principles of Emergence

Suicide researchers have increasingly argued that suicide is best understood as an emergent property of complex systems (Bryan et al., 2020; De Beurs et al., 2021; de Beurs et al., 2023; Franklin, 2019). A system can be defined as a set of coherently organized and interconnected components or parts that produce a usual or typical pattern of behaviors (Meadows, 2008). Systems are considered complex when their overall behavior cannot be readily modeled or predicted based on the behavior of their individual parts. This is because the system's components are interdependent, meaning the behavior of one component influences the behavior of (and may, in turn, be influenced by) the behavior of other components. Said another way, A influences B and C but B and C also influence A; moreover, B may also influence C and C may influence B in return. As applied to suicide, we know that suicide can result from a multitude of interrelated and mutually influential factors and processes like thoughts (hopelessness, perceived burdensomeness), emotions (depression, anger), biological processes (sleep disturbance, agitation), behaviors (substance use, social withdrawal), and environmental circumstances (relationship problems, financial strain). These various components of the human condition are perpetually pushing and pulling on each other, leading to a wide range of human behaviors and experiences that cannot be readily explained by any single component or combination of components.

As applied to suicide, change in any given risk factor or component therefore does not necessarily yield a proportional change in probability of suicidal behavior. A 10% increase in depression, for instance, does not necessarily increase the risk of suicide by 10%; a 10% decrease similarly does not necessarily decrease the risk of suicide by that same amount. For this reason, most people will not try to kill themselves even when experiencing an increase in risk factors and, conversely, suicides sometimes occur among people who are experiencing improvements in their risk factors (e.g., they die despite "getting better"). This nonproportionality arises from the interdependencies of the system's components and the tendency of systems to maintain equilibrium over time, such that change in one part of the system is often counteracted by change in another part of the system. By itself, changing depression thus does not necessarily translate directly to a proportional change in suicide risk because change in our emotional state is interconnected with our life circumstances, thoughts, behaviors, and biological processes. When depression increases, our thoughts, biological processes, and behaviors will typically react to this change a way that counteracts that increase, "pulling" depression back to its typical levels and returning the system to its homeostatic equilibrium. In response to a transient increase in depression, for instance, someone may experience an internal drive to contact friends or loved ones, leading to a new external context that competes with the depressive state. Over time, these complex interactions among a system's many components fall into usual or typical patterns, allowing for a reasonable degree of stability and predictability in their behavior over time. Occasionally, however, unexpected and (in some cases) never-before-seen behaviors occur—someone may attempt suicide, for instance. This departure from the usual and typical pattern is the essence of emergence—the coming into being of something that did not previously exist.

To illustrate, consider a simple example: water. Water is made up of many interacting molecules and has three distinct states: solid (ice), liquid (water), and gas (vapor or steam). The state that water is in at any given time is controlled by two key variables—temperature and pressure. When in its solid state (ice), water's molecules bond together and are arranged in a rigid tetrahedral structure. As the temperature increases, water remains in its solid state until the temperature reaches 0 degrees Celsius (32 degrees Fahrenheit). At this temperature, the heat energy flowing into the ice surpasses the strength of the molecular forces that hold the water molecules together and a new behavior pattern emerges: the water molecules begin breaking apart and recombining over and over, falling out of their previously rigid tetrahedral structure. This newly emergent pattern marks the transition from one state (solid) to a new state (liquid). Water molecules continue to behave in this new way until the temperature reaches 100 degrees Celsius (212 degrees Fahrenheit), at which point another behavior pattern emerges—the water molecules break apart completely but do not recombine, such that the individual molecules can move independently. This newly emergent pattern marks yet another transition from liquid to gas.

The thresholds that separate water's three states are not dictated by temperature alone; the boundaries that separate the three states are also influenced by air pressure. As air pressure rises, water's melting point changes very little but its evaporating point quickly increases. At 2 atmospheres, for instance—approximately double the typical air pressure we experience on Earth—the threshold for transitioning from liquid to gas (water's boiling point) increases from 100 to 120 degrees Celsius; more heat energy than usual is therefore needed for the state transition to occur. Conversely, at 0.5 atmospheres—approximately half the typical air pressure we experience on Earth—water's boiling point drops to 81 degrees Celsius, meaning less heat energy than usual is needed for the state transition to occur. Interestingly, under very extreme conditions—when air pressure is less than 0.06 atmospheres, or just 6% of the typical air pressure we experience on Earth—water transitions directly from its solid state to its gas state, skipping over the liquid state completely, a process known as sublimation. Note that transitions from one state to another are not caused by the interacting molecules themselves; how and when water transitions from one state to another therefore cannot be readily explained by the behavior of its constituent molecules. Instead, emergent patterns of interaction, governed by two external variables, dictate the state transitions. Change in the overall behavior of water thus arises from external global conditions rather than its internal components.

Like water, suicide risk has multiple distinct states that are characterized by qualitatively unique patterns of interactions among its components—instead of molecules, however, the components that give rise to suicide are thoughts, emotions, biological processes, and behaviors. Because suicide is binary—people are either trying to end their life (we will call this the high-risk state) or they are not (we will call this the low-risk state)—at least two suicide risk states must exist. It is possible that more than two states exist but for the sake of parsimony and clarification, we limit ourselves in this chapter to only two states. According to the principles of emergence, the ways in which a person's thoughts, emotions, biological processes, and behaviors interact when they are attempting suicide will differ from how these components interact when someone is *not* attempting suicide. Just as the behavior of individual water molecules reveals information about its current state and can provide information about vulnerability to a state change, the behavior a person's thoughts, emotions, biological processes, and behaviors can also reveal information about a person's current suicide risk state and provide information about when a state change may occur. Suicidal ambivalence, which is marked by conflicting desires to live and die, is especially well-suited for characterizing the patterns that differentiate low- and high-risk states.

6.3 Suicidal Ambivalence

Suicidal ambivalence has been defined in multiple ways by various researchers, all of which include some form of intrapsychic struggle between two competing motives: the wish to die, which pushes people toward suicide, and the wish to live, which pulls people away from suicide. This fluctuating state of ambivalence has come to be seen by many suicide researchers as one of the most important and defining psychological features of the suicidal state (Evans & Farberow, 2003; Harris et al., 2010; Kovacs & Beck, 1977; Shneidman, 1998; Teismann et al., 2024). Shneidman (1998), for instance, argued that suicidal ambivalence "occurs in almost every case of suicide" (p. 129). Indeed, around half of those who are trying to die by suicide report experiencing ambivalence at the time of their suicide attempt (Kovacs & Beck, 1977) and over 90% of those with suicidal ideation describe feeling this ambivalence (Harris et al., 2010).

Central to ambivalence is the presence of conflicting perspectives or feelings. Consistent with this view, suicide researchers have adopted a model of suicidal ambivalence that places the wish to live and the wish to die on opposing ends of a unidimensional continuum, with ambivalence falling between these two extremes (Figure 6.1). Researchers have found that the relative balance between the wish to live and the wish to die can be a useful indicator of someone's risk for suicide. Brown et al. (2005), for instance, reported that risk of suicide death was much higher for people reporting a strong wish to die with no wish to live (i.e., located on the far right of the continuum) as compared to people reporting suicidal ambivalence (i.e., located in the center of the continuum) or a strong wish to live with no wish to die (i.e., located on the far left of the continuum). These findings are generally consistent with clinical best practices in suicide risk assessment, which emphasize weighing the relative balance of the factors that promote suicide to the factors that protect against suicide as a strategy for characterizing a patient's level of suicide risk (Bryan & Rudd, 2010).

Moreover, research also implicates the balance of a person's wish to live relative to their wish to die as an important factor that is specific to suicide risk. Indeed, Brown et al. (2005) found that ambivalence scores predicted death by suicide but no other manner of death (i.e., natural causes, homicide, or accident). These findings suggest that ambivalence may not be simply a *correlate* of suicide risk severity but rather a core

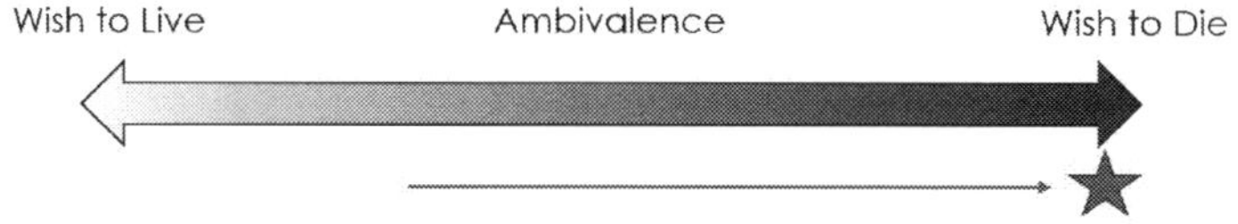

Figure 6.1 Suicidal ambivalence as a unidimensional continuum anchored by a strong wish to live combined with an absence of wish to die on one end, a strong wish to die combined with an absence of wish to live on the other end, and suicidal ambivalence in the middle. Using this approach, increasingly negative values and increasingly positive values represent reduced ambivalence in competing directions. Accordingly, suicide can only be approached from a single direction (from the left), corresponding to an increase in the wish to die and decrease in the wish to live.

Source: Figure by Craig Bryan.

process that influences suicide's emergence. If true, suicide could potentially be prevented not only by reducing someone's wish to die but also by strengthening their wish to live, even if only modestly. Thus, if someone is located on the far right of the continuum in Figure 6.1, where most (if not all) suicides occur, it may not be necessary to move them all the way to the left end of the continuum to prevent their suicide; moving them to center (or close to it) may be good enough. Understanding how and why the wish to live and the wish to die change over time is therefore critical for understanding when someone is vulnerable to attempting suicide and how to reduce this vulnerability.

Implicit in this view is the assumption that the wish to live and the wish to die are dynamic. This notion of suicidal ambivalence as a variable in constant flux aligns with broader theory and empirical findings showing that suicide risk is an inherently dynamic construct. Indeed, people are not *always* suicidal—they *become* suicidal—consistent with state transitions and the principles of emergence. Unfortunately, our understanding of these change processes is limited because, historically, suicidal ambivalence has been measured at only a single point in time. Emerging research suggests that the relative balance between the wish to live and wish to die fluctuates, however. Contemporary research methodologies like ecological momentary assessment (EMA), which facilitates repeated measurement of psychological (e.g., suicidal ideation, mood) and contextual (e.g., location, time) suicide-related variables in real-time, has revealed important information about how various aspects of suicide risk naturally occur in the real world. A key finding of this research is that people move in and out of suicidal states, with state transitions often occurring suddenly and rapidly. In one study, for instance, around 90% of participants reported a one standard deviation or larger increase in the intensity of suicidal ideation within only a few hours (Kleiman et al., 2017), indicating rapid shifts from low-risk to high-risk states. These studies have also shown that suicide risk is multidimensional, with some facets of suicide risk changing more quickly than others. Suicidal desire, for example, ebbs and flows gradually over many hours and days whereas the urge to kill oneself—often referred to as suicidal intent—erupts suddenly within a matter of minutes to hours and then just as quickly resolves (Coppersmith et al., 2022).

Preliminary evidence also shows that the wish to live and the wish to die are similarly dynamic, although the nature and time scale of these changes remain poorly understood and understudied. Consistent with the unidimensional continuum model depicted by Figure 6.1, it is generally thought that the wish to live and wish to die fluctuate together in opposing directions, such that individuals with higher wish to live have a lower wish to die and vice versa. Research suggests that this assumption may not be supported in all circumstances, however. In one study of suicidal ambivalence (Bryan et al., 2016), researchers repeatedly measured the wish to live and the wish to die among suicidal adults every few months during and after mental health treatment. Consistent with the idea of suicidal ambivalence as a dynamic construct, both the wish to live and the wish to die fluctuated over time, but not in a way that fully aligned with the continuum model. In that study, the wish to live and the wish to die were negatively correlated with one another on average, meaning the wish to live was usually elevated when the wish to die was reduced, and vice versa. Over time, however, change in the wish to live and change in the wish to die disconnected from one another, such that when the wish to live increased, the wish to die sometimes decreased but other times increased and still other times did not change at all. The same was true in the reverse direction—an increase in the wish to die sometimes corresponded to a decrease, sometimes an increase, and other times no change in the wish to live.

This finding suggests that suicidal ambivalence sometimes behaves like a unidimensional continuum but other times it behaves instead as though it is a two-dimensional variable wherein the wish to live and the wish to die function independently. This two-dimensional model is depicted in Figure 6.2 as a Cartesian-like plane with the wish to live and the wish to die as separate axes, which allows each motive to change independently of the other. One implication of the two-dimensional model is the potential existence of qualitatively distinct states of ambivalence. For example, the co-occurrence of a strong wish to live and a strong wish to die—corresponding to the upper right corner of Figure 6.2—may characterize a subjective state of inner turmoil or struggle related to these competing motives. By comparison, the co-occurrence of a weak (or absent) wish to live and a weak (or absent) wish to die—corresponding to the lower left corner—may instead characterize a subjective state of indifference about living and dying. In contrast, the co-occurrence of a strong wish to live and a weak wish to die—corresponding to the lower right corner—may indicate a strong and largely unwavering certainty about living while the co-occurrence of a weak wish to live and a strong wish to die—corresponding to the upper right corner—may reflect the experience of heightened suicidal resolve and heightened risk for making a suicide attempt. It is in this upper left corner that we would expect most, if not all, suicidal behaviors to occur.

An advantage of the two-dimensional model relative to the unidimensional model is the potential to account for a much broader range of risk trajectories. If we assume that most (if not all) suicidal behaviors occur when someone experiences a strong wish to die combined with a diminished wish to live, suicidal behavior will generally be located on the right side of Figure 6.1 and the bottom right corner of Figure 6.2. In the unidimensional model, suicide can emerge from only a single direction—moving from the left to the right of the continuum, corresponding to an increase in the wish to live and decrease in the wish to die. Though intuitive, this single process does not account for the multitude of qualitatively distinct trajectories that are known to precede suicide. Some suicides occur quickly without much forethought, for example, while others are carefully planned over lengthy periods of time (Bryan et al., 2023; Chaudhury et al., 2016; Conner, 2004; Conner et al., 2007; Jeon et al., 2010), and some suicides occur after very long periods of persistently negative emotions whereas other suicides occur during emotional tumult and instability (Bryan et al., 2019; Kleiman et al., 2018; Kleiman et al., 2017).

Unlike the unidimensional model, the two-dimensional model allows for this variability. In Figure 6.2, the upper left corner can be approached from multiple angles and directions. These various trajectories are, in turn, associated with the different types of suicidal ambivalence described above.

Although it is theoretically possible for suicide to emerge from any trajectory and ambivalence state, it is likely that some presentations of ambivalence are more conducive to becoming suicidal than others. For

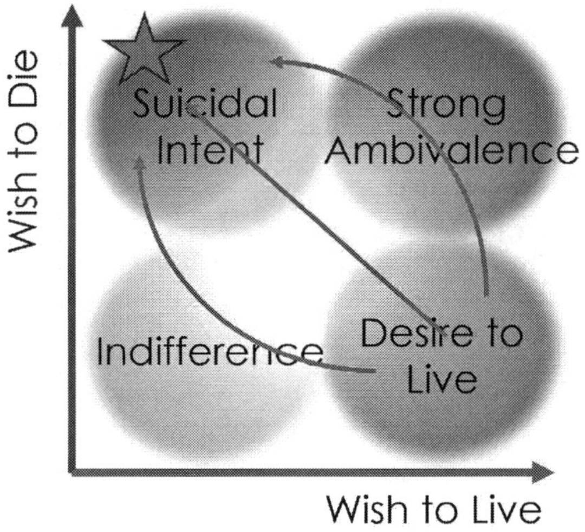

Figure 6.2 Suicidal ambivalence as a two-dimensional construct. A consequence of this model is the potential existence of multiple "types" of suicidal ambivalence and multiple potential pathways or trajectories to suicide that traverse these different types of ambivalence. Although there are potentially infinite pathways to suicide, some pathways will be more probable than others. By extension, some types of suicidal ambivalence will be more conducive to suicide than others.

example, individuals with a strong, certain sense about their wish to die with almost no wish to live may be more prone to experience a higher level of suicide risk in general. In contrast, individuals who are in a state of ambivalence characterized by strong inner turmoil may be more reactive to life events—being more likely to experience an increase in suicide risk or make a suicide attempt in the presence of a triggering event or significant life stressor, or even, conversely, a reduction in suicide risk if life circumstances shift more positively. However, given that states of ambivalence are found across the spectrum of suicide risk—among individuals who are having suicidal thoughts and even among those who have made an attempt (Harris et al., 2010; Kovacs & Beck, 1977)—it is likely that there are other factors that must occur together with suicidal ambivalence to galvanize the emergence of higher suicide risk states within which suicidal behaviors are especially probable.

6.4 Suicidal Ambivalence as Competing Forces to Preserve or Disrupt Equilibrium

As noted previously, a central assumption of emergence is the existence of multiple discrete states of being. Because suicide is binary—it either occurs or it does not—suicide requires at least two states of being: one in which someone is attempting suicide (i.e., high-risk state) and another in which someone is not attempting suicide (i.e., low-risk state). Each of these states is distinguished by qualitatively distinct interrelationships among key processes. Preliminary research supports this important point: different suicidal states are characterized by qualitatively distinct patterns of interactions among thoughts, emotions, biological processes, and behaviors (Kaurin et al., 2022). Understanding how the wish to live and the wish to die interact with each other (and other variables) in each state could therefore advance our ability to recognize when someone is especially vulnerable to suicide.

To illustrate, consider the three hypothetical trajectories to suicide depicted in Figure 6.2, representing three different ways that someone could transition from the low-risk state in the lower right to the high-risk state in the upper left. Because humans never or only rarely try to end their life, low-risk states can be understood as the "default setting" for humans. People will therefore spend nearly all their time experiencing a strong wish to live combined with a weak wish to die. Furthermore, if they move away from this location owing to a momentary decrease in their wish to live (movement to the left) and/or a momentary increase in their wish to die (upward movement), they will usually return to their starting point because complex systems are designed to maintain stability and equilibrium. In systems language, these forces of equilibrium are called *attractor dynamics* because they resist change and hold the system together, like gravity. The wish to live and the wish to die are therefore anchored to this location. As people spend more and more time in the lower right area, the attractor dynamics that maintain the default setting strengthen, contributing to the long-term coherence and stability of the low-risk state (Prigogine & Stengers, 2018). When attractor dynamics are strong, the system therefore resists change and rapidly returns to its default setting whenever its typical pattern is disrupted. Under these conditions, movement away from the lower right region, therefore, occurs infrequently, is small in magnitude, and short in duration.

Conversely, when attractor dynamics are weak, the system is easier to change and takes longer to return to its default setting; movement away from the lower right region is therefore more probable, larger in magnitude, and longer in duration. Many possible factors can influence the strength of these attractor dynamics: interpersonal conflict, financial strain, occupational stress, abuse, victimization, and/or loss could, for example, temporarily diminish the wish to live and/or increase the wish to die, pushing people away from their default setting. Factors that disrupt a state's typical pattern are called *perturbations*. Over time, repeated exposure to perturbations can disrupt the low-risk state's usual and typical patterns, weakening its attractor dynamics and increasing the probability of transitioning to a high-risk state and suicidal behavior. Under these conditions, suicidal ambivalence will be experienced more often. The low-risk state's typical patterns can also be disrupted by perturbations that are so sudden and forceful that the attractor dynamics are quickly overridden. Under these circumstances, people may transition to a high-risk state so quickly that they experience suicidal ambivalence for only a brief moment before they are trying to end their life.

To illustrate these concepts, note how all three state transitions depicted in Figure 6.2 pass through some form of ambivalence running from the lower right to the upper left of the figure. As the boundary that separates the low-risk and high-risk states, this region of suicidal ambivalence also serves as the boundary that separates their unique attractor dynamics. Within this region of ambivalence, the attractor dynamics that govern each state reach their limit of influence—once someone crosses this threshold, the influence of one state is overtaken by the influence of the other, just as the molecular forces that hold water molecules together are overtaken by the forces of heat when the temperature crosses 0 degrees Celsius—water's melting point. Once the threshold is passed, a new set of rules apply and the system changes. Because of this, the emergence of suicide is expected to progress through several phases that can serve as signals or "warning signs." First, as someone moves away from their default setting in the lower right, they will experience increased inner tension or unease—a feeling that something is "off" or "not right." This reflects the inability of the low-risk state's attractor dynamics to pull the person back to their default setting and re-establish equilibrium. The person feels "off" because their usual or typical pattern has been disrupted.

As the person continues to move toward the region of ambivalence, their wish to live and wish to die will next begin to fluctuate. These fluctuations will increase in frequency and intensity as they approach the boundary separating the two states, reflecting the weakening influence of the low-risk state's attractor dynamics that continue to pull the person toward the lower right, albeit with greatly diminished force, and the growing influence of the high-risk state's attractor dynamics that pull the person toward the upper left. At this point, the person will likely report feeling like they are "on a roller coaster" of ups and downs. The tension between opposing forces continues to mount until the threshold separating the two states is reached. Here, tension between the two states' competing forces is maximized and the person is likely to describe experiencing an internal debate or suicidal "mulling" (e.g., "Should I do it or not?")—the very essence of ambivalence. If the threshold separating the two states is crossed, the high-risk state's attractor dynamics overrides the attractor dynamics of the low-risk state, and the person rapidly moves toward the upper left region and attempts suicide.

These "stages" in the trajectory toward suicide align with empirical findings. In a study aimed at understanding suicidal trajectories, for instance, Millner et al. (2017) interviewed people soon after they attempted suicide and found that ambivalence or "mulling," which was defined as "strongly considering attempting suicide, perhaps going back and forth in one's mind about whether to do it or not" (p. 357), was commonly experienced in the time before a suicide attempt. Interestingly, Millner et al. found that this ambivalent state tended to occur either days to weeks before the attempt or less than a few minutes to hours before the attempt, suggesting two very different pathways to suicide—one that involves a longer transition (and therefore possibly more readily detectable in advance) and one that involves a rapid and sudden transition (and therefore less difficult to detect in advance). Ambivalence thus appears to coincide with a "tipping point" of sorts, consistent with the notion of a threshold or boundary between two states characterized by different forces.

Within the context of emergence and complex systems, these findings preliminarily suggest that information about a person's current risk state (e.g., where are they located) and the stability of their current risk state (e.g., are they able to quickly return to their default setting?) reveal clues about their vulnerability to suicidal behavior (e.g., are they approaching or moving away from a threshold separating two states?).

6.5 Implications for Suicide Prevention

Viewing suicidal ambivalence as a conceptual threshold or tipping point that must be crossed for someone to attempt suicide implicates the possibility of ambivalence serving as an early indicator or "warning sign" of emerging suicidal behavior and method for optimizing the effectiveness of prevention and treatment strategies. Treatments and interventions that strengthen the attractor dynamics of low-risk states could reduce long-term vulnerability to suicidal behavior, for instance. Consider as well how the three trajectories depicted in Figure 6.2 might implicate different strategies for preventing a state transition. The upper pathway that first moves up then curves to the left may benefit the most from an intervention that reduces the wish to die. By comparison, the lower pathway that first moves left then curves up would instead benefit the most from an intervention that strengthens the wish to live. Finally, the middle pathway that moves straight up and to the left may benefit from either or both. Multiple distinct strategies are therefore needed to achieve the shared goal of returning as many people as possible to their default setting in the lower right.

Now imagine three different people who are also experiencing suicidal ambivalence after they tried to take their own lives. In these cases, the three trajectories move in the *reverse* directions, from the upper left to the lower right. Owing to this difference in context, "resolving ambivalence" takes on a very different meaning. In the immediate aftermath of trying to take one's life, "resolving ambivalence" could inadvertently strengthen the attractor dynamics of the high-risk state, pulling the trajectories back to the upper left region and slowing the return to a low-risk state—the opposite of the desired effect. In these cases, achieving the desired outcome of returning the person to their default setting in the lower right might require interventions that initially *induce* ambivalence. After the transition from high-risk to low-risk state occurs, interventions that serve to *resolve* ambivalence could then be implemented. This distinction in ambivalence induction versus resolution appears to underlie the effects of brief cognitive behavioral therapy (BCBT) for suicide prevention, a specialized psychotherapy that has been shown to significantly reduce suicidal behaviors (Baker et al., 2024; Diefenbach et al., 2025; Rudd et al., 2015; Sinyor et al., 2020). In a study investigating patterns of change in the wish to live and the wish to die in BCBT and other mental health treatments (Bryan et al., 2016), researchers found that BCBT patients who did not go on trying to kill themselves displayed a unique change pattern suggesting the treatment facilitated return to low-risk states and increased resistance to high-risk states. Suicidal behavior was therefore prevented not only because people had an increase in their wish to live and a decrease in their wish to die, but also because the "pull" of the low-risk state's default state was magnified while the "pull" of the high-risk state was diminished.

6.6 Summary

Suicidal ambivalence is a psychological state commonly experienced prior to many suicidal behaviors. Often experienced as an "inner debate" between competing motives to live and die, ambivalence involves fluctuations in the wish to live and the wish to die. Although it has historically been conceptualized as a unidimensional continuum wherein the wish to live and the wish to die nullify or "cancel out" one another, newer thinking and research based on complexity theory and the concept of emergence suggest suicidal ambivalence may be better understood and modeled as a two-dimensional construct, where the wish to live and the wish to die can change independently. This perspective implicates the existence of multiple trajectories to suicide, suggests suicidal ambivalence could reflect the process of transitioning from low-risk to high-risk states, and implicates the need for more nuanced consideration of how interventions and strategies should be designed and implemented to effectively prevent suicide. In the end, suicidal ambivalence is more than just the tension that arises from competing motives to live and die; it also reflects the tension that arises from competing forces that serve to maintain versus disrupt the patterns of thoughts, emotions, biological processes, and behaviors that typify low-risk states.

References

Baker, J. C., Starkey, A., Ammendola, E., Bauder, C. R., Daruwala, S. E., Hiser, J., ... & Bryan, C. J. (2024). Telehealth brief cognitive behavioral therapy for suicide prevention: A randomized clinical trial. *JAMA Network Open*, 7(11), e2445913–e2445913.

Brown, G. K., Steer, R. A., Henriques, G. R., & Beck, A. T. (2005). The internal struggle between the wish to die and the wish to live: A risk factor for suicide. *American Journal of Psychiatry*, *162*(10), 1977–1979.

Bryan, C. J., Allen, M. H., Wastler, H. M., Bryan, A. O., Baker, J. C., May, A. M., & Thomsen, C. J. (2023). Rapid intensification of suicide risk preceding suicidal behavior among primary care patients. *Suicide and Life-Threatening Behavior*, *53*(3), 352–361.

Bryan, C. J., Butner, J. E., May, A. M., Rugo, K. F., Harris, J. A., Oakey, D. N., Rozek, D. C., & Bryan, A. O. (2020). Nonlinear change processes and the emergence of suicidal behavior: A conceptual model based on the fluid vulnerability theory of suicide. *New Ideas in Psychology*, *57*, 100758.

Bryan, C. J., Rozek, D. C., Butner, J., & Rudd, M. D. (2019). Patterns of change in suicide ideation signal the recurrence of suicide attempts among high-risk psychiatric outpatients. *Behaviour Research and Therapy*, *120*, 103392.

Bryan, C. J., & Rudd, M. D. (2010). *Managing suicide risk in primary care.* Springer Publishing Company.

Bryan, C. J., Rudd, M. D., Peterson, A. L., Young-McCaughan, S., & Wertenberger, E. G. (2016). The ebb and flow of the wish to live and the wish to die among suicidal military personnel. *Journal of Affective Disorders, 202*, 58–66.

Chaudhury, S. R., Singh, T., Burke, A., Stanley, B., Mann, J. J., Grunebaum, M., Sublette, M. E., & Oquendo, M. A. (2016). Clinical correlates of planned and unplanned suicide attempts. *The Journal of Nervous and Mental Disease, 204*(11), 806.

Conner, K. R. (2004). A call for research on planned vs. unplanned suicidal behavior. *Suicide and Life-Threatening Behavior, 34*(2), 89–98.

Conner, K. R., Hesselbrock, V. M., Meldrum, S. C., Schuckit, M. A., Bucholz, K. K., Gamble, S. A., Wines, J. D., & Kramer, J. (2007). Transitions to, and correlates of, suicidal ideation, plans, and unplanned and planned suicide attempts among 3,729 men and women with alcohol dependence. *Journal of Studies on Alcohol and Drugs, 68*(5), 654–662.

Coppersmith, D. D., Ryan, O., Fortgang, R., Millner, A., Kleiman, E., & Nock, M. (2022). Mapping the timescale of suicidal thinking. *Proceedings of the National Academy of Sciences, 120*(17), e2215434120

De Beurs, D., Bockting, C., Kerkhof, A., Scheepers, F., O'Connor, R., Penninx, B., & van de Leemput, I. (2021). A network perspective on suicidal behavior: Understanding suicidality as a complex system. *Suicide and Life-Threatening Behavior, 51*(1), 115–126.

de Beurs, D., de Winter, R. F., Helbich, M., & Bockting, C. (2023). Suicidal behavior from a complex system perspective: Individual, dynamical, and contextual. In M. Pompili (Ed.), *Suicide risk assessment and prevention* (pp. 1281–1294). Springer.

Diefenbach, G. J., Collett, S., Black, S., Rudd, M. D., Gueorguieva, R., & Tolin, D. F. (2025). The effect of inpatient brief cognitive-behavioral therapy for suicide prevention on post-discharge emergency department utilization: Secondary analysis of a randomized clinical trial. *General Hospital Psychiatry, 93*, 73–79.

Evans, G., & Farberow, N. L. (2003). *The encyclopedia of suicide, 2nd Edition.* Facts on File.

Fazel, S., & O'Reilly, L. (2020). Machine learning for suicide research–Can it improve risk factor identification? *JAMA Psychiatry, 77*(1), 13–14. https://doi.org/10.1001/jamapsychiatry.2019.2896

Franklin, J. C. (2019). Psychological primitives can make sense of biopsychosocial factor complexity in psychopathology. *BMC Medicine, 17*(1), 1–8.

Goldstein, J. (1999). Emergence as a construct: History and issues. *Emergence, 1*(1), 49–72.

Harris, K. M., McLean, J. P., Sheffield, J., & Jobes, D. (2010). The internal suicide debate hypothesis: Exploring the life versus death struggle. *Suicide and Life-Threatening Behavior, 40*(2), 181–192.

Jeon, H. J., Lee, J.-Y., Lee, Y. M., Hong, J. P., Won, S.-H., Cho, S.-J., Kim, J.-Y., Chang, S. M., Lee, H. W., & Cho, M. J. (2010). Unplanned versus planned suicide attempters, precipitants, methods, and an association with mental disorders in a Korea-based community sample. *Journal of Affective Disorders*, *127*(1–3), 274–280.

Kaurin, A., Dombrovski, A. Y., Hallquist, M. N., & Wright, A. G. (2022). Integrating a functional view on suicide risk into idiographic statistical models. *Behaviour Research and Therapy*, *150*, 104012.

Kleiman, E. M., Coppersmith, D. D. L., Millner, A. J., Franz, P. J., Fox, K. R., & Nock, M. K. (2018). Are suicidal thoughts reinforcing? A preliminary real-time monitoring study on the potential affect regulation function of suicidal thinking. *Journal of Affective Disorders*, *232*, 122–126. https://doi.org/10.1016/j.jad.2018.02.033

Kleiman, E. M., Turner, B. J., Fedor, S., Beale, E. E., Huffman, J. C., & Nock, M. K. (2017). Examination of real-time fluctuations in suicidal ideation and its risk factors: Results from two ecological momentary assessment studies. *Journal of Abnormal Psychology*, *126*(6), 726.

Kovacs, M., & Beck, A. T. (1977). The wish to die and the wish to live in attempted suicides. *Journal of Clinical Psychology*, *33*(2), 361–365.

Meadows, D. H. (2008). *Thinking in systems: A primer*. Chelsea Green Publishing.

Millner, A. J., Lee, M. D., & Nock, M. K. (2017). Describing and measuring the pathway to suicide attempts: A preliminary study. *Suicide and Life-Threatening Behavior*, *47*(3), 353–369.

O'Connor, R. C., & Kirtley, O. J. (2018). The integrated motivational–volitional model of suicidal behaviour. *Philosophical Transactions of the Royal Society B: Biological Sciences*, *373*(1754), 20170268.

Prigogine, I., & Stengers, I. (2018). *Order out of chaos: Man's new dialogue with nature*. Verso Books.

Rudd, M. D., Bryan, C. J., Wertenberger, E. G., Peterson, A. L., Young-McCaughan, S., Mintz, J., Williams, S. R., Arne, K. A., Breitbach, J., & Delano, K. (2015). Brief cognitive-behavioral therapy effects on post-treatment suicide attempts in a military sample: Results of a randomized clinical trial with 2-year follow-up. *American Journal of Psychiatry*, *172*(5), 441–449.

Schafer, K. M., Kennedy, G., Gallyer, A., & Resnik, P. (2021). A direct comparison of theory-driven and machine learning prediction of suicide: A meta-analysis. *PloS One*, *16*(4), e0249833.

Shneidman, E. S. (1998). *The suicidal mind*. Oxford University Press.

Sinyor, M., Williams, M., Mitchell, R., Zaheer, R., Bryan, C. J., Schaffer, A., Westreich, N., Ellis, J., Goldstein, B. I., & Cheung, A. H. (2020). Cognitive behavioral therapy for suicide prevention in youth admitted to hospital following an episode of self-harm: A pilot randomized controlled trial. *Journal of Affective Disorders*, *266*, 686–694.

Teismann, T., Siebert, A. M., & Forkmann, T. (2024). Suicidal ambivalence: A scoping review. *Suicide and Life-Threatening Behavior*, *54*(5), 802–813.

Van Orden, K. A., Witte, T. K., Cukrowicz, K. C., Braithwaite, S. R., Selby, E. A., & Joiner Jr, T. E. (2010). The interpersonal theory of suicide. *Psychological Review*, *117*(2), 575.

7 Situated Suicidality

Taking the Environment Seriously

Zuzanna Rucińska, Lieke Asma, and Sabrina Coninx

Razors pain you
Rivers are damp
Acids stain you
And drugs cause cramp.
Guns aren't lawful
Nooses give
Gas smells awful
You might as well live.
"Résumé" by Dorothy Parker (1926)

7.1 Introduction

Suicide is one of most common causes of death around the world (World Health Organization, 2024), yet as a phenomenon it is still not well understood. The topic of this anthology, suicidal ambivalence, reflects the fact that suicidal agents are torn between what is described as "the wish to live" and "the wish to die", and are simultaneously holding those opposing desires (Schneidman, 1998). Suicidal ambivalence is not resolved in many cases of those who attempt suicide, looking at the number of 911 calls (112 in Europe) that suicidal agents made right before their attempts, or following interviews with survivors of highly lethal suicide attempts (such as jumping from the Golden Gate bridge in San Francisco) who consistently remark that they have changed their mind about their suicidal attempt mid-jump (Steel, 2006). While at times the decision to attempt suicide is preceded by many years of suicidal ideation, at other times the decision looks to be made "spontaneously", made within a time window of only five minutes.[1] Also that decision is often not made "wholeheartedly", which means, with absolute resolve of ambivalence; instead, the wish to die seems to fluctuate even until the very end (Bryan, 2021).

For us, the central *puzzle of suicidal ambivalence* is then the following: without resolved ambivalence about wanting to live or die, how

DOI: 10.4324/9781003616221-10

can we explain that suicidal people eventually do make an attempt to end their lives? Moreover, why do suicidal people switch so rapidly between these "incompatible desires" or make apparently spontaneous decisions to attempt to end their lives? And why does access to lethal means contribute to reaching the "tipping point" of one's decision to end one's life, as discussed in the previous chapter (Chapter 5)? We propose that looking at the environment and contextual factors provides valuable insights to answer these questions. This move is strongly motivated by the fact that interventions on contextual factors, such as means restriction, constitute potentially the single most effective strategy to prevent suicide, in comparison to approaches focusing on individual factors.

In this chapter, we will attempt an answer to the puzzle of suicidal ambivalence from the perspective of situated cognition. Situated cognition is a theory in cognitive science and philosophy of mind that emphasizes the role of the environment and context in shaping cognitive processes (Robbins & Aydede, 2008; Newen, De Bruin, & Gallagher 2018). Situated cognition can therefore be used to understand how the decision to end one's life is made, by not focusing solely on the internal states of the agent (e.g., wish to live vs. wish to die), but by looking at how the decision is shaped by the context of the act itself, such as its sociocultural and material constraints or the physical presence of other people. From this perspective, the answer to the puzzle of suicidal ambivalence will be that there is no need for a decision to be made by the agent wholeheartedly and "in their head", with a resolved ambivalence about it; that decision is always made in a situated context. The environment plays a role in making the decision, and therefore the decision can often be made even without resolved ambivalence.

This chapter proposes to examine suicidality and suicidal ambivalence through the lens of situated cognition, looking at how contextual factors can actively influence and shape the decision-making process, planning, and behavior of a person in the context of suicide. It focuses on the impact of means restriction and other people in public spaces. Rethinking suicidality from the perspective of situated cognition, particularly applying the relational concept of affordances, offers valuable insights for our understanding of suicidality and suicidal ambivalence, as it is well placed to address *both* the physical and the social context of the suicidal person. Further, it inspires rethinking currently prevailing approaches to suicidal ambivalence and decision-making, accounting for the effectiveness of environmental interventions, and opening new avenues for research.

We will motivate understanding suicidality through situated cognition by first addressing the fact that purely internalistic approaches seem to systematically overlook crucial elements of explaining suicidal ambivalence and decision-making (Section 7.2) and then by looking at the multitude of empirical findings on the importance of the contextual and environmental factors that impact suicidality that are not seriously integrated in mainstream literature on suicide-related decision-making or in explanations of suicidality (Section 7.3). We then explain the key concepts behind situated cognition relevant to understanding suicidality, and propose how the situated perspective can make a pragmatic difference by providing an affordance-based explanation for how the environment plays a role in one's suicidal decision-making process (Section 7.4). Finally, we consider new questions and avenues for therapeutic interventions and further research that stem from the situated perspective (Section 7.5).

7.2 Suicide as a "Wicked Problem"

In this section, we start by showcasing some of the main characteristics of the problem of suicide, which raise the worry of the difficulty of explaining the occurrence of suicide using solely internalistic approaches. This is centrally related to the fact that suicide is a "wicked problem" (Bryan, 2021), characterized by a high level of inherent complexity that makes it particularly difficult to solve or eliminate. This becomes apparent in three characteristics.

First, suicide has long been understood through a mental illness-based model, which assumes that approximately 90% of individuals who die by suicide were struggling with mental illness (e.g., mood disorder, substance use disorder, psychotic disorder) (Cavanagh et al., 2003). This fosters a strong focus on the individuals and their clusters of symptoms as the "root cause" for suicide and the target for intervention. However, there is only a weak correlation between mental illness and suicide (attempts) (Franklin et al., 2017). Many individuals suffering from mental illness do not engage in suicide-related behavior, and a larger percentage of suicides than commonly assumed may occur in the absence of mental illness. More generally, it seems that several broad categories of potential risk factors—whether related to psychiatric symptoms or also demographic factors (e.g., age, education, ethnicity, socioeconomic status)—failed to accurately predict suicide far above chance levels (Franklin et al., 2017).

Similar considerations apply to the prominent interpersonal model of suicide (Van Orden et al., 2010). This model proposes to explain why people die by suicide by focusing on the interplay of specific psychological and interpersonal factors that contribute to suicidal ideation and behaviors, which include perceived burdensomeness (belief that one is a burden to others), thwarted belongingness (feeling disconnected from others), and the capacity for suicide (one's ability to hurt oneself). However, other studies show that the average correlation for perceived burdensomeness, thwarted belongingness, and capability for suicide (factors that are central to the interpersonal theory of suicide) is only weak to moderate (see, e.g., Chu et al., 2017).

Second, suicide manifests as an exceedingly complex phenomenon arising from a potentially infinite combination of interacting factors, including biological predispositions, psychiatric issues, emotional distress, but also socioeconomic pressures, access to healthcare, and histories of abuse. The way these factors influence each other and contribute to or prevent the emergence of suicide also depends on the situation in which a person is in. This concerns the process to making the decision to kill oneself, including the potentially shorter or longer process leading up to this decision, and the local context in which a person acts upon the decision. As Bryan writes: "We cannot meaningfully separate the decision to make a suicide attempt from the circumstances within which the choice is presented" (2021, p. 112). It seems therefore clear that there are sociocultural and socioeconomic factors (economic insecurity, access to mental health care, discrimination, lack of social support, etc.) that have a significant influence on the larger decision-making process (Bryan, 2021, pp. 179–180).

Approaches, such the interpersonal model of suicide as well as similar approaches (e.g., the integrated motivational-volitional theory, suicide crisis syndrome theory, or the three-step theory) that focus exclusively on individualistic factors tend to systematically overlook these contextual factors (Kirmayer, 2022). As Kirmayer shows, "suicide is not simply a psychological problem that can be characterized in terms of individual risk and protective factors (understood in the context of a biography and life trajectory), but is fundamentally shaped by social and cultural context" (Kirmayer, 2022, p. 4), and while "suicidology conventionally considers the interplay of psychological and interpersonal processes, these are often described as though they are independent of the social-structural and cultural contexts in which they occur" (Kirmayer, 2022, p. 5). This fits the picture that the context is classically seen as something happening "in the background" of cognition, whereas it should not be.

Third, and connected to the puzzle of suicidal ambivalence, suicidal thoughts fluctuate significantly over time, making it a dynamic phenomenon. Many people experience significant shifts in suicidal thinking over periods ranging from months to weeks, or even hours (Kleiman et al., 2017). Consequently, intra-individual differences in suicidal thinking may be more significant than inter-individual differences when identifying individuals at risk of suicide (Bryan et al., 2016). Furthermore, some individuals who attempt suicide may not report having any thoughts about death a week before the event (Simon et al., 2013). Several studies also indicate that a substantial number of individuals attempting suicide deny having serious suicidal ideation or engage in planning to kill themselves until shortly before the attempt (Simon et al., 2001; Wyder & de Leo, 2007). In fact, in half of all suicide attempts, individuals report to have made the final decision to act only within a timeframe of 5 to 20 minutes before the attempt (Miller et al., 2017, Williams et al., 1980). As such, *half of all suicides may appear almost spontaneous or impulsive.* For these groups of people, screening for suicidal ideation or planning of suicide might be of little to no use.

To summarize, it is very difficult to predict which individuals are more likely to attempt suicide based solely on the presence of mental illness, demographic factors, or prolonged reports of wanting to die or kill oneself. Potentially, there simply are no informative patterns to distinguish between those who attempt suicide and those who do not. It is also challenging to predict which changes in risk or protective factors will lead to specific outcomes in relation to a particular individual, as there may be disproportionate effects of various factors. As emphasized by Bryan (2021), while we cannot precisely identify who is most likely to attempt suicide, we can intervene on broader contextual factors to minimize the probability of suicide attempts or reduce their lethality. Indeed, rather than focusing and intervening on unreliable individual factors, great success has been achieved by concentrating on the environmental factors that contribute to suicide. We will turn to identifying these environmental factors in the next section.

7.3 Empirical Findings on the Role of the Environment

In this section, we list some of the main empirical findings on the difference that the environmental factors seem to make in intervention strategies, focusing particularly on means restriction and the presence of others.

Scholars in the field agree that means restriction is an important method to prevent suicide (e.g., Azrael & Miller, 2016; Britton, Bryan, & Valenstein, 2016; Daigle, 2005; Knipe et al., 2017; Yip et al., 2012). In some sense, the effectiveness of means restriction seems obvious: if you do not have access to the means to kill yourself, you will end up not doing it. However, the role of means restriction is more significant and complex than this.

For instance, the central role of means-restriction and the environment in the process of decision-making and action in the context of suicide is clearly identified in Chapter 5 of this book where the authors look at the role of the environment in entering a state of imminent suicide risk (uncertainty and transition phases) and further the enactment of suicidal behavior (action phase) from an empirical perspective. They convincingly lay out that the behavior of suicidal individuals is hard to predict, while there is insufficient evidence that specific internalistic factors, such as felt burdensomeness, are solely of causative importance. Instead, they propose that access to lethal means is one of the most important factors within the transition to suicidal behavior, and restricting access to lethal means one of the most effective methods of suicide prevention (see Chapter 5 of this book).

This close relation between suicide attempts and means restriction can be seen in various studies. For example, people do not use a different method when their preferred method or place is not available (see, e.g., Clarke & Lester, 1989; Daigle, 2005; Yip et al., 2012). Reisch and Michel (2005) found that installing a protective net at a well-known terrace in Berne, Switzerland, not only led to no suicides at that site, but also reduced the overall number of people jumping from high places in Berne (including bridges) compared to the years before. Another example comes from the UK, where between the late 1950s and early 1970s, coal gas was replaced with natural gas from the North Sea wells, which contained a lower amount of carbon monoxide. This replacement was followed by a steady and prominent decrease in fatal gassing and overall suicide rate in the UK (Kreitman, 1976; Thomas, Chang, & Gunnell, 2011); similar results were found in Japan (Lester & Abe, 1989) and the USA (Lester, 1990). Also, a study by Yip et al. (2010) showed that removing bags of charcoal in one district of Hong Kong (a popular method of attempting suicide by the youth at the time in Hong Kong), from self-service access to locked storage, did not prohibit purchase, but lead to a decline in suicide compared to other districts without such measure but a similar population size and socioeconomic status.

Studies on pesticide ingestion, which is responsible for a substantial number of suicides globally (Gunnell et al., 2007), support these findings as well. Research has shown that banning certain pesticides in South Korea not only reduced pesticide suicide mortality, but also overall suicide mortality (Cha et al., 2016). Knipe et al., (2017) found that overall suicide mortality was also diminished by banning certain pesticides in Sri Lanka, even though there was a small rise in the use of other methods there. What is more, as an earlier study by Gunnell et al. (2007) has shown, the reductions in suicide mortality did not appear to be associated with unemployment, alcohol misuse, divorce, pesticide use, and the years associated with Sri Lanka's Civil war. A study by Kong and Zhang (2010) in China also showed that easy access to highly toxic pesticides is an independent risk factor for suicide, even after controlling for mental disorder, marital status, income, and education level.

The independent role means seem to play in suicide is also supported by research on the relationship between firearms ownership and suicide. A study by Hemenway and Miller (2002) shows that not only handgun ownership and suicide rate were positively correlated across nine regions in the U.S., but that this correlation was still significant even after controlling for lifetime prevalence of major depression, suicidal thoughts, urbanization, education, unemployment, and alcohol consumption. What is more, even though a higher number of handguns is correlated with lower rates of nonfirearm suicide, it still amounts to higher levels of overall suicide.[2]

While we have to be careful in drawing causal conclusions from these kinds of ecological studies,[3] these studies, conducted across a variety of cultures and types of means for suicide, point out two interesting insights. First of all, means restriction seems to not only reduce suicide by a specific means, but it also often leads to an overall reduction in suicide. Second, availability of certain means seems often to be a stronger predictor of suicide than other individualistic factors like low mental disorder, socioeconomic status, or alcohol misuse. This suggests that when it comes to suicide, means are more than just means: the availability itself seems to have an impact on the decision to attempt suicide. Merely having a handgun, pesticides, or poisonous gas readily available seems to make a difference to the decision-making process.

How can these insights best be understood? As Britton et al. (2016) point out in their paper on means restriction and motivational interviewing, the mechanism by which means restriction exactly works is still unclear (p. 52). Eddleston and Bateman suggest that this has to do with the strength of intent: having these pesticides available at home makes "acts of self-harm, with low intention, fatal events" (2011, p. 1), while alternative common methods in Sri Lanka, such as hanging, drowning, burning, and walking in front of trains "probably require relatively higher levels of intent and more planning" (Eddleston & Bateman, 2011). Relatedly, after arguing that tackling availability is an important suicide prevention strategy, Hawton (2007, p. 9) ends his article by stating that "[w]hile not addressing the underlying causes of suicide, it is a policy that may have significant impact on overall suicide rates". We will return to how to interpret these findings from the perspective of situated cognition in section 6.4.

What we need to acknowledge is also the crucial role that the social context can play for suicidality, including the actual presence of others as well as the cognitive accessibility of their presence for the suicidal individual. Various social events, and sometimes mere coincidences, can influence suicidal decision-making or interrupt a suicide attempt: a phone call or a poster that evokes memories of a loved one, or a simple interaction with a passerby. For instance, consider the study of Owens, Dergens, and Abraham (2019) on the influence of passersby on preventing suicides of those attempting to end their lives in public places. Through both verbal and nonverbal communication (e.g., speaking to the person or just being present), they can help bring a suicidal person out of a trance-like state and guide them back to the present moment. This reconnection—with themselves, those around them, and the everyday world—can be a crucial step in preventing suicide attempts. Interestingly, the bystanders did not require any special training in spotting or engaging with suicidal individuals to provide effective measures of intervention (see the discussion in section 4.3).

In summary, empirical research on suicidality has long recognized the importance of the environmental context in constraining and shaping suicidal behavior. However, classical models mostly focus on properties of individuals (e.g., psychiatric conditions, feelings of burdensomeness, thwarted belongingness, pervasive feeling of entrapment and defeat, or capacity for suicidal behavior (Kirmayer, 2022), treating the physical and social contexts at best as a mere background factor. We do not propose that these psychological factors are *not* of importance, or that they cannot be the main drivers of suicidal action; this can be the case and will be dependent on each individual circumstance. We simply want to point out that focusing on psychological factors *alone* tend to overlook the close interconnection between those psychological states and the environment in which the suicidal person is embedded. While psychological research has clearly seen the importance of environmental factors, it tends to not do justice to this importance in their theory-building, which also has practical consequences in limiting therapeutic interventions that are built on those theories. In the following we show that by adopting a situated perspective, we can shed new light on why and how context matters. It provides both more conceptual clarity and new ideas for effective intervention options. This chapter cannot provide a complete situated theory of suicidality, but we aim to illustrate how insights from situated cognition can help us to address the puzzle of suicidal ambivalence and reframe the role of means restriction and other people in suicide, enriching both explanation and intervention strategies.

7.4 Understanding Suicidality through the Lens of Situated Cognition

In this section, we first delineate the key concepts of the situated cognition framework and introduce the concept of affordances, so that we can apply it to better understand suicidal decision-making and ambivalence.

Situated cognition is a theory in cognitive science and philosophy of mind that emphasizes the role of the environment in shaping cognitive processes. Unlike traditional cognitive theories that view cognition as primarily occurring inside the brain, situated cognition posits that thinking and learning are fundamentally tied to the material and social context in which they occur. Situated cognition is aligned with the 4E Cognition framework (cognition being embodied, enacted, embedded, and extended; see Newen et al., 2018), which suggests a different outlook on the relationship between the environment and our cognition. Situated cognition sees cognition as an instantiation of strong coupling of the individual organism with its natural, social, and cultural environment (Robbins & Aydede, 2008). It thereby proposes to take seriously the idea that thinking, planning or decision-making is also a collaborative, dynamic process that involves interaction with materials and other people.

In the context of suicide, this perspective puts a stronger emphasis on studying and understanding why environmental factors act as powerful means-restrictions (Bryan, 2021; Daigle, 2005; Britton et al., 2016), and why the presence of other people can constrain suicidal decision-making (Owens et al., 2019). One explanatory approach starts with the assumption that the material environment and larger sociocultural context shape the perception of *affordances* (or possibilities for action) for taking one's life. Affordances are possibilities for actions stemming from the particular relations between subjects and their environment (Gibson, 1977). For instance, when you are thirsty, a cup of tea affords drinking, partly because of the material properties of the cup (the graspability of its hold in relation to your hand), but partly because of the situational context (*your* cup of tea, and not a cup of another, affords drinking to you). Rietveld and Kiverstein (2014) introduce a useful distinction between the *landscape* and a *field* of affordances, where the landscape delineates all the possibilities available to you as a human being (drinkability from a cup), and a field of affordances points to the relevant possibilities for action that a particular individual is responsive to in a concrete situation, depending on the individual's abilities and concerns (drinking from *that specific* cup at a *specific* time). While we may share the landscape of affordances, or what is possible to do for humans in certain contexts, our fields of affordances will differ between us, and change depending on our current state of mind. Notably, some affordances may have a particularly inviting character (Withagen, Araújo, & de Poel, 2017): one affordance can "call for action" more strongly than another (e.g., a door that is already open vs. one that needs to be opened tends to be more often chosen for passing, as they are more inviting for engagement).

Affordances feature in many texts in the context of mental health. Some examples include Ratcliffe's (2018, p. 129) work on how many people with depression "often experience the world as bereft of the relevant types of possibilities"; or De Haan's (2020) analysis that for many clinically depressed individuals, no affordances tend to be inviting any more than others, whereas for a person diagnosed with Obsessive-Compulsive Disorder, only one affordance (such as compulsive washing of one's hands) stands out and calls for action.

We also wish to emphasize the relational conceptualization of affordance that we endorse in this chapter. As Chemero (2009) pointed out, affordances are relational: they always point to the organism and the environment at the same time. Other people can also change the situation, and make us open to affordances. As Ratcliffe (2018, p. 132) notes, "A substantial body of evidence indicates that actual and anticipated interactions with others, and even the mere presence of others, influence the perceptual and practical salience of one's surroundings in a pre-reflective fashion". Interactions with others, but also sometimes their mere presence, can make a difference in what possibilities for action we as individuals are responsive to.[4] As an everyday example, assume that we may perceive a piano as "lift-able" only when others are in the room with us, and we may see a dark park as less threatening when we know that there are other people in it (McKitrick, 2003; Rucińska, 2017).

With our new conceptual toolkit, we will now turn to applying it to understand the puzzle of suicidality in a novel way. We propose that the situated cognition framework can offer a different, richer perspective on suicidal ambivalence. Furthermore, it can offer an explanation of why the environment plays an important role in one's suicidality as it does. We will first focus on how the social and the physical environment can increase the perception of "suicidal affordances" (7.4.1), then use this concept to address the puzzle of suicidal ambivalence (7.4.2), and finally offer a way to rethink intervention strategies by looking at how to use the social and physical environment to open up new affordances in intervention strategies (7.4.3).

7.4.1 Suicidal Affordances

The specific environment, with its available means and the presence of others, makes a difference in the *perception of affordances for suicide*, or what we will call "suicidal affordances". These are possibilities for actions to die by suicide that the suicidal agent is responsive to. In a simplified manner, we could say that a high bridge with low railing provides a potential affordance for suicide to human beings who could climb over the railing (making it part of their landscape of affordances), but this affordance is only salient (part of the field of affordances) to some. Thus, being in a certain state of mind changes how the world appears to us, and what possibilities for action we perceive as inviting. What actions become available and how we are affected changes when we are in different situations, triggered by different environmental and interpersonal constraints. So at a specific moment in time, in a specific context, attempting suicide can be experienced as the most salient option to end one's suffering, and the smallest shifts in one's situation (availability of preferred means, alignment of situational factors, or negative interpersonal exchanges) can trigger or call for action.

It is crucial to stress again that following the relational view of affordances, suicidal affordances are not special, "general" features of the environment. Affordances are here better thought of as emergent properties of the situation, deeply contextualized and tied to one's state of mind *and* the social and environmental setting and constraints to be found within that situation. Since affordances are relational, it means that we have two *relata*: the person and their internal states as well as the environment. So to understand suicidality we need to address both of these aspects. Some people might be more responsive to suicidal affordances, more or less irrespective of the material and social environment (e.g., perceiving every object as means to end their life), while some places might be more inviting to the perception of suicidal affordances, which is less dependent of personal tendencies (e.g., thinking about and recognizing the possibility to jump when standing on top a tall building, even without having suicidal tendencies).

It follows that whether suicidal affordances stand out depends partly on the state of mind one is in (compare a person in a suicidal episode and a person who is not), and partly on the features of the environment itself. For instance, in a stressful situation, an agent could perceive affordances for attempting suicide, and interpreting any objects in sight as possible means. A good case in point is Clancy Martin's report of being coerced into a mental institution after a failed suicide attempt. In the context of having his freedom taken away, Martin saw a regular mirror in the bathroom as a means to self-harm: he saw the possibility of smashing it to cut his own throat with a sliver of glass (2023, p. 10), just as he saw the affordances of harming himself with scissors, window blinds, or a simple fork. These materials formed Martin's "field of affordances"; as a person living with suicidal thoughts, Martin made sense of these basic objects in a specific, potentially-good-for-suicide way.

At the other side of the coin, the perception of affordance is shaped by the structure of the sociocultural environment, for example, which objects or situations are perceived as "inviting" actions related to suicide. Suicidal affordances are cultural and context dependent. For example, consider again the "trend" of the teenagers to engage in suicide via charcoal inhale in Taiwan, functioning like a Werther effect, which explains why in certain countries at certain times, some means for action are more prevalent and perceived as affording suicide. Research on the context of suicide makes it clear "how much both intrapsychic and interpersonal processes depend on cultural meanings and practices expressed in social norms and maintained by social institutions and practices" (Kirmayer, 2022, p. 5), such as strong association of suicidality with experiences of shame in Cuba (Schneider et al., 2022), or structural inequalities and injustices in China (Chang et al., 2019).

Notably, the role of the personal state of mind and the environment are closely intertwined in these processes as they can reinforce and effect one another, dynamically changing the responsiveness to suicidal affordances. Say, a particular environment can make affordances stand out in a different manner in different phases, such as in the phase of preparing to act and action phase (see Chapter 5). For instance, during the "uncertainty" phase, taking actions such as getting close to the ledge of a bridge, or during the "preparation" phase, taking actions such as preparing a gun, rope or medications open up further doors for perceiving suicide-related actions as more inviting. In the "action" phase of suicidality, the environmental opportunities can play a role as well: an empty park can invite hanging, or a high bridge jumping. What is important is that once we acknowledge the relevance of material and sociocultural factors in the perception of suicidal affordances, they can become crucial elements in the understanding of and intervention on suicide, as we will discuss more in section 6.4.3 below.

In short, from the situated perspective, suicidality cannot be understood by focusing on a decontextualized agent alone. Suicidality is always to be understood in addressing the agent in their physical and social environment, in order to capture the complex and dynamic nature of the interactions in which they find themselves in, and suicidal affordances that those interactions might open.

7.4.2 *Rethinking Ambivalence*

We framed the puzzle of suicidal ambivalence in the following way: without resolved ambivalence about wanting to live or die, how can we explain that suicidal people eventually do make an attempt to end their lives? And why does it seem that many people take apparently spontaneous decisions to end their lives by suicide, without fully solving their state of ambivalence through a whole-hearted decision? Situated cognition can give us a new perspective of how to address this puzzle.

By taking the context seriously, we have reasons to think that there can exist a dissonance between the two "wishes" (the wish to live and wish to die), which shows up in acts such as collecting means to have them "ready to hand" (e.g., a gun), and getting oneself ready to use them, but at the same time resisting this action in anticipation of pain or disfigurement, or causing hurt to another. Since acts of suicide commonly require overcoming the fear of bodily self-harm, it is further understandable why there is ambivalence about going through the act until the end; the decision that is being made is clashing with the bodily anxiety and so it is both made and "not really made" until the very last moment. As these "incompatible" wishes can actually happen at the same time, there is no real "switching" between these states. Ambivalence can continue to permeate the suicidal experience as it does with other experiences. The wish to die and wish to live can thereby occur at the same time.

But what is important for us is that the decision to end one's life can be made without resolution to that ambivalence, dependent among others on what "invites" one to suicidal action in a particular context. We want to explain an agent's action in the midst of ambivalence. Situated cognition invites us to already think differently about the *desire* to end one's life to begin with, as already a desire that is situated and even shaped by other people. The difference our perspective makes is that we see the suicidal person as not necessarily entering a risky situation with a "wish to die", which is then "enabled" or "blocked" by the environmental constraints or restricted means. Instead, we see one's wish to die as dynamically shaped by the available possibilities and constraints that are meaningful parts of the decision-making process. The decision to end one's life can therefore be made in the midst of the activity, without fully resolved ambivalence. Ambivalence about the wish to live or die can be seen as having a dynamic quality of its own. Such ambivalence is stronger when there are other possibilities for action that the person is responsive to (that do not amount to suicide), but weaker in situations where suicidal affordances are in sight and experienced as especially inviting.

The process of decision-making is not going to be a linear process, whereby a decision is first made (in the head), and then acted (or not acted) upon in the behavior (see Rucińska, 2021). Instead, how the current situation is interpreted, and what affordances it opens, will shape the decision about ending one's life. And that decision will not be detached from the longer history of interactions of the agent, or her sociocultural context, for the past experiences and longings influence the current perception of possibilities (such as, to end one's life) in an ongoing way.[5] This can also explain why the last-minute changes in the situation (the dynamically changing "external factors") are important in swaying someone off their suicide attempt and can form aspects of an intervention. We will turn to these interventions now.

7.4.3 *Rethinking Interventions*

What is the pragmatic value of taking the situated approach? We propose that situated cognition can help us better understand the success and failures of existing interventions.

The situated perspective can first shed new light on how to make sense of motivational interviewing for means restriction (e.g., Britton et al., 2016). The idea behind motivational interviewing is to strengthen the person's desire to live, while reducing the desire to die, which may provide them with reasons to restrict their access to lethal means and take safety precautions as well (Britton et al., 2016, p. 53). As Britton et al. note, "the way in which means restriction works, especially in reducing overall suicide, remains unclear" (2016, p. 52). However, we can see now that one of the reasons for this is that the desire to live and desire to die, and reasons to intervene, are treated as internal psychological states, in which means restriction appears as a mere external blockage, restricting the person to act on their intention. From the perspective of situated cognition, deciding to restrict your access to means and to take safety precautions implies changing your motivation and your relationship to the world as well. Means restriction in itself may strengthen the wish to live, or diminish the wish to die, and could accordingly diminish the agent's tendency to attempt suicide. But as the decision-making process is heavily dependent on the situation, a stronger wish to live that is experienced right after interventions like motivational interviewing may still change rapidly. Thus, the environmental factors must still be acknowledged and brought into existing interventions. There is a tendency to choose between environmental and personal factors (see Yip et al., 2012), but the situated perspective provides a way to integrate them.

A wider acceptance of a more interactive picture of cognition may have positive effects in practice as well. According to Britton et al. (2016, p. 3), many care workers do not seem to believe in means restriction. There is an assumption among clinicians that patients are not willing to restrict their means, and that they will use a different method if one is restricted. Many of the respondents believed that every single jumper would have found another way to complete suicide than the one whose means were blocked. 40% believed that "most" would have completed suicide using other means. This belief in the inevitability of suicide may be a political impediment to adopting potentially effective suicide prevention efforts. Care workers and clinicians might have a certain picture of cognition and how persons come to decide to attempt suicide, as the decision that is done outside of the context of the act. With a different picture of that decision-making process, means-restriction could be given more salience by the practitioners.

We contend that, particularly in the context of suicide prevention, situational approaches are highly valuable: means restrictions appear to reduce suicide rates by approximately 30–60%, whereas suicide-focused treatments seem to reduce the suicide rate by only 15–20% (Bryan, 2021, p. 171).[6] Thus, we may achieve greater success by strongly integrating intervention strategies concentrating on situational factors that contribute to suicide, such as eliminating or *significantly reducing access* to the most frequently used means for suicide, or aiming to make suicide attempts *less lethal* by modifying potential means. Situational factors shape individual factors, as both are equally implied in the notion of affordance. Thus changing the situational factors will have an effect on individual factors, and vice versa.

We should also put the means "out of sight" (such as when storing firearms in a safe, but preferably not in one's house at all), since the mere presence of a firearm in a house can significantly increase the risk for suicide, also for those without mental illnesses (Brent et al., 1993; Kellermann et al., 1993). Why do safe storage practices work? They may slow down individuals enough to overcome intense episodes of suicidal thinking, and they might reduce the "cognitive access" of firearms as a perceived means (or perceived affordance) for suicide (Bryan, 2021, pp. 171–175; Khazem et al., 2015). For instance, seeing a firearm may remind the agent of the fact that they *could* kill themselves, which would not have been on their minds if it wasn't in sight.

Aside means-restriction that focuses on taking away the negative affordances, we should further consider how to open up positive affordances for *not* attempting suicide, that is, strategies that reinforce a person's perception for actions related to reasons for living. What kinds of interventions would those be? These could be all kinds of environmental measures that induce, for example, thoughts about reasons not to die by suicide (Bryan, 2021, pp. 191–196). Telephones on the bridges or posters with information on how to get help might fall into this category, as they open up positive affordances for not going through with the act. Those can also be interventions by others in critical phases, to which our perspective provides a new explanation of why bypassers are successful interveners. Even the smallest changes, such as a concerned look and questions from a stranger, can act as an affordance for not attempting suicide. Owens et al.'s (2019) study showed this most clearly. They found that passing strangers, who managed to prevent suicides of those attempting to end their lives in public places, had no "specialist skills", but were ordinary people who, just by their presence and engagement with the suicidal person (by being authentic, calm and compassionate) made the suicidal person feel "safe, connected and validated" (p. 1). This suggests that other people can impact our perception of affordances to end one's life too. As such, they can act as positive buffers to *not* attempt suicide.

Location was also an important clue in the same study, which described the interveners as "distinguished only by a high level of social awareness, combined with a readiness for social action" (Owens et al., 2019, p. 1), but our affordance-based re-description points to something else. We can doubt if a high level of social awareness is really needed here, as that presupposes some empathy on the side of the intervener. What the interveners actually exhibited seems to be a certain level of *attunement to the situational factors*. The interveners showed that they could recognize the person being at risk, primarily through their location: the person "either appeared to have placed themselves in immediate physical danger or was judged to be out of place, giving rise to curiosity and concern" (Owens et al., 2019, p. 3). The study noted that the specific features of the situation were described by the interviewers as feeling "weird", which they knew how to spot. The situated perspective that reconsiders the significance of the environment does not consider these findings perplexing. In fact, it can make good sense of it, by suggesting that a bypasser can spot potential "suicidal affordances" of another. How that works requires more explanation in future work.

7.5 Conclusion and Follow-Up

In this chapter, we proposed to consider the role of the context through the perspective of situated cognition, which provides a new outlook on how to think of our environment and behaviors in it. We attempted to re-examine means restriction and suicidal ambivalence from the perspective of situated cognition, according to which the distinction between the mind and the environment is not as sharp as in classical theories of agency that focus on the contradictory content of desires. The situated perspective claims that agency is already situated in a certain environment, and one's decision-making process and the desires one might have are actively shaped by the material and sociocultural environment and the affordances in it. We also proposed that the situated perspective can make a pragmatic difference by opening up a new outlook on why context-based interventions work. While the role of context within which suicide occurs has always been seen as somewhat important by the scholars of suicide, it has not played a key role in understanding the ambivalence and the decision-making of suicidal agents, which we now hope to have remediated. We have also showed that suicidal ambivalence need not be resolved for one to be drawn to act on suicidal affordances; in fact, such ambivalence might be a dynamic feature of the person's experience.

We believe there can be many fruitful insights that stem from taking on the situated perspective. For instance, it can open up new pragmatic questions and avenues for further research, such as:

1 How to further the notion of suicide-inviting situations or places? Our previous consideration indicates that there are at least some situations or places that make the perception of suicidal affordances highly probable, because of the material structure in relation to our physical condition as human beings (e.g., heights) and our sociocultural upbringing (e.g., guns, hanging by rope, or jumping on train tracks).
2 Can we see another person's affordances for attempting suicide? Asking this opens up the door for considering that anyone can see suicidal

affordances—even some interveners—and not just people who "are suicidal". Assuming this is possible, how can seeing of others' suicidal affordances be integrated into existing or new intervention strategies? And how to develop or train such sensitivity?

3 How can we create spaces whose material and social properties make the perspective of suicidal affordances less likely, or to prevent transitions from preparation to action phases in the process of suicide? How can we for example make use of empirical insights on means restriction and the presence of others to improve suicide preventions, especially when focusing on risk factors of individuals seem not as effective? Consider again the instance of introducing free phone booths on bridges so as to afford reaching out to a friend or an expert prevention strategist at a time of crisis.

Here the situated approach is not inventing new methods for suicide intervention, but it is motivating research in this promising direction of measures to open up individuals to perceive more affordances to live than to die by suicide.

From a theoretical perspective, situated cognition as applied to the topic of suicidality can also help up rethink some of the attitudes we have toward suicidal people's agency, rationality, responsibility, or epistemic injustice, by making us rethink these terms. For instance, the situated approach will make a difference to understanding suicidal *agency*, as the "behavior" of the suicidal person, such as her response to the environmental trigger, or the decision she makes within five minutes, is not a mere "reaction" to available means, or simply an effect of the desire to end one's life. Through actions such as that of coming closer to the train tracks, collecting pills, or reaching for the phone, suicidal people are still *making sense* of their situation and deciding whether they want to go ahead with their plan. The suicidal agent might perceive the environment differently, but still meaningfully, which explains why certain places or means play such a powerful role in their suicidality, while at the same time does not take away from their agency. Exploring suicidal agency, rationality and responsibility from situated perspective is a topic for future research.

Notes

1 We qualify this statement with "looks to be", as in many instances, the suicidal decision is not coming out of nowhere, but reflects years of pain or "self-ache" (see Webb, 2010; Martin, 2024).

2 An earlier study by Brent et al. (1991) points in the same direction, as do studies by Azrael, Miller, and colleagues (see Azrael & Miller, 2016, pp. 652–654 for discussion).

3 Other factors may have contributed to these findings (see, e.g., Azrael & Miller, 2016; Daigle, 2005, p. 630; Florentine & Crane, 2010 for discussion), and the findings seem to vary among different social groups (see, e.g., Yip et al., 2012, p. 2395).
4 There are multiple studies that support this, such as the study of Schnall et al. (2008), who found that the climbability of a hill (and judgement of its steepness) changed when the climber was walking with another person.
5 For more on how to understand integrating different timescales in perception of affordances, see Gallagher and Rucińska (2021).
6 It should be noted that we are not claiming that promising treatment measures—so-called suicide-focused treatments such as Dialectical Behavior Therapy, Cognitive Behavioral Therapy for Suicide Prevention, or Crisis Response Planning—are rendered useless. These approaches share the common aim of enabling individuals to make decisions in the context of intense emotional stress in a less extreme manner, thereby avoiding reliance on suicidal behavior. We are not suggesting that these treatments are ineffective. We simply want to give the situational approaches their due.

References

Azrael, D., & Miller, M. J. (2016). Reducing suicide without affecting underlying mental health: Theoretical underpinnings and a review of the evidence base linking the availability of lethal means and suicide. In R. C. O'Connor & J. Pirkis (Eds.), *The international handbook of suicide prevention* (pp. 637–662). Wiley Blackwell. https://doi.org/10.1002/9781118903223.ch36

Brent, D. A., Perper, J. A., Allman, C. J., Moritz, G. M., Wartella, M. E., & Zelenak, J. P. (1991). The presence and accessibility of firearms in the homes of adolescent suicides: A case-control study. *Journal of the American Medical Association, 266*(21), 2989–2995. https://doi.org/10.1001/jama.1991.03470210057032

Brent, D. A., Perper, J. A., Moritz, G., Baugher, M., Schweers, J., & Roth, C. (1993). Firearms and adolescent suicide: A community case-control study. *American Journal of Diseases of Children, 147*(10), 1066–1071. https://doi.org/10.1001/archpedi.1993.02160340052013

Britton, P. C., Bryan, C. J., & Valenstein, M. (2016). Motivational interviewing for means restriction counseling with patients at risk for suicide. *Cognitive and Behavioral Practice, 23*(1), 51–61. https://doi.org/10.1016/j.cbpra.2014.09.004

Bryan, C. J. (2021) *Rethinking suicide: Why prevention fails, and how we can do better*. Oxford University Press. https://doi.org/10.1093/med-psych/9780190050634.001.0001

Bryan, C. J., Rudd, M.D., Peterson, A. L., Young-McCaughan, S., & Wertenberger, E. G. (2016) The ebb and flow of the wish to live and the wish to die among suicidal military personnel. *Journal of Affective Disorders, 202*, 58–66. https://doi.org/10.1080/13811118.2017.1319313

Cavanagh, J. T., Carson, A. J., Sharpe, M., & Lawrie, S. M. (2003). Psychological autopsy studies of suicide: A systematic review. *Psychological Medicine, 33*(3), 395–405. https://doi.org/10.1017/s0033291702006943

Cha, E. S., Chang, S. S., Gunnell, D., Eddleston, M., Khang, Y. H., & Lee, W. J. (2016). Impact of paraquat regulation on suicide in South Korea. *International Journal of Epidemiology, 45*(2), 470–479. https://doi.org/10.1093/ije/dyv304

Chang, Q., Yip, P. S., & Chen, Y. Y. (2019). Gender inequality and suicide gender ratios in the world. *Journal of Affective Disorders, 243,* 297–304. https://doi.org/10.1016/j.jad.2018.09.032

Chemero, A. (2009). *Radical embodied cognitive science.* MIT Press.

Chu, C., Buchman-Schmitt, J. M., Stanley, I. H., Hom, M. A., Tucker, R. P., Hagan, C. R., Rogers, M. L., Podlogar, M. C., Chiurliza, B., Ringer, F. B., Michaels, M. S., Patros, C. H. G., & Joiner, T. E. (2017). The interpersonal theory of suicide: A systematic review and meta-analysis of a decade of cross-national research. *Psychological Bulletin, 143*(12), 1313–1345. https://doi.org/10.1037/bul0000123

Clarke, R., & Lester, D. (1989). *Suicide: Closing the exits.* Springer Verlag.

Daigle, M. S. (2005). Suicide prevention through means restriction: Assessing the risk of substitution: A critical review and synthesis. *Accident Analysis & Prevention, 37*(4), 625–632. https://doi.org/10.1016/j.aap.2005.03.004

De Haan, S. (2020). *Enactive psychiatry.* Cambridge University Press. https://doi.org/10.1017/9781108685214

Eddleston, M., & Bateman, D. N. (2011). Major reductions in global suicide numbers can be made rapidly through pesticide regulation without the need for psychosocial interventions. *Social Science & Medicine, 72*(1), 1–2. https://doi.org/10.1016/j.socscimed.2010.10.013

Florentine, J. B., & Crane, C. (2010). Suicide prevention by limiting access to methods: A review of theory and practice. *Social Science & Medicine, 70*(10), 1626–1632. https://doi.org/10.1016/j.socscimed.2010.01.029

Franklin, J. C., Ribeiro, J. D., Fox, K. R., Bentley, K. H., Kleiman, E. M., Huang, X., Musacchio, K. M., Jaroszewski, A. C., Chang, B. P., & Nock, M. K. (2017). Risk factors for suicidal thoughts and behaviors: A meta-analysis of 50 years of research. *Psychological Bulletin, 43*(2), 187–232. https://doi.org/10.1037/bul0000084

Gallagher, S., & Rucińska, Z. (2021). Prospecting performance: Rehearsal and the nature of imagination. *Synthese, 199*(1–2), 4523–4541. https://doi.org/10.1007/s11229-020-02989-2

Gibson, J. J. (1977). The theory of affordances. In R. E. Shaw, & J. Bransford (Eds.), *Perceiving, acting and knowing. Toward an ecological psychology* (pp. 67–82). Routledge. https://doi.org/10.4324/9781315467931

Gunnell, D., Eddleston, M., Phillips, M. R., & Konradsen, F. (2007). The global distribution of fatal pesticide self-poisoning: Systematic review. *BMC Public Health, 7,* 357. https://doi.org/10.1186/1471-2458-7-357

Gunnell, D., Fernando, R., Hewagama, M., Priyangika, W. D. D., Konradsen, F., & Eddleston, M. (2007). The impact of pesticide regulations on suicide in Sri Lanka. *International Journal of Epidemiology, 36*(6), 1235–1242. https://doi.org/10.1093/ije/dym164

Hawton, K. (2007). Restricting access to methods of suicide: Rationale and evaluation of this approach to suicide prevention. *Crisis, 28*(S1), 4–9. https://doi.org/10.1027/0227-5910.28.S1.4

Hemenway, D., & Miller, M. (2002). Association of rates of household handgun ownership, lifetime major depression, and serious suicidal thoughts with rates of suicide across US census regions. *Injury Prevention, 8*(4), 313–316. https://doi.org/10.1136/ip.8.4.313

Kellermann, A. L., Rivara, F. P., Rushforth, N. B., Banton, J. G., Reay, D. T., Francisco, J. T., Locci, A. B., Prodzinski, J., Hackman, B. B., & Somes, G. (1993). Gun ownership as a risk factor for homicide in the home. *New England Journal of Medicine, 329*, 1084–1091. https://doi.org/10.1056/NEJM199310073291506

Khazem, L. R., Houtsma, C., Gratz, K. L., Tull, M. T., Green, B. A., & Anestis, M. D. (2015). Firearms matter: The moderating role of firearm storage in the association between current suicidal ideation and likelihood of future suicide attempts among Unites States military personnel. *Military Psychology, 28*, 25–33. https://doi.org/10.1037/mil0000099

Kirmayer, L. J. (2022). Suicide in cultural context: An ecosocial approach. *Transcultural Psychiatry, 59*(1), 3–12. https://doi.org/10.1177/13634615221076424

Kleiman, E. M., Turner, B. J., Fedor, S., Beale, E. E., Huffman, J. C., & Nock, M. K. (2017). Examination of real-time fluctuations in suicidal ideation and its risk factors: Results from two ecological momentary assessment studies. *Journal of Abnormal Psychology, 126*(6), 726–738. https://doi.org/10.1037/abn0000273

Knipe, D. W., Chang, S. S., Dawson, A., Eddleston, M., Konradsen, F., Metcalfe, C., & Gunnell, D. (2017). Suicide prevention through means restriction: Impact of the 2008-2011 pesticide restrictions on suicide in Sri Lanka. *PLOS ONE, 12*(3), e0172893. https://doi.org/10.1371/journal.pone.0172893

Kong, Y., & Zhang, J. (2010). Access to farming pesticides and risk for suicide in Chinese rural young people. *Psychiatry Research, 179*(2), 217–221. https://doi.org/10.1016/j.psychres.2009.12.005

Kreitman, N. (1976). The coal gas story. United Kingdom suicide rates, 1960-71. *Journal of Epidemiology & Community Health, 30*(2), 86–93. https://doi.org/10.1136/jech.30.2.86

Lester, D. (1990). The effects of detoxification of domestic gas on suicide in the United States. *American Journal of Public Health, 80*(1), 80–81. https://doi.org/10.2105/AJPH.80.1.80

Lester, D., & Abe, K. (1989). The effect of restricting access to lethal methods for suicide: A study of suicide by domestic gas in Japan. *Acta Psychiatrica Scandinavica, 80*(2), 180–182. https://doi.org/10.1111/j.1600-0447.1989.tb01324.x

Martin, C. (2024). *How not to kill yourself: A portrait of the suicidal mind.* Vintage.

McKitrick, J. (2003). A case for extrinsic dispositions. *Australasian Journal of Philosophy, 81*(2), 155–174. https://doi.org/10.1080/713659629

Millner, A.J., Lee, M. D., & Nock, M.K. (2017). Describing and measuring the pathway to suicide attempts: A preliminary study. *Suicide and Life-Threatening Behavior, 47*, 353–369. https://doi.org/10.1111/sltb.12284.

Newen, A., De Bruin, L., & Gallagher, S. (Eds.). (2018). *The Oxford handbook of 4E cognition.* Oxford University Press. https://doi.org/10.1093/oxfordhb/9780198735410.001.0001

Owens, C., Derges, J., & Abraham, C. (2019). Intervening to prevent a suicide in a public place: A qualitative study of effective interventions by lay people. *BMJ Open, 9*(11), e032319. https://doi.org/10.1136/bmjopen-2019-032319

Ratcliffe, M. (2018). The interpersonal structure of depression. *Psychoanalytic Psychotherapy, 32*(2), 122–139. https://doi.org/10.1080/02668734.2018.1455729

Reisch, T., & Michel, K. (2005). Securing a suicide hot spot: Effects of a safety net at the Bern Muenster Terrace. *Suicide and Life-Threatening Behavior, 35*(4), 460–467. https://doi.org/10.1521/suli.2005.35.4.460

Rietveld, E., & Kiverstein, J. (2014). A rich landscape of affordances. *Ecological Psychology, 26*(4), 325–352. https://doi.org/10.1080/10407413.2014.958035

Robbins, P., & Aydede, M. (2008). A short primer on situated cognition. In P. Robbins & M. Aydede (Eds.), *The Cambridge handbook of situated cognition* (pp. 3–10). Cambridge University Press. https://doi.org/10.1017/CBO9780511816826

Rucińska, Z. (2017). The role of affordances in pretend play. In C. Durt, T. Fuchs, & C. Tewes (Eds.), *Embodiment, enaction, and culture: Investigating the constitution of the shared world* (pp. 257–277). MIT Press. https://doi.org/10.7551/mitpress/9780262035552.001.0001

Rucińska, Z. (2021). Enactive planning in rock climbing: Recalibration, visualization and nested affordances. *Synthese, 199*(1), 5285–5310. https://doi.org/10.1007/s11229-021-03025-7

Schnall, S., Harber, K. D., Stefanucci, J. K., & Proffitt, D. R. (2008). Social support and the perception of geographical slant. *Journal of Experimental Social Psychology, 44*(5), 1246–1255.

Schneider, B. H., Sanz Martinez, Y., Koller, S. H., D'Onofrio, P. A., Puricelli, D., Lalota, G., & Lu, R. (2022). Hopelessness and shame in relation to suicide attempts by Cuban adolescents. *Transcultural Psychiatry, 59*(1), 28–36. https://doi.org/10.1177/1363461520963924

Schneidman, E. S. (1998). Perspectives on suicidology: Further reflections on suicide and psychache. *Suicide and Life-Threatening Behavior, 28*(3), 245–250.

Simon, G. E., Rutter, C. M., Peterson, D., Oliver, M., Whiteside, U., Operskalski, B., & Ludman, E. J. (2013). Does response on the PHQ-9 Depression Questionnaire predict subsequent suicide attempt or suicide death? *Psychiatric Services, 64*(12), 1195–1202. https://doi.org/10.1176/appi.ps.201200587

Simon, O. R., Swann, A. C., Powell, K. E., Potter, L. B., Kresnow, M. J., & O'Carroll, P. W. (2001). Characteristics of impulsive suicide attempts and attempters. *Suicide and Life-Threating Behavior, 32*(1 Suppl.), 49–59. https://doi.org/10.1521/suli.32.1.5.49.24212.

Steel, E. (Director). (2006). *The Bridge* [Film]. Produced by Eric Steel. "Suicide". World Health Organisation (2024). Retrieved on August 21, 2024 from www.who.int/news-room/fact-sheets/detail/suicide

Thomas, K., Chang, S. S., & Gunnell, D. (2011). Suicide epidemics: The impact of newly emerging methods on overall suicide rates—a time trends study. *BMC Public Health, 11*, 314. https://doi.org/10.1186/1471-2458-11-314

Van Orden, K. A., Witte, T. K., Cukrowicz, K. C., Braithwaite, S. R., Selby, E. A., & Joiner Jr, T. E. (2010). The interpersonal theory of suicide. *Psychological Review, 117*(2), 575–600. https://doi.org/10.1037/a0018697

Webb, D. (2010). Thinking about suicide: Contemplating and comprehending the urge to die. *Psychotherapy in Australia, 16*(4), 28–33.

Williams, C. L., Davidson, J. A., & Montgomery, I. (1980). Impulsive suicidal behavior. *Journal of Clinical Psychology, 36,* 90–94. https://doi.org/10.1002/1097-4679(198001)36:1<90::AID-JCLP2270360104>3.0.CO;2-F

Withagen, R., Araújo, D., & de Poel, H. J. (2017). Inviting affordances and agency. *New Ideas in Psychology, 45*, 11–18. https://doi.org/10.1016/j.newideapsych.2016.12.002

World Health Organization. (2024, August 21). Suicide. www.who.int/news-room/fact-sheets/detail/suicide

Wyder, M., & De Leo, D. (2007) Behind impulsive suicide attempts: Indications from a community study. *Journal of Affective Disorders, 104*(1–3), 167–173. https://doi.org/10.1016/j.jad.2007.02.015.

Yip, P. S., Caine, E., Yousuf, S., Chang, S. S., Wu, K. C. C., & Chen, Y. Y. (2012). Means restriction for suicide prevention. *The Lancet, 379*(9834), 2393–2399. https://doi.org/10.1016/S0140-6736(12)60521-2

Yip, P. S. F., Law, C. K., Fu, K. W., Law, Y. W., Wong, P. W., & Xu, Y. (2010). Restricting the means of suicide by charcoal burning. *The British Journal of Psychiatry*, 196(3), 241–242. https://doi.org/10.1192/bjp.bp.109.065185

Part 3

The Value of Ambivalence

8 The Benefits of Ambivalence and the Context of Suicide Intervention

Elizabeth Ventham and Sabrina Coninx

8.1 Introduction

We all have times when we want to avoid ambivalence. When we are stuck on a decision – whether it is big or small – we usually prefer to have one clear direction to go in, rather than oscillating between two equally tempting paths and being conflicted about what to do. There are even times when we know what we would like to feel or what we would like to be motivated towards doing (e.g., editing a paper, going on a run, confronting the problematic friend), but we just cannot help to also feel pulled in the opposite direction, hindering our potential progress.

This chapter aims to join an ongoing philosophical investigation into whether – and to what extent – ambivalence is detrimental to a person and their agency. The answer to this question carries critical implications for how we should theorize about ambivalence, but also how it should be practically approached, both generally and in cases of ambivalence about suicide. Despite the intuitive appeal of viewing ambivalence as harmful, we will focus on its potential benefits. We argue that ambivalence can, under certain circumstances, contribute positively to well-functioning agency. Furthermore, we establish a reciprocal relationship between the literature on ambivalence and suicide intervention. That is, research on the benefits of ambivalence can inform research on suicide, and *vice versa*. We suggest that the philosophical exploration of ambivalence offers significant insights into the ethical considerations surrounding suicide intervention, while psychological research on suicidal agents provides valuable case studies that are important for our understanding of the nature and value of ambivalence. This is particularly evident in research suggesting that there are no straightforward ways to 'resolve' ambivalence in suicidal cases and that, in some instances, fostering ambivalence may be beneficial for suicide prevention.

The chapter is structured as follows. Section 8.2 provides a concise introduction to our understanding of desire and ambivalence. Section 8.3

DOI: 10.4324/9781003616221-12

establishes the criteria we consider most appropriate for evaluating the potential harms and benefits of ambivalence. Section 8.4 presents a more nuanced and positive account of the relationship between ambivalence and agency, challenging the assumption that ambivalence is necessarily detrimental or only beneficial when appropriately resolved. Section 8.5 explicitly connects these reflections to the domain of ambivalence about suicide, both from the internal perspective of the agent and the external perspective of intervention, highlighting the reciprocal insights that emerge. Section 8.6 concludes.

8.2 Desires and Ambivalence

This section introduces the notion of ambivalence as we understand it alongside the notion of desire.[1] To begin, it is important to clarify that our focus is on *volitional ambivalence* – a phenomenon characterized by the presence of two or more conflicting desires.[2] For example, an ambivalent agent is not just one whose feelings on a topic are mixed, but one whose feelings can be explained in part by desires that pull in different directions. It is not just that I might feel both positively and negatively about a sibling, but instead I must have something like a desire for their success and also for their failure. It follows from this understanding that to be ambivalent about suicide is characterized by both a desire to die by suicide and a desire to live.

To get clearer on the matter, the notion of 'desire' itself requires some elaboration. 'Desire' for us serves as a broad term encompassing phenomena such as preferences, volitional tendencies, motivations, longings, or inclinations. Furthermore, desires can in principle take various forms: they may be long-standing or fleeting, carefully considered or spontaneous, conscious, or unconscious.[3] However, not all types of desires are pertinent to the notion of ambivalence we aim to address.

Harry Frankfurt – one of the authors most critical of the benefit of ambivalence – famously characterizes ambivalence as:

> (…) conflicting volitional movements or tendencies, either conscious or unconscious, that meet two conditions. First, they are inherently and hence unavoidably opposed; that is, they do not just happen to conflict on account of contingent circumstances. Second, they are both wholly internal to a person's will rather than alien to him; that is, he is not passive with respect to them.
>
> (Frankfurt, 1992, p.8)

Put succinctly, an agent is ambivalent when they hold two conflicting desires of a specific kind.

First, these desires must conflict for reasons beyond mere contingent facts. For instance, my desire to have a scoop of pistachio ice cream may conflict with my desire to have a scoop of lemon sorbet, but this conflict arises only due to circumstantial limitations – such as the amount of money in my pocket or the dimensions of the ice cream cone preventing me from having both. There is nothing inherent to the two desires that precludes the possibility of enjoying both under different circumstances.

Second, in Frankfurt's conception of ambivalence, it is essential that the conflicting desires are not alien to the agent: they must genuinely belong to them. Justin Coates (2022) refines this criterion by emphasizing that the considered desires must be integral to the agent's *practical identity*: ambivalence arises between desires where, regardless of how the conflict is resolved, the agent is forced to relinquish something deeply meaningful to them. Independent of the exact conceptualization, fleeting or superficial desires, such as the preference between ice cream flavours mentioned above, are less likely to qualify as instances of genuine ambivalence in this sense. In contrast, the conflicting desire to die by suicide and the desire to continue living are unavoidably opposed and will often (insofar as we are interested in them here) fulfil the criteria of being such that the person identifies with or cares about them in a relevant sense.

Part of the reason for our focus on this kind of ambivalence is because of its particularly strong and possibly problematic nature. If we want to provide a defence of ambivalence, then such a defence would be most interesting and most successful if it targets one of the strongest kinds of ambivalence. Furthermore, we think there is a lot of interesting progress to be made in understanding the implications of this kind of ambivalence, in part because of the important role that desires play in our mental lives. Desires are not mere isolated mental states that float freely within an agent's mind; rather, they exert a profound influence on various aspects of a person's wider mental life, cognitive, affective, epistemic, or hermeneutical. A person's desires can shape their beliefs, intentions, perception, attention, emotions, and other attitudes, serving as a driving force behind their actions and decisions.

Desires motivate behaviour, providing a foundation for reasoning and deliberation. When a particular desire becomes salient, it often shapes and constrains the agent's mental landscape, prompting reflection and planning. For example, a desire for ice cream might cause a person to start considering a new route home that goes via the gelateria – sometimes even distracting the person from whatever they're supposed to be working on instead. Or consider someone committed to receiving a PhD in philosophy, who might dedicate years to studying, choose their academic and personal priorities based on this goal, and constantly reflect on how their decisions align with their broader aspirations. Furthermore, desires exert a significant influence that extends beyond conscious and voluntary mental behaviours, affecting us "(1) through involuntary shifts in attention, (2) through changing dispositions to learn and recall, (3) through changes in subjective confidence, and (4) through distortion by emotions and wishes" (Arpaly & Schroeder, 2014, p. 227). Desires impact imagination, attention, and the vividness with which things are mentally represented to agents.[4] When a person's desires centre around a particular subject, their attention is involuntarily drawn to related instances, their memory of relevant information is heightened, and their learning about it is shaped accordingly. Desire imbues the world with a distinctive salience and character that would otherwise remain absent. When the person wants an ice cream, this might be as simple as meaning that they're more likely to notice signs for ice cream shops, to imagine the different flavours, to remember a particularly good place for waffle cones, etc. For the prospective PhD, we can imagine similar changes over the longer term: the desire to get a higher education degree in philosophy can increase their chances of noticing relevant information, cause them to imagine and plan more, make the possibilities more vivid, etc.

If anything, this important role of desire serves to highlight how difficult things can be when we are ambivalent in the manner that Frankfurt and Coates describe. In the next section, we look at this difficulty in more detail.

8.3 Ambivalence and Agency

Harry Frankfurt (1992, 2004) is interested in the *intrinsic value or disvalue* of ambivalence. In particular, he argues that ambivalence has disvalue because ambivalent agents lack unity of will, and their decisions can therefore never fully reflect their will. For Frankfurt, unity means that an agent's will is free from internal conflict and directed towards a singular commitment. Wholeheartedness requires that the agent's will is structured such that it is 'unequivocally clear' which motive the agent identifies with and 'stands behind'. Unity and wholeheartedness ensure that an agent's decisions and actions are genuinely their own. Otherwise, the agent's will is divided, leading to incoherence, self-defeat, and self-betrayal. Consequently, the agent fails to effectively pursue and attain their goals and to fully endorse their desires and resulting actions. For these reasons, Frankfurt characterizes ambivalence as an 'illness of the will'. The inherent disvalue of ambivalence in the realm of volition lies equivalent to the disvalue of self-contradiction in the realm of beliefs: it necessarily requires accepting and rejecting the same judgement, with this inconsistency setting the agent up for failure (Frankfurt 1992, 2004).

Justin Coates (2017) challenges Frankfurt's view, arguing that the two compared realms of conflicting volitions and beliefs are fundamentally distinct: while a divided will may lack internal coherence, an agent torn between two incompatible courses of action experiences a conflict very different from believing a logical contradiction such as p and $\neg p$. In particular, ambivalence does not necessarily set an agent up for failure in their practical capacities in the same way as they are set up for failure in cognitive capacities when holding contradicting beliefs. If this is true, then there might be nothing inherently disvaluable about ambivalence. Furthermore, authors such as Justin Coates (2017, 2022) and Patricia Marino (2011) highlight the broader benefits ambivalence may have for a well-functioning agent, proposing that in some circumstances, unity or wholeheartedness could itself represent defects in agency.

We hope for this chapter to contribute to ambivalence's defence, largely in the next section, by saying something more about the ways in which it can both be better for us and better for us *as agents*. That is, it is not just that being ambivalent happens to work out well for us, and that spending time being pulled two ways can happen to end up leading to a better outcome – more or less accidentally. Rather, we want to emphasize how ambivalence is an integral *part* of the rational process – not a flaw to be overcome or avoided, but a normal part of agency that contributes to its functioning.

Before proceeding to this next step, we will say something a bit more about what we mean when we say the ways in which ambivalence could be good for us or us *as agents*.

It seems most useful to adopt a broad definition of the value or disvalue of ambivalence that allows for a multidimensional analysis, incorporating various criteria that are considered in the debate (Coates 2017, 2022; Feldman & Hazlett, 2021; Marino, 2011; Rorty, 2014). We therefore propose evaluating ambivalence, in contrast to wholeheartedness, based on how it undermines or supports the following four intertwined conditions:

- **Rationality:** A well-functioning agent forms the right sorts of mental states given the input they receive from the world. They form good beliefs in terms of the evidence they are given, appropriate desires given the values that things in the world have, etc. The agent's internal state coheres well with the world as they see it and they are responsive to reasons.
- **Agential Effectiveness:** A well-functioning agent is not hindered by paralyzing effects of indecisiveness or ineffective cycles of contradicting actions. Agential effectiveness is understood as the agent's ability to perform coherent actions based on reasons and thus directly relates to the practical success of an agent's actions.

- **Autonomy:** A well-functioning agent is able to govern themselves, to make decisions, and to act in accordance with their own reasons, free from external coercion.
- **Authenticity:** A well-functioning agent does not experience pervasive alienation from their choices but experiences them as an expression of who they consider themselves to be. Authenticity refers to the alignment between desires and actions with the subject's 'true' self – what they deeply care about and consider representative of who they are.

These criteria are not supposed to carve out clear and distinct boundaries of different kinds of agency and rationality. They are overlapping, and a full analysis of the ways in which they interact would be more work than we are able to provide here. We also do not mean for these to be the only ways to understand the above terms – rationality, for example, being particularly controversial. For now, we simply wish to emphasize some of the ways in which we can evaluate the functioning of agency. In the next section, we argue how ambivalence can benefit the agent in each of these ways.

8.4 Benefit and Harm: Wholeheartedness vs. Ambivalence

Based on the different ways of thinking about well-functioning agency discussed in the previous section, we now argue in greater detail for the claim that ambivalence is not necessarily disvaluable and, in some cases, can even be beneficial, regardless of whether it is ultimately resolved through wholehearted decisions. Furthermore, we identify cases in which unity of will and wholeheartedness in decision-making can themselves prove detrimental. As the analysis of cases will demonstrate, there is rarely a rigid or absolute verdict to be made: the evaluation of benefits and harms is a gradual and dynamic manner. Nonetheless, we particularly aim to show what Patricia Marino phrased as follows: "Valuational inconsistency is not dangerous, and can be worth keeping; the valuationally inconsistent person may have an internally divided self, but an internally divided self can be a fully rational and good self" (2011, p. 53). In the sections, we will systematically argue for this claim in reference to the proposed criteria of (1) rationality, (2) agential effectiveness, and (3) autonomy and authenticity.

8.4.1 Rationality

At first glance, it might seem that ambivalence renders the agent irrational, as they are holding two desires that are in themselves contradictory. If a person cannot have both A and B, how can it be rational to want both?

This question implicitly assumes a definition of rationality based on the internal structure of mental states, specifically, the avoidance of contradictory desires. From *this* perspective, ambivalence appears irrational and, therefore, undesirable. However, this approach risks assuming the very conclusion it seeks to establish. Instead, we propose a more productive framework of understanding rationality in terms of an agent's capacity to respond to good reasons for or against a given action.[5] Based on *this* understanding, we argue that conflicting desires can, in certain contexts, positively contribute to an agent's rationality.

And while we concede that there is a sense in which ambivalence is disvaluable, we want to argue that there are additional ways that these same opposed desires can contribute positively to a person's rationality. In some cases, it is warranted to be ambivalent when there is a genuine tension among our desires, mirroring complexities in the world as it relates to our own values and goals. Ambivalence, in this sense, can be seen as fitting: life situations and decisions are often multifaceted, layered, and contradictory (Feldman & Hazlett, 2021). As such, we can have good reasons to hold conflicting corresponding desires.

Consider the example of an academic, called Aoife, who deeply values her work and has invested substantial effort in building her career. To advance in her field, she must relocate to a new institute in Italy, a move that suits her adventurous character but conflicts with her equally deep desire to remain close to her family, friends, and partner in her hometown. Both desires – the pursuit of a fulfilling career and the commitment to her relationships – are central to her identity and unavoidably exclusive. This situation illustrates how ambivalence can reflect the multifaceted nature of Aoife's circumstances and identity rather than a flaw in her will. These two conflicting potential lives are both valuable in a way that speaks to important aspects of her character. That she desires both speaks well to the way her desires are responsive to reasons.

Properly functioning as an agent in this context means acknowledging and endorsing the reasons on both sides. In fact, an agent who fails to experience this ambivalence might demonstrate an insensitivity to the significant values at stake. As Coates (2017) notes, such insensitivity would result in a failure to take seriously the residue of unchosen alternatives. If Aoife were not torn between her career and her relationship, she would risk disregarding the genuine value of one of these options. This lack of ambivalence would suggest a failure to fully engage with the moral and practical dimensions of her situation, thus making her irrational.

Ambivalence can not only be an expression of rational agency, but increasing ambivalence can in some cases make an agent more epistemically responsible, as it allows them to evaluate more carefully the range of available options. Remember the variety of ways that desire influences an agent's mental landscape – not just affecting her decisions but also the things in the world she pays attention to, the ease with which she learns about particular options, and the imaginative capacities she has in regard to what effects her decisions might have. Having desires that pull in different directions can be a vital tool in understanding what those directions really look like. Ambivalence therefore can allow agents to explore and evaluate their options more thoroughly. It not only facilitates the acquisition of propositional knowledge but also enhances the ability to vividly imagine and emotionally connect with the realities of each choice. Ambivalence can signal an agent's ability to hold multiple perspectives and carefully weigh competing outcomes.

Let us reconsider the example of Aoife, torn between moving to Italy, which excites her sense of adventure and career ambition, and staying in her hometown, where she enjoys close personal relationships. Her ambivalence might compel her to learn more about both options, making her more sensitive to relevant facts about Italy and her hometown alike. She is more likely to listen in on conversations about Italy, pay attention to tourist adverts, or ruminate over what she would be missing when she leaves. By desiring both outcomes, Aoife can better imagine the practical and emotional aspects of each possibility, simulating what life would be like in each scenario. This vivid imagining helps her appreciate the full depth of each choice. Without ambivalence, she might fail to recognize the emotional weight or significance of either path. Thus, ambivalence is not always an obstacle to rational decision-making, but can be a valuable tool for navigating complex, value-laden decisions.

That said, ambivalence can sometimes mislead agents, causing them to overestimate the availability or benefits of a particular option. For instance, being torn between the indicated two options might be misleading for Aoife, in case she later discovers that the position in Italy no longer exists or does not offer the adventurous benefits initially expected. Such mistakes, however, can happen whether or not the agents are ambivalent. As long as it can sometimes give agents a new tool to act rationally with, then our point stands.

8.4.2 Agential Effectiveness

A serious concern about ambivalence is that it can paralyze an agent, trapping them in indecisiveness or leading to cycles of contradictory actions that negate one another. This criticism is rooted in the idea that ambivalence undermines the agent's ability to make decisions and act effectively towards their goals, which is central to being a well-functioning agent. Again, Harry Frankfurt provides a strong critique of ambivalence along these lines:

> In order for a conflict (…) to be resolved, so that the person is freed of his ambivalence, it is not necessary that either of his conflicting impulses disappear. It is not even necessary that either of them increase or diminish in strength. Resolution requires only that the person become finally and unequivocally clear as to which side of the conflict he is on. The forces mobilized on the other side may then persist with as much intensity as before; but as soon as he has definitely established just where he himself stands, his will is no longer divided and his ambivalence is therefore gone. He has placed himself wholeheartedly behind one of the conflicting impulses, and not at all behind the other.
>
> (Frankfurt 2004, p. 91)

Thus, for Frankfurt, episodes of ambivalence require a wholehearted resolution – a complete alignment of one's actions with one's values and goals by committing to one of the conflicting desires as one's own. Consider the example of Aoife again: if she remains ambivalent about her choice, she might be at risk of becoming unable to make any decision or of vacillating between both options, such as taking the job in another country but continuously travelling back to her hometown – thus leaving her worse off in terms of her new job as well as her relationships. From Frankfurt's perspective, resolving this ambivalence by committing wholeheartedly to one path would restore the scholar's capacity to act decisively and effectively in line with her core values.

This critique emphasizes the potential risks of ambivalence. However, the necessity of resolving ambivalence through wholehearted commitment remains a subject of debate. Not all reasonable resolutions of ambivalence require fully endorsing one option at the expense of the other. Coates (2017) suggests that individuals can navigate ambivalence without unifying their will, instead choosing to prioritize one desire as the basis for action in a given context while continuing to identify with the alternative. For instance, Aoife might weigh the reasons for and against each option and make a practical decision for taking the new job. What matters, then, is not the unification of the will or wholehearted commitment to a single option but the agent's ability to *constructively* manage ambivalence. Securing agential effectiveness involves finding sufficient reasons to act in one direction or another, and this could happen wholeheartedly or not.

Still, would it not be better to resolve ambivalence in a wholehearted manner, even if it is not strictly required? Not necessarily. As we discussed in the previous sub-section, wholeheartedly committing to one option can, in some cases, be irrational because it risks making the agent insensitive to valid reasons for reconsidering their decision. The desires that are not selected as the basis for action should not always be entirely discarded, as their continued presence allows the agent to remain open to new information or changing circumstances that might warrant reevaluating their choice. In this sense, maintaining some engagement with the rejected alternatives ensures that the agent's decision-making remains sensitive to their axiological truth and reflective of the complexities of their situation (Rorty, 2014).

We agree that there are indeed circumstances where wholeheartedly committing to one option might be most beneficial. Fully embracing a decision can reduce psychological stress, limit the cognitive burden of ongoing deliberation, and alleviate the grief associated with lost opportunities, or prevent regret over past decisions. For example, our protagonist Aoife might decide to commit entirely to her career ambitions if the process of maintaining ambivalence becomes emotionally exhausting or disrupts her ability to focus or engage in actions related to either option. Thus, such wholehearted resolutions can sometimes be beneficial for a well-functioning agent, and as such an agent can have good reasons to strive for wholeheartedness.

Our aim has not been to deny the value of wholehearted resolutions of ambivalence altogether but rather to challenge the assumption that ambivalence necessarily undermines agential effectiveness. When approached constructively, ambivalence can foster richer engagement with one's values and promote reasons-based decision-making. The critical point is that the harm or benefit of ambivalence depends thereby on how it is managed and not on the ambivalence itself (also see Chapter 9). For example, cases of chronic indecisiveness, where individuals struggle to make choices, do not reflect a flaw in ambivalence itself. Instead, they highlight the need for effective strategies to navigate ambivalence.[6] Importantly, mastering ambivalence does not always require a wholehearted resolution. It requires the ability to act on reasons and navigate complex decisions without being paralyzed by indecision – wholeheartedly or not.

8.4.3 Autonomy and Authenticity

We define autonomy as the capacity of a well-functioning agent to govern themselves and to act in accordance with their own reasons. Harry Frankfurt (2004) argues that unresolved ambivalence threatens autonomy by dividing the self, thereby preventing the agent from fully endorsing any particular course of action as genuinely their own. If autonomy is about self-governance and the identification with one's own action, then this might seem impossible in case the agent is ambivalent. However, we aim to also highlight ways in which ambivalence can support the self in this way.

Ambivalence can enhance autonomy by making different options more salient, imaginatively vivid, and emotionally accessible, encouraging deeper reflection on the values and reasons behind each choice. For instance, her ambivalence might force Aoife to engage thoughtfully with both possibilities which makes her final decision more an action of her own than spontaneously but wholeheartedly committing to one option over the other. Similarly, Marino observes: "An inconsistent person may be more obviously acting autonomously than a consistent one, since an inconsistent person must reflect before acting, whereas a consistent person—especially an unconflicted one—may be acting simply on impulse" (2011, p. 56).

Similar considerations apply to the condition of authenticity. Authenticity, as understood here, entails not only regarding one's reasons for acting as one's own but also aligning them with the values and goals that constitute one's 'true self', that is, those aspects that are considered most central to one's identity. At first glance, ambivalence might appear incompatible with authenticity: conflicting desires may seem inherently self-defeating or self-betraying, preventing the agent from living in alignment with the core aspects of their identity. Moreover, being torn between opposing desires might seem fundamentally problematic, undermining the coherence and clarity that often characterize an authentic sense of self. For instance, if Aoife feels equally drawn to both staying in her hometown and moving to Italy, it might initially appear that her inability to wholeheartedly pursue either path compromises her ability to act in a way that reflects her true self.

This interpretation is misguided, as ambivalence does not necessarily undermine authenticity (Poltera, 2010). On the contrary, decisions made through reflective deliberation prompted by ambivalence may not only demonstrate autonomy but also be profoundly authentic to the individual. Authentic decisions often arise from a genuine engagement with conflicting values, rather than the absence of ambivalence or an impulsive, wholehearted choice of one alternative over the other. Moreover, remaining ambivalent does not inherently preclude authenticity. If a person deeply identifies with two conflicting desires as integral to their identity, then their ambivalence may itself reflect their most authentic self. While such inner conflict may sometimes give rise to negative emotions – such as self-doubt, self-hatred, or anxiety – this does not make the person less authentic. Importantly, this kind of psychological distress is not a necessary consequence of ambivalence. For instance, our protagonist Aoife may decide to pursue one path, such as moving to Italy, while still valuing the alternative and making peace with the fact that life often entails difficult choices that preclude 'having it all'.

8.5 Suicidal Ambivalence

Finally, we aim to connect the previous discussion of the ways in which ambivalence can be beneficial for agents with one particular case study: that of suicidal ambivalence. Suicidal ambivalence characterizes a person's desire to die by suicide and the conflicting desire to continue living. This is a useful case to focus on, because these two research areas can both inform each other, as indicated in the introduction. That is, understanding the benefits of ambivalence can tell us something about the ethics of intervention in cases of suicide, and looking at cases of suicide can help us to consider the more theoretical merits of ambivalence.

One point of clarification before developing the previous claim in more detail. We take it that some cases of suicide are worth preventing. This does not mean that in all possible instances an agent is better off in some relevant sense if their suicide is prevented. However, we assume that at least sometimes they are. These are the cases that we believe to be most important when it comes to questions such as the ethics of intervention, and that is the reason for our focus on it here.

8.5.1 The Benefit of Ambivalence and Suicide Intervention

In terms of demonstrating why work on the value of ambivalence is useful when it comes to theorizing about the ethics of suicide prevention, a lot of the work has been done already. We have argued, above, that ambivalence can be beneficial for well-functioning agency. It is not just that it can work out well for them, but it can be an important and valuable part of being a rational creature.

Recent research suggests that ambivalence as we have described it is common in suicidal ideation and behaviour.[7] Thus, ambivalence might shape the decision-making process before, during, and after suicidal behaviour, making it a crucial element in understanding and addressing suicide.[8]

If we only pay attention to the ways in which ambivalence is bad for an agent – the ways that ambivalence might make an agent less rational, functional, autonomous, etc. – then this might make suicide interventions more justifiable than they would be otherwise. Agents who demonstrate ambivalence might therefore be more at risk of particular kinds of paternalistic intervention that would not affect non-ambivalent agents. Of course, it might be that certain kinds of paternalistic intervention are impermissible in any case, or that there are some kinds of intervention that are worth putting in place for everyone, and that are not particularly intrusive.[9] But if there are some kinds of intervention that *are* intrusive – and that only become justifiable if the agent in question appears to not be acting rationally or functioning well as an agent – then we have shown that ambivalence, on its own, is not enough to do that justificatory work. Ambivalence is *not* a clear defect in agency, but can be a sign of an agent's proper functioning – a way of properly responding to the values in the world that might accurately reflect both a complicated world and a complicated but authentic agent. There may be other factors that make an agent more worthy of such interventions, such as the desire to die on its own. But ambivalence is not it.

There are other reasons why understanding the benefits of suicidal ambivalence might have an impact on suicide prevention, and that is through thinking about the process of how such prevention works. Bryan (2022), for example, emphasizes the importance of increasing ambivalence in individuals feeling driven to take their own lives. When someone is overly determined or even wholeheartedly committed to end their life, they might shift in a rapid manner from uncertainty/ambivalence to certainty. This partly relies on the dynamic nature of suicidal ideation that is hard to predict. Encouraging ambivalence in this context, limiting a person's means to kill themselves, or making means less lethal can be lifesaving, as it prevents individuals (maybe not from attempting) but from dying by suicide and thus provides time and space to re-introduce ambivalence through interventions.[10]

Ambivalence can initiate a crucial period of self-reflection and reconsideration, helping individuals see that their current state is not permanent or that there are other viable paths and solutions. This ambivalence can disrupt the tunnel vision that often accompanies suicidal ideation (Shneidman, 1998), where the individual sees death as the only solution to their problems. The ultimate goal in cases of suicidal intervention is to resolve the ambivalence in a direction that supports life and well-being. This is not about achieving wholeheartedness in the decision to live or die, but rather about guiding the resolution of ambivalence towards choosing life (see studies on motivational interviewing by Britton 2012; Britton et al., 2020).

Interestingly, there is an asymmetry in the will to live and the will to die. The wish to live and the wish to die do not behave like two ends of the same pole pushing in two different directions and being equally relevant for suicidal behaviour. As Bryan et al. (2016) argue, suicidal behaviour is primarily driven by the absence of a strong will to live rather than the presence of a strong will to die. Moreover, research suggests that a strong wish to live serves as a protective factor against suicide, whereas a weaker wish to die does not necessarily predict suicidal behaviour (Bryan, 2022, pp. 188–189). Patients whose wish to live is equal to or greater than their wish to die are less likely to die by suicide (Brown et al., 2005).

Finally, further insight might be gained by considering research on ambivalence in medical and clinical settings (Moore et al., 2021), for example, when patients reveal contradictory or oscillating attitudes towards treatment choices. In such cases, we may encounter genuine ambivalence, where patients simultaneously endorse multiple, incompatible options while also seeking ways to reconcile them. Similarly, discussions on self-illness ambiguity – where individuals struggle to distinguish between their own agency and the influence of their illness in decision-making (Dings & de Haan, 2022) – might offer valuable insights. These perspectives could enhance our understanding of how ambivalence relates to rationality, agential effectiveness, authenticity, and autonomy, also in the context of suicide.

8.5.2 Learning from Cases of Suicidal Ambivalence

In this second part, we argue that considerations on suicidal ambivalence can teach us something valuable about ambivalence more generally. In particular, it is an important example of the real-life difficulties of resolving ambivalence.

Non-idealized agents cannot resolve ambivalence from an objective standpoint. When an agent chooses between two desires that they have, they cannot appeal to what is objectively better for them or what is objectively best overall. The best the agent can do is make a judgement about the options from what they believe from their perspective. Even if they were able to do that much, sometimes this will point them towards what is objectively best, and other times it will fail to do so. Our perspectives, after all, are not always correct.

This problem with resolving ambivalence has been brought up in the literature before. Jacqui Poltera (2010), building on work from David Velleman (2006), discusses an example of a homosexual man growing up in hostile surroundings.[11] He is caught between the desire to embrace his sexuality and the desire to repress it. From an external perspective, it might seem easier to see the right thing to do – the thing that would be best for him overall and that would be the best reflection of his authentic self: to embrace it. But it is hard to see what we would be able to point to (in terms of the agent's own perspective) that would cause the agent to resolve their ambivalence that way. The internalized homophobia might make it very difficult for the agent to identify with his identity, and it might seem to him that the right thing to do is to repress his sexuality instead. This is true even when the agent is trying to do the right thing and trying to be authentic to what he really wants.

Research on suicidal agents gives us another important example of how misleading our own attempts to resolve ambivalence can be. It is notoriously difficult to predict which patients will attempt suicide out of the number who are at risk, and there are no clear or agreed-upon factors. One potential candidate for a (albeit weak to moderate) correlation, according to Teismann et al (2016) and Chu et al (2017), is 'perceived burdensomeness'. If an agent conceptualizes themselves as being more of a burden on others, this is one possible factor, among many others, that could make them more likely to move from thinking about suicide to attempting it. But this means that when such an agent tries to resolve their suicidal ambivalence, then thinking about what their moral obligations are, or what might be better for people overall, will point them in a direction that might not prove better for them overall: towards, instead of away from, suicide. Where the best thing for them and others might be to live, there might not be a clear internal route that they are able to take while perceiving themselves in that way. The reality of our inability to resolve ambivalence in a way that works out well for us is made clearer by the case of suicidal ambivalence. This is another good cautionary point, then, against in principle supporting wholeheartedness over ambivalence.

8.6 Concluding Remarks

In this chapter, we made a case in favour of ambivalence's place in properly functioning, rational agency. Even in cases of ambivalence about suicide, we argued that there is nothing inherent about the ambivalence itself that is a sign of poorly functioning agency or irrationality. This means that one potential ground for intervention is taken away. If intervention is justified, it must be on other grounds, such as facts about the desire to die itself, regardless of whether the agent is ambivalent about it. It is important, we think, not to ascribe irrationality to someone without good enough justification.

In terms of what this tells us about ambivalence, the practical facts of the desires of suicidal agents also give us reasons why, in real life, ambivalence can be better than wholeheartedness and ambivalence should not always be something we look to resolve. When an agent is ambivalent, it is important to recognize that ambivalence for its value in decision-making and in its value for helping them see the complicated world as it really is. This can be better than just choosing to resolve the ambivalence in a wholehearted but overall harmful manner.

Notes

1 See Chapter 2 for a more detailed examination of the philosophical debate surrounding the notion of ambivalence.
2 See Chapter 3 for the discussion of other types of ambivalence.
3 See Schroeder (2020) for these and more distinctions of different types of desires. There are also more controversial aspects to the nature of desire, on which we remain agnostic for current purposes. For example, the ontological status of desires remains an open question. Some theories conceptualize desires as dispositions, such as to act or to experience pleasure (Schroeder, 2020); others regard them as learning systems (Arpaly and Schroeder, 2014) or even as

a kind of belief (Gregory 2021). While these debates are significant overall, they will not directly influence the argument presented here.

4 See, for example, Sinhababu 2017 for how desire has this impact but also Myers 2021 and Badura 2021 for on how imagination itself is epistemically important

5 We are aware that this is not the only relevant way rationality can be understood, while this functional reading seems most crucial to us for the context at hand. Responsiveness to reasons is also sometimes discussed as important for agents being in control, such as in McHugh (2017).

6 See also Chapter 9 on unmastered ambivalence.

7 See Chapter 2 on the empirical state of art on suicidal ambivalence.

8 See Chapter 2 for an in-depth discussion on the ethics of suicide prevention in the light of ambivalence.

9 See Chapter 11 for a more in-depth discussion on ambivalence and paternalistic suicide prevention.

10 For more, see Chapter 11.

11 The case used is a real one, inspired by Stephen Fry's autobiography *Moab is my washpot* (1998).

References

Arpaly, N., & Schroeder, T. (2014). *In praise of desire*. Oxford University Press.

Badura, C. (2021). How imagination can justify. In *Epistemic uses of imagination* (1st ed., p. 19). Routledge. https://doi.org/10.4324/9781003041979

Britton, P. C., Conner, K. R., Chapman, B. P., & Maisto, S. A. (2020) Motivational interviewing to address suicidal ideation: A randomized controlled trial in veterans. *Suicide and Life Threatening Behavior*, *50*(1), 233–248. https://doi.org/10.1111/sltb.12581

Britton, P. C., Conner, K. R., & Maisto, S. A. (2012). An open trial of motivational interviewing to address suicidal ideation with hospitalized veterans. *Journal of Clinical Psychology*, *68*(9), 961–71. https://doi.org/10.1002/jclp.21885

Brown, G. K., Steer, R. A., Henriques, G. R., & Beck, A. T. (2005). The internal struggle between the wish to die and the wish to live: a risk factor for suicide. *American Journal of Psychiatry*, *162*(10):1977–1979. https://doi.org/10.1176/appi.ajp.162.10.1977

Bryan, C. J. (2022). *Rethinking suicide: Why prevention fails, and how we can do better*. Oxford University Press.

Bryan, C. J., Rudd, M. D., Peterson, A. L., Young-McCaughan, S., & Wertenberger, E. G. (2016). The ebb and flow of the wish to live and the wish to die among suicidal military personnel. *Journal of Affective Disorders*, *202*, 58–66.

Chu, C., Buchman-Schmitt, J. M., Stanley, I. H., Hom, M. A., Tucker, R. P., Hagan, C. R., Rogers, M. L., Podlogar, M. C., Chiurliza, B., Ringer, F. B., Michaels, M. S., Patros, C. H. G., & Joiner, T. E. (2017). The interpersonal theory of suicide: A systematic review and meta-analysis of a decade of cross-national research. *Psychological Bulletin, 143*(12), 1313–1345. https://doi.org/10.1037/bul0000123

Coates, D. J. (2017) A wholehearted defense of ambivalence. *The Journal of Ethics, 21*(4), 419–444. https://doi.org/ 10.1007/s10892-017-9257-x

Coates, D. J. (2022). *In praise of ambivalence*. Oxford University Press.

Dings R., & de Haan, S. (2022). The role of self-illness ambiguity and self-medication ambiguity in clinical decision-making. *The American Journal of Bioethics*, *22*(6), 58–60. https://doi.org/10.1080/15265161.2022.2063436

Feldman, S. D. & Hazlett, A. (2021). Fitting inconsistency and reasonable resolution. In B. Brogaard & D. E. Gatzia (eds.), *The philosophy and psychology of ambivalence: Being of two minds* (pp. 131–146). Routledge.

Frankfurt, H. (1992). The faintest passion. *Proceedings and Addresses of the American Philosophical Association*, 66, 5–16.

Frankfurt, H. (2004). *The reasons of love*. Princeton University Press

Fry, S. (1998). *Moab is my washpot*. Arrow Books.

Gregory, A. (2021). *Desire as belief*: A study of desire, motivation, and rationality. Oxford University Press.

Marino, P. (2011) Ambivalence, valuational inconsistency, and the divided self. *Philosophy and Phenomenological Research*, *83*, 41–71.

Moore, B., Nelson, R. H., Ubel, P. A., & Blumenthal-Barby, J. (2021). Two minds, one patient: Clearing up confusion about 'ambivalence'. *The American Journal of Bioethics*, *22*(6), 37–47. https://doi.org/10.1080/15265161.2021.1887965

McHugh, C. (2017). Attitudinal control. *Synthese*, 194(8), 2745–2762.

Myers, J. (2021). *Reasoning with imagination*. In *Epistemic uses of imagination* (1st ed., p. 19). Routledge. https://doi.org/10.4324/9781003041979

Poltera, J. (2010). Is ambivalence an agential vice? *Philosophical Explorations*, 13(3), 293–305.

Rorty, A. (2014). The ethics of collaborative ambivalence. *The Journal of Ethics*, *18*, 391–403. https://doi.org/10.1007/s10892-014-9184-z

Schroeder, T. (2020). Desire. In E. N. Zalta (Ed.), *The Stanford encyclopedia of philosophy* (Summer 2020 Edition). Retrieved from https://plato.stanford.edu/archives/sum2020/entries/desire/

Shneidman, E. (1998). *The suicidal mind*. Oxford University Press.

Sinhababu, N. (2017). *Humean nature: How desire explains action, thought, and feeling*. Oxford University Press.

Teismann, T., Forkmann, T., Rath, D., Glaesmer, H., & Margraf, J. (2016). Perceived burdensomeness and suicide ideation in adult outpatients receiving exposure therapy for anxiety disorders. *Behaviour Research and Therapy*, 85, 1–5.

Velleman, J. D. (2006). *Self to self: Selected essays*. Cambridge University Press.

9 Unmastered Ambivalence

Friedrich Hausen and Martin Weichold

9.1 Introduction

For a long time, in philosophy ambivalence has been regarded as something harmful, something to be avoided. In psychology, it has even been linked to pathological states. For example, Eugen Bleuler (1911/2014), who coined the term, used it to describe characteristic mental states in schizophrenia. Following the traditional philosophical perspective, Harry Frankfurt (2004, p. 95) refers to ambivalence as "a disease of the mind". According to Frankfurt, ambivalence leads to self-defeat and undermines a person's well-functioning agency and coherent self-affirmation, both of which are crucial for well-being.

More recently, however, Justin Coates has, in his influential book *Praise of Ambivalence*, presented a more positive approach to ambivalence. He persuasively highlights the advantages of ambivalent states in certain contexts. Coates argues that personal integrity does not necessitate the absence of ambivalence. Moreover, Coates contends that even an extremely painful ambivalence can sometimes reflect deeper moral integrity and normative competence, suggesting that "ambivalence rather than whole-heartedness can signify well-functioning agency" (Coates, 2023, p. 73).

Thus, we are confronted with conflicting views on ambivalence. Some of these tensions may stem from conceptual differences,[1] but they may also reflect a genuine conflict.[2] Both perspectives offer valuable analyses of ambivalence. On one hand, in certain situations – particularly dilemmatic ones – deep ambivalence, involving a partial sacrifice of wholeheartedness, may be necessary for maintaining an open-minded, context-sensitive, and balanced relationship with people, things, options, and the world. On the other hand, in some cases, the link between ambivalence and serious threats to personal integrity or certain mental disorders is evident. Recent research on disorders with high suicide rates, such as borderline personality disorder and schizotypal disorders, suggests a strong association with

DOI: 10.4324/9781003616221-13

ambivalence (cf. Kwapil et al., 2022). In these contexts, highly ambivalent states are not merely epiphenomena but are often considered symptoms and, in some cases, contributing factors to the disorders (cf. Maiese 2016).

Against this background, the central question of this paper emerges: Is there a systematic way of distinguishing between those cases of ambivalence that are harmful and those cases that are praiseworthy? The answer which we want to suggest and discuss is the following thesis (T):

T: An instance of ambivalence is directly harmful for the ambivalent person to the extent that it instantiates unmastered, strong, and temporally extended ambivalence (USTA).

We will elaborate on thesis (T) and the concepts encompassed by "unmastered, strong, and temporally extended ambivalence" (USTA) in the following sections. As we will argue, strong unmastered ambivalence poses a significant threat to a person's integrity – though not necessarily in the manner Frankfurt suggests. While recent discussions of ambivalence in relation to suicide often highlight the life-sustaining potential of suicidal ambivalence (the ambivalence between the preference for life and death), our paper will concentrate on certain highly ambivalent states that exert a pressure of suffering and might motivate suicidal thought and behavior.

Our paper is structured as follows. In the next step, we want to characterize USTA (Section 9.2), in order to make clear which cases of ambivalence are praiseworthy and which are harmful according to our account. Then, we will point to certain problems in the story Harry Frankfurt tells about the relation between ambivalence and integrity (Section 9.3). In the following three sections, we will argue that USTA does indeed pose a threat to integrity, but that ambivalence and integrity have to be rethought in a more organic, gradualist, and context-sensitive way. In Section 9.4, we will revisit the idea of ambivalence, and in Section 9.5, we will revisit the idea of integrity. In Section 9.6, we will explore how exactly USTA threatens integrity. In Section 9.7, we use our organically coherentist conception for making a suggestion about what it means to master strong ambivalence. Finally, we end with a conclusion (Section 9.8).

9.2 Unmastered, Strong, and Temporally Extended Ambivalence

In this section, we will point out how those cases of ambivalence that are harmful can be characterized. According to our thesis (T), these are those cases of ambivalence that are unmastered, strong, and temporally extended. In this section, we will explain what we mean by "unmastered", "strong", and "temporally extended". And we will give examples of such cases of ambivalence, showing that they result in harm. In the following sections, we will search for a deeper reason for why exactly cases of USTA are cases of harmful ambivalence, reasons that will lead us to the topic of threats of integrity.

As we argue in another chapter in this book (Chapter 3), ambivalence is:

Ambivalence: Subject S is ambivalent about X if and only if S values X both in a positive and in a negative way.

When considering cases where ambivalence plays a significant role in mental suffering, the question arises: What is truly harmful? Is it the ambivalence itself, as Harry Frankfurt emphasizes, or is it the inability to competently manage it, as Justin Coates suggests, perhaps due to a lack of preparation for ambivalent states? It seems both trivial and accurate to say that harmful ambivalence is characterized by a person's inability to deal with it in an integral way. This allows us to distinguish between ambivalences that are managed with integrity and those that are not. We can refer to an instance of ambivalence that is managed with integrity as "mastered ambivalence" and an instance that is not as "unmastered ambivalence". In the following, we will discuss the features of (a) strength, (b) endurance, and (c) unmasteredness of ambivalence in more detail:

a Let the term "strength of ambivalence" serve as a general concept that encompasses degrees of intensity, the extent of felt pain, the range of relevant influence, and the depth of personal involvement. The strength of ambivalence can vary significantly. Similarly, a person's ability to manage strong ambivalence can also vary. Depending on factors such as the specific situation, individual preparation, and available resources, ambivalences may either be manageable or too overtaxing to be mastered. In brief, we can note (Chapter 3):

Strong ambivalence: Subject S is strongly ambivalent about X if and only if S has an experience of valuing X both in a positive and in a negative way, resulting in a strong inner conflict.

Weak ambivalence: Subject S is weakly ambivalent about X if and only if S values X both in a positive and in a negative way, resulting only in a weak or no inner conflict.

Not all ambivalences are strong or harmful. For example, you might have ambivalent feelings toward a distant colleague, fluctuating between trust and mistrust, or between high and low esteem. While such feelings may be unpleasant, if the relationship is relatively superficial and its consequences are insignificant, you might choose not to invest the effort required to master this ambivalence or to find a more coherent way to cope with it. You might simply tolerate the ambivalence without suffering any harm due to the relationship's lack of importance.

However, if you experience deep ambivalence toward someone more significant in your life, such as a beloved partner, there is a strong reason to seek clarity in the relationship. Let's suppose that you share trust, enchantment, and warm feelings in important realms of your relationship on the one hand, but there are, on the other hand, other aspects provoking deep disgust or feelings of humiliation, which increasingly are challenging and poisoning the relationship, eroding its realms of love and trust. In such cases, it seems intuitive that investing in inner clarification and working on mastering the ambivalence becomes crucial, whether this leads to a divorce or to finding a better way to manage the relationship.

b The notion that unmastered, strong ambivalence must be "temporally extended" to be harmful can be understood through the following analogy: Imagine a person exposed to a temperature of 80°C in dry air. Under normal conditions, enduring this heat for 10 minutes is bearable and not harmful. However, if the exposure extends beyond 30 minutes, it becomes life-threatening. Similarly, experiencing a state of strong, unmastered ambivalence for a brief period may not necessarily cause harm. However, if this state persists for an extended period – months or even indefinitely – it becomes detrimental.[3]

For example, consider the following two variations of the famous example of *Sophie's choice*: Sophie sees her two small daughter twins drowning in deep water and knows that she can only rescue one of them and has to decide fast to avoid the death of both. In another situation in a less developed country Sophie's two twins both suffer from a heart defect, and in the years, it increases to a threat to the life of both. But she can only afford to pay the money for one heart surgery, not for both. So she has to decide who will have a chance to survive. And after the extremely painful decision, she lives together for months with the daughter that will die, who knows that she will die and that her sister probably will survive. And the mother, in deep struggle, questions her decision, but doesn't change it. After the heart surgery and sufficient recovery, the other child comes back from hospital. And some months later, the other child dies. The second situation with the long-lasting dilemma is more likely to bring out a long-lasting ambivalence that may be a threat to the mother's self-esteem, to her ability to love and to appreciate life at all.

c Concerning the difference of mastered and unmastered ambivalence, we can say, borrowing again from our other chapter in this book (Chapter 3):

Mastered ambivalence: Subject S manifests mastered ambivalence about X if and only if S values X both in a positive and in a negative way and copes with this in a way that preserves well-functioning agency.

Unmastered ambivalence: Subject S manifests unmastered ambivalence about X if and only if S values X both in a positive and in a negative way, but does not cope with this in a way that preserves well-functioning agency.

Mastering ambivalence means integrating a state of ambivalence into one's web of attitudes and self-governed agency in a coherent and functioning way. Staying within ambivalence and mastering it often demonstrates greater normative competence compared to simply escaping from it. This is illustrated in Justin Coates' discussion of Agamemnon's tragic dilemma and his decision to kill his daughter (Coates, 2023, p. 117).

Agamemnon faces a tragic dilemma when the goddess Artemis demands the sacrifice of his daughter Iphigenia to allow the Greek fleet to sail to Troy. Torn between his duty as a leader and his love as a father, he must choose between betraying his army's cause and committing an unthinkable act against his own child. Agamemnon ultimately decides to sacrifice Iphigenia, prioritizing his role as commander and the success of the war. This decision reveals the tragic conflict between personal loyalty and public duty, highlighting the devastating cost of leadership and the inescapable nature of fate in Greek tragedy. Coates argues that it might have been rational for Agamemnon to sacrifice Iphigenia. However, Coates describes problematic aspects of the way he does it. Agamemnon abruptly resolves his ambivalence without deeper troubles of ambivalence, disconnecting from his love for his daughter (Coates, 2023, p. 124). According to Coates, this immediate shift in his practical identity shows a lack of integrity and normative competence. Here lies a deep problem. On the one hand, remaining in such a strong ambivalence and working to master, it may show integrity. On the other hand, staying in a state of unmastered ambivalence can pose a threat to a person's integrity and agency. Thus, the challenge lies in navigating ambivalence in a way that preserves one's integrity.

So far, we have made clear what we mean by USTA. In the rest of this section, we want to give some examples of such cases of ambivalence, illustrating how harmful they are. This is also meant as a reminder for keeping in view how much suffering can be caused by ambivalence.

Cases of harmful ambivalence, specifically instances of USTA, are not uncommon. Some particularly striking examples can be found in cases of "double binds", as described by Bateson (1956) and Watzlawick et al. (1967). These paradoxical relationships involve deep existential dependence and contradictory expectations and communication structures, which can result in severe psychological consequences, including schizophrenia.[4] In such cases, psychosis may emerge as a means of escaping the painful paradoxes inherent in the relationship.

A classic example of a double bind involves a boy in a psychiatric clinic who is visited by his mother. When he approaches her to show affection, she stiffens and withdraws, nonverbally indicating that she does not want to be hugged. Confused, the boy hesitates but still hugs her. In response, the mother verbally scolds him, saying things like, "Don't you love me?" or "Why are you so distant?" This creates a no-win situation for the boy: If he doesn't hug her, he's accused of being unloving; if he does, he disregards her nonverbal cues, such as her stiffening and withdrawing. Against the background of the evoked toxic relationship, this ambivalent experience results in the spontaneous development of a psychosis.

This double bind traps the boy in a situation where any response leads to negative feedback, fostering confusion and emotional distress. This example vividly illustrates how contradictory communication can lead to psychological issues, as theorized by Bateson (Bateson et al., 1956) and Watzlawick (Watzlawick et al., 1967). The boy's inability to master the enduring ambivalence inherent in the double bind may contribute to significant psychological harm, demonstrating the destructive potential of USTA.

Another example of harmful ambivalence, or cases of USTA, can be found in instances of dissociative identity disorder (DID), as argued by Michelle Maiese (2016). According to Maiese, DID can result from extreme emotional ambivalence. This form of ambivalence involves deeply conflicting needs, often connected to traumatic experiences with close individuals during childhood, and can be overwhelming, leading to dissociation. The mechanisms of dissociation serve as an unconscious strategy to manage such intense and contradictory feelings. Maiese's analysis provides a framework not only for understanding DID but also for examining how strong ambivalence can contribute to other disorders characterized by strong suffering.

Maiese contends that DID does not involve a splitting of the personality into different selves, but rather a disruption of self-awareness, resulting in discontinuity and high internal barriers within the self. DID is seen as the outcome of an unconscious attempt to cope with a dilemmatic situation. Maiese's characterization of extreme emotional ambivalence not only aids in understanding the causes of DID but also sheds light on other disorders linked to painful ambivalence and the intense suffering that can arise from strong ambivalences.

By now, we have exemplified what USTA is, and we have illustrated by examples how cases of USTA are cases of harmful ambivalence. In the next steps, we are searching for a deeper explanation for the harmfulness of USTA. In the next section, we will argue that Harry Frankfurt is on the right track in this regard, but that his account has blind spots. In the following sections, we will shed light on those blind spots.

9.3 Problems with Basic Concepts of Ambivalence and Integrity in Frankfurt's Account

Regarding Frankfurt's view, probably the most prominent account of ambivalence, we see some major problems and desiderates:[5]

a *Intellectualism.* Frankfurt views all cases of ambivalence as cases of reflective second-order attitudes. According to his account, it is not enough for a person, P, to have conflicting first-order desires to be considered ambivalent. There must be a deeper connection that involves the person more strongly. In Frankfurt's framework, this connection is a second-order attitude of identification with the conflicting first-order desires. This view allows us to meaningfully say that a "whole person" is ambivalent.

   However, critics argue that there are numerous cases of ambivalence where second-order level attitudes are not involved, or not exclusively so. For example, Michelle Maiese (2016, p. 230) highlights cases of ambivalence experienced in vulnerable states of early childhood, where such reflective attitudes are unlikely to be present. The experience of being pulled in different directions seems independent of second-order attitudes. Additionally, as discussed in our other chapter in this book (Chapter 3), there are cases of ambivalently suicidal individuals who might have a second-order level volition only regarding their wish to die, but not concerning their wish to live. These situations are prototypical examples of ambivalence that Frankfurt's account does not adequately capture. A more nuanced understanding of ambivalence should avoid overestimating the role of reflective attitudes and self-awareness.

b *Perfectionism.* Harry Frankfurt's concept of integrity is deeply tied to the notion of wholeheartedness. "Wholeheartedness" refers to a state of coherence of affirmative attitudes, where a person fully identifies with and is unified around their desires, commitments, and values, without conflict or ambivalence. However, as Justin Coates critiques, Frankfurt's account might overstate the need for affirmative unity and demand excessive inner consistency. By being principally intolerant of ambivalent states, Frankfurt's model fails to recognize that such states can exemplify and even enhance well-functioning agency. Yet, at the same time, Frankfurt's emphasis on affirmation and its role in a person's unification has deeply plausible aspects. A sufficiently coherent web of affirmative attitudes appears to be a fundamental condition for self-governed agency and the experience of self-efficacy. Therefore, in arguing for thesis (T), it seems helpful to develop a refined concept of integrity, which is sensitive to cases of ambivalence that can contribute to well-functioning agency. We will develop such a conception in Section 5.

These two topics point to relevant blind spots and open questions in Frankfurt's account and accounts that are inspired by his thinking. In the next three sections, we will rethink Frankfurt's take on these three topics, resulting in a more context-sensitive account of ambivalence, integrity, and the threat of ambivalence to integrity. This will yield our answer to the question of *why* it is exactly cases of USTA that are harmful, namely by threatening integrity.

9.4 Rethinking Ambivalence

As we discuss in our other chapter in this book, ambivalence is a multifaceted phenomenon. Different concepts of ambivalence can be used as conceptual tools for focusing on different aspects of this multifaceted phenomenon (Chapter 3). In this section, we want to discuss how a concept of ambivalence can look like that is helpful for our discussion of how certain cases of ambivalence, but not others, are harmful for human beings. We will argue that for these purposes, it is helpful to follow Frankfurt in some, but not in other respects.

We can start our discussion by coming back to the work of Michelle Maiese. Facing blind spots of a narrow concept of ambivalence, Maiese (2016) argues that a concept of ambivalence which emphasizes emotional aspects may help to understand a broader range of relations internal to a person's experience of ambivalence. She elaborates (2016, p. 230):

> In cases of extreme ambivalence, conflict is widespread and involves various elements of the psyche, including not just volitions, but also bodily feelings, impulses, and patterns of attention. Thus, it is not simply that the ambivalent subject is volitionally conflicted, but also that she *feels torn* and *pulled in different directions*. However, there is a worry that Frankfurt's volitional account downplays the affective dimension of ambivalence.

In characterizing extreme emotional ambivalence, she proposes a "Frankfurt-style" concept of ambivalence, which, however, allows ways of identification with conflicting desires *below* the level of self-awareness and will. This concept integrates conflicting affective attitudes and associated bodily feelings, recognizing the experience of being pulled in different directions. Following Maiese, a de-intellectualized concept, where reflective second-order states are not necessary for ambivalence, allows us to model mixed feelings and experiences of this type, which can be crucial for cases of DID.

We might be in the realm of Maiese's idea, when we claim that such a concept includes not only conflicting attitudes, but conflicting webs of attitudes, which constitute parts of the person's overall web of attitudes. Such overall web of attitudes contains states and dispositions such as impressions, beliefs, epistemic expectations, questions, evaluative attitudes, wishes, wills, affective and motivational attitudes, impulses and dispositions, and needs. Many of these states can cohere or conflict with others in a deeply person-involving way, without being focused in a reflective second-order-level attitude. The potential of deep involvement arises from the fact that not only single states, but also groups of states connected together build cohering or conflicting parts of the personality. Impulses, if not integrated into or conflicting with a web of attitudes, might be experienced as alien, that is, as in some sense not belonging to oneself. By contrast, even in the case of conflicting attitudes, the broader the range of attitudes involved is, the more natural it is to experience them as belonging to oneself. Against this background, we can offer the following characterization of ambivalence with identification[6]:

Ambivalence with Identification: Subject S is ambivalent with identification if and only if S has integrated conflicting pro- and contra-attitudes toward X, where each of them is connected with supporting surroundings of other states, abilities, and attitudes, building together unities of conflicting webs of attitudes.

This description fits Maiese's explanation of DID. If ambivalence is constituted in this way that particular webs of attitudes build coherent unities conflicting with other particular webs, then some cases of DID may be explained as a result of some extreme ambivalence.[7]

To sum up, while "ambivalence" can be used to refer to different aspects of a multi-facetted realm of phenomena (Chapter 3), we have developed in this section a particular characterization of ambivalence with identification that does not require reflection or self-awareness, nor *explicit* identification. Still, even according to our account, persons can be strongly ambivalent as whole persons, because the conflicting states they have are – on our take – each connected with core webs of attitudes of the persons and thus involve the person deeply.

9.5 Rethinking Integrity: Organic Coherence-Maximization under Non-Ideal Conditions

As the next step, we want to characterize a view of integrity that is less intellectualistic and less perfectionist than Frankfurt's view (at least according to many interpretations of Frankfurt's texts), preparing the next section, where we will describe in more detailed ways how USTA, as analyzed in the previous sections, threatens integrity.

Integrity can be understood as a state of wholeness and unity, where a person's actions, thoughts, and attitudes are in harmony, reflecting a coherent character. A certain degree of integrity is a necessary condition for self-governance. To capture this, we propose that the notion of coherence should play a central role.

What does coherence mean in this context? A Frankfurtian concept of volitional coherence – focused on evaluative and volitional attitudes with propositional content – may be too narrow to account for all relevant aspects of coherent self-governance. Instead, we require a more organic conception of coherence, one that integrates volitional, motivational, cognitive, and emotional dimensions.

Maiese's concept of "emotional ambivalence" points us in the right direction for considering the emotional dimensions of ambivalence and of coherent identities. The organic overall coherence that includes emotional coherence itself does not merely involve conscious acceptance or identification but also encompasses subconscious pro- and contra-attitudes that influence motivation. These may encompass states and dispositions like impressions, beliefs, epistemic expectations, questions, evaluative attitudes, wishes, affective and motivational attitudes, impulses, and needs. Such a broader perspective, which contains reflective, motivational, and affective attitudes, enhances the descriptive power of coherentist accounts. The degree of coherence of a person's web of attitudes depends on the degree of consistency, on the density of connection, and of supporting relations between the affective, cognitive, and practical attitudes.[8]

The idea of organic coherence implies that we organize our webs of attitudes not merely by explicit reasoning but also by adjusting our mental states to fit each other as harmoniously as possible. To maximize coherence, in situations with conflicting constraints individuals decide along the weight of constraints, accept the higher weighting, and negate the lower weighting constraint. For example, consider Paul, a hiker injured during an expedition in the wild. With each step, he feels pain – a signal to avoid burdening the injured foot. However, for Paul, who maximizes coherence, this pain is not an imperative but a constraint. He must care for his foot, but he also needs to focus on other priorities, such as leaving the wilderness before nightfall. To survive, he must reconcile his goal of reaching safety with the limitation imposed by his injury. He attempts to ignore the pain to some extent to weaken its inhibiting effect and concentrates on moving forward – yet the pain persists, and he stays aware of it.

In the next sub-sections, we want to model integrity as a coherent web of attitudes in feeling, thinking, and doing (a), consider bridges between coherence and adequacy related to needs (b), then highlight the crucial role of affirmation (c), and make explicit the non-perfectionist view of coherence-maximization under non-ideal conditions (d).

a Feeling, Thinking, and Doing as Dimensions in a Web of Attitudes

Feeling, thinking, and doing are deeply interconnected yet can be conceptually distinguished – like icebergs that appear separate above water but are linked beneath the surface. Against this background, we distinguish these dimensions in a phenomenological way.

The terms *cognitive* and *thinking* refer to mental contents and processes, including images, propositional content, associations, thoughts, impressions, and reasoning. *Affective* and *feeling* denote qualitative experiences of varying intensity, which are themselves more or less preferable. *Practical attitude*, *doing*, and *action* encompass motivational forces and dispositions that either bring about tangible changes in the environment or manifest as self-imposed inertia. Affective, cognitive, and practical attitudes cohere to varying degrees, depending on how strongly they are connected and how much they support one another.

b Needs and Cognitive Contents as Bridges Between Coherence and Adequacy

In the coherentist analysis, conditions of integrity are linked with conditions of adequacy, such that coherence-maximization is a probability raiser of adequate action. There is also a connection between internal states and the external environment: Feelings, motivations, and thoughts can represent needs, affordances, and objective states.

Feeling*:* Needs – both basic and conditional – are represented in desires and feelings of satisfaction (e.g., happiness, relief, enthusiasm, liking, love) or dissatisfaction (e.g., hunger as a response to lack of food, loneliness to lack of social warmth, self-contempt to lack of success or practical meaning, and self-blame to failing to meet obligations). Bodily sensations, such as physical pain, serve a signaling function.

Thinking: Our impressions, beliefs, and expectations are more or less attuned to what supports our well-being or that of our loved ones. Subjective horizons of relevance are shaped by situational contexts and the conditions necessary for well-being and effective agency.

Doing: Our plans, motivations, intentions, desires, and impulses are generally oriented toward fulfilling needs. However, feelings, thoughts, and actions are often shaped by narratives rather than genuine needs. Nevertheless, in principle, we are capable of self-correction.

Thus, coherence-maximization can involve adaptation to situational demands. What defines the coherentist approach to integrity is its focus on analyzing internal structures in terms of consistency, density of connections, and the degree of mutual support among its elements.

c Analyzing Organically Coherent Webs of Attitudes in Feeling, Thinking, and Doing in Terms of Affirmation

While we have analyzed integrity in terms of organically coherent webs of attitudes, we now will examine coherence in terms of affirmation. What is affirmation and why is it so crucial for integrity? Frankfurt (2004) highlights the role of affirmation in his account and argues in line with Nietzsche when he speaks of "volitional necessity that constrains us in what we love" (p. 49). We are constrained to act according to the affirmed and cannot coherently wish and act against it. In its broadest sense, "affirmation" can be understood as the most general term for positive evaluation.[9] Basically everything can be affirmed in this sense: parts of the environment, inner states, goals, actions, etc. Preferences inherently contain a degree of affirmation, a sensitivity – whether conscious or subconscious – to the affirmed and to options for realizing them. Affirmation is involved in identification in Frankfurt's sense. It does not need to be explicit; self-esteem, for instance, involves an implicit affirmation of one's ability to contribute to a fulfilling life. When faced with failures, the motivation to improve requires self-trust and the belief that one can learn and do better. A certain degree of self-affirmation is even necessary to enable fruitful self-criticism. The general role of affirmation in coherence of a person's web of attitudes is basic, because it is crucial for action and self-identification. In a broad sense, doing is moving toward the preferred. Self-determination or self-efficacy, from a non-intellectualistic standpoint, can be seen as a movement toward what is agreeable and away from what is disagreeable. For instance, an organism might seek shade when the sunlight becomes too hot or move back into the sun when the shade becomes too cool.[10]

Coates appears only partially convinced about Frankfurt's rhetoric of affirmation (cf. Coates, 2023, p. 94) and instead highlights the role of normative competence and well-functioning agency for one's practical identity. He argues that "what makes our actions *ours* is that they are the result of an exercise of normative competence that makes us the rational agents we are" (Coates, 2023, p. 73). This general claim seems accurate. But it also can be claimed that our actions are *ours*, because we affirm it *because* our normative competence expressed by it supports the satisfaction of our own needs and those of others we care about. We affirm it because rational agency facilitates the attainment of what we prefer. Thus, what Coates calls "practical identity" may be held together by affirmation and self-affirmation, suggesting that affirmation could serve as a grounding relation for it.

It seems quite convincing to say that what makes actions truly one's own is that they are not only caused by external factors, but represent the organism's movement toward the preferred. Motivational attitudes and impulses, which constantly fail to play a supporting role in this movement toward the preferred, may be felt as un-affirmable and experienced as strange and ambiguous in their relation to the person. Integrity, therefore, depends on a sufficient degree of coherence of affirmative attitudes. This coherence of affirmative states can be analyzed in the relations between feeling, thinking, and doing: Feeling, thinking, and doing entail relations of affirmation: Feelings are positive or negative. Thinking is directed to cognitive value or practical value. Doing is directed toward the affirmed. So in more detail, the relations can be described as it follows:

Feelings represent the fulfillment of objects of pro-attitudes, the wished, wanted, or needed in positive feelings such as happiness, relief, pride, satisfaction, and respect. Conversely, they signify harm (and potential harm) in negative feelings such as bodily pain, fear, disgust, hate, contempt, indignation, and cognitive dissonance. Feelings are inherently connected with intentional objects (e.g., fear with danger, sadness with loss) and with tendencies to act (e.g., fear to avoidance or flight, contempt to dishonoring).

Thinking might be considered as oriented at first glance in cognitive values, such as truth and understanding and at second glance in relation to practical concerns: We look for reliable thoughts, impressions, or images of situations, in order to make fitting plans, decisions, and so on. We implicitly and explicitly affirm positively adequate descriptions of situations and options, which seem to support successful practice. Our thinking adapts to our needs, motivational tendencies, wishes, pro-attitudes, resources, and external situation factors. It more or less satisfies constraints that emerge from feelings, drives, and motivational orientations.

Doing – encompassing planning, practical commitments, action tendencies, and impulses – is inherently directed toward values and goals and is thus guided by implicit affirmation. The strength and direction of action impulses are influenced by the intensity and orientation of feelings, as well as by their positive or negative valence. Moreover, they are shaped by situational representations, propositional knowledge, and beliefs about what is valuable or harmful in a given context.

Together, the distinct phenomenological differences and deep interconnections between feeling, thinking, and doing enable an analysis of organic coherence with regard to affirmative attitudes.

d Non-Perfectionist Coherence-Maximization

Another issue with Frankfurt's account of integrity concerns the perfectionism which Frankfurt has apparently built into his theory. According to this perfectionism, a person has to be unified by a perfectly harmonious, ambivalent-free affirmation of their desires. Some critics of Frankfurt, like Coates, argue that this is too demanding. Against this background, it is reasonable to understand integrity in a non-perfectionist way. A perfectionist account of coherence might reject any ambivalence, demanding wholeheartedness in every aspect of will. However, a more organic concept of integrity claims that a person's integrity hinges on a positive attitude toward a significant proportion of actual internal factors, allowing the person to accept, or at least potentially accept, their thoughts and actions without resorting to self-deception.[11] This concept allows, to some extent, to actually be in an inner conflict that involves contradicting evaluations of options and actual inner states while keeping integrity.

A context-sensitive concept of coherence-maximization must account for the non-ideal conditions of life. Consider, in detail, the example of Paul, the hiker. While trekking through mountainous wilderness, he falls and injures his foot. Soon after, a weather change is forecasted, bringing an impending snowstorm. Staying put is not an option – he must press forward as quickly as possible. His pain signals him to avoid putting weight on his foot, yet his awareness of the situation urges him to move swiftly. He finds himself in a state of ambivalence: One impulse calls for caution, the other for urgency. Despite this, he pushes forward. He acknowledges the pain but strives to minimize its influence, focusing instead on the necessity of his task. When the pain becomes particularly intense, he briefly hesitates, feeling the pull of conflicting inclinations. Yet he remains convinced that continuing forward is the right course of action. This scenario illustrates coherence-maximization under non-ideal conditions because:

A The value supported by the behavior (surviving) tops the value of the sacrificed (health of a part of the body and its impact on action-ability) in terms of relevance of dependence relations. And Paul knows that.

B Adequate prioritization is an aspect of a well-functioning agency and so basically preferable (reason for self-affirmation), while the opposite decision would not be. So, in prioritizing surviving over protection of his injured foot, Paul acts in accordance with deep-rooted conditions for affirmation of actions and himself as an agent.

C The pain in his foot is a crucial signal of bodily harm and the desirability of minimizing strain. Paul, despite his urgency, can affirm both the pain and his ambivalence as expressions of important bodily and psychological capacities.

D Despite his ambivalent feelings, he remains motivated to act according to the present priorities. So, in acting in this way, he constitutes himself as an effective agent. Against this background, he can affirm his action and himself as an agent. Thereby, he maximizes coherence of his affirmative attitudes.

So, he stays in mixed feelings; he stays sensitive to the important signals of body feelings and the impulses and motivations they support (he accepts their role), despite his consequent acting against the signals and impulses. This case may be not an example of USTA, but it exemplifies relevant structures of coherent affirmation which can tolerate ambivalence.

In manageable situations where conflicting values are both deeply rooted in one's needs and practical identity but to differing degrees – coherence-maximization entails sacrificing the less fundamental value for the more fundamental one, without disregarding the significance of what is sacrificed. A coherence-maximizing will, therefore, may be compelled to tolerate or even appreciate ambivalence when it reflects a sensitive and well-balanced engagement with the world. In such cases, the partial incoherence that comes without ambivalence may be more disruptive than the dissonance inherent in ambivalence.

This is why even the cases Coates discusses as instances of "wise inconsistency" can be understood as coherence-maximization under non-ideal conditions. By contrast, Agamemnon sacrifices diachronic coherence for a form of immediate coherence – one that lacks not only ambivalence but also connection to his deeply rooted personal commitments and the socially shared values and norms he had previously upheld. In doing so, he abandons a deeper coherence for a more superficial but temporally synchronized one.[12]

9.6 Rethinking How Unmastered, Strong, and Temporally Extended Ambivalence Is a Threat to Integrity

According to our thesis (T), cases of USTA are harmful. Now, we found the deeper reason for this: They are harmful because they affect the overall coherence of a person's attitudes. We expect that they affect the overall unity of what a person can affirm and result in long-lasting strongly inconsistent attitudes, which the person cannot deal with in a satisfying way. To explain, we will discuss the immediate effects of strong unmastered ambivalence on a person's integrity (a) and reflect on what distinguishes inner ambivalence from outer dilemmas (b).[13]

a The Immediate Threat to Integrity

Let us begin with our second variation of the well-known dilemma of *Sophie's choice:* Sophie in the dilemma with her twins with heart defects and economic pressure, so that she only can afford one heart surgery and has to decide, who of the two will survive. After some deep struggle, she decides in favor of Anna, who is a little bit stronger than Betty, and seems more likely to recover fully, and so, Betty has to die. Anna gets the heart surgery and recovers, and 1 year later, Betty eventually dies. For months, Sophie has seen Betty and has cared about her, knowing that she decided to let her die. And she has been tormented in seeing her, knowing that Betty knew that her fate would be to die early, due to the advantage of survival of her sister. And Sophie never overcomes the loss of Betty. She often recalls Betty's expressions of deep resignation – at times, as if silently blaming her. Sofie regrets *deciding* and not *dicing* and merely *accepting* an unavoidable fate. Had the choice been out of her hands, Betty's death might have felt like pure misfortune rather than a sacrifice. Sophie now perceives her decision as a failure of moral integrity – the most profound failure of her life. Additionally, Sophie blames herself for not finding a way to save both daughters and imagines Betty resenting both her and Anna for the sacrifice.

As a result, she loses trust in her own agency, no longer affirming her capacity to act. Although she experiences moments of love and gratitude for Anna's survival, a persistent undercurrent of non-acceptance lingers. The knowledge that Betty was sacrificed for Anna distances her emotionally from the daughter she saved. Despite her explicit motivation to care for Anna and raise her with a mother's love, emotional warmth often eludes her. She has internalized Betty's (real or imagined) silent reproach toward her sister. At times, Sophie acts toward Anna like a stranger. Consequently, Anna does not receive the emotional support she needs to cope with the loss of her twin. This leaves her deeply ambivalent about her own existence, reinforcing Sophie's own self-doubt and self-reproach – ultimately fueling a cycle of self-contempt.

In this case, a form of psychological damage emerges, which can be analyzed in terms of coherent self-affirmation. Sophie's deep-seated need for sufficiently strong indicators of her own affirmation-worthiness – particularly her ability to see herself as a good, loving, and caring mother – remains unfulfilled by her experiences, attitudes, and actions. The absence of these necessary indicators of affirmation-worthiness results in negative feelings, thoughts, and action tendencies toward herself and her concerns.

Our coherentist account suggests that USTA results in long-lasting strongly inconsistent attitudes which the person cannot deal with. As a consequence, particularly in serious cases, even a minimal coherence of their attitudes may be at risk. The coherence of attitudes which makes up a person is extremely weakened or even dissolved. As a result, the person herself dissolves to a relevant degree. In the light of coherentism, a probable effect of a loss of self-efficacy and well-functioning agency is a loss of self-affirmation. And a loss of self-affirmation might explain cases of loss of motivation toward self-awareness and self-care or cases of tendencies to self-punishment or even tendencies to suicide.

Persons who experience USTA may have to face crucial dissolutions of the coherence of the webs of attitudes that constitute themselves and, as a result, are confronted with a lot of suffering. This can even be the cause of mental health issues characterized by disintegrated personality like DID or schizophrenia, as discussed by Maiese (2016) and Bateson (Bateson et al., 1956) and Watzlawick (Watzlawick et al., 1967). Pragmatic aspects of the suffering which USTA causes can be these: It can lead to a paralysis of activity, to a seesawing between options, to a sabotaging of one's projects in the wake of this seesawing, and to a state where one becomes unpredictable to others, resulting in social conflicts and loneliness. Phenomenal aspects of the suffering which USTA causes can be mental pain in being torn and negative feelings concerning one's own inconsistencies, like self-contempt or self-hate. Such negative feelings can lead to self-punishment, drug abuse, loss of self-care, and mental disorders. In this regard, Maiese, as well as Bateson and Watzlawick, describe mental disorders like DID or schizophrenic psychosis as a kind of attempt to escape unbearable painful ambivalence. In the case of DID, persons try to escape from the ambivalence by creating heightened barriers between different parts of the self, such that they do not have to experience and cope with the ambivalence in just one part of the self.[14]

b In What Respects Does Inner Ambivalence Differ from a Dilemma as a Cause of Harm?

However, we might argue that it is the dilemma itself, rather than the ambivalence, that compromises Sophie's integrity – and perhaps even that of her surviving daughter. While both the dilemma and her inner ambivalence contribute to the psychological damage, they are phenomenologically distinct.

Unmastered ambivalence has specific experiential qualities: an acute perception of a high-value gap, diachronic fluctuations in evaluations, contradictions that coexist synchronically, and an absorbing nature that constrains agency. Sophie's experience of loss and guilt is shaped not only by the tragic dilemma but also by the way her ambivalence absorbs all circumstances into a single, undifferentiated emotional reality, manifesting in her ambivalent relationship to her remaining daughter.

These qualitative features are not part of the dilemma itself but rather of the ambivalent experience – and they may trap a person in painful ambivalence. In sum, key features of unmastered ambivalence include high intensity of conflicting values ("high-value gap"), diachronic fluctuations, ambiguity, globality (the entire experience reality of the object is affected by ambivalence), and absorption. Let's look at these features in more detail:

1 The high intensity of ambivalence often leads to an overwhelming emotional gap between the things that are evaluated positively and negatively. In the case of *Sophie's choice*, the dramatic meaning of both

options and their positive and negative aspects can overtax the capacity to deal with the ambivalence.

2 Diachronicity reflects the unpredictable fluctuations in evaluations over short time intervals, hindering the development of a coherent epistemic and practical perspective.
3 Ambiguity involves conflicting expectations based on the relevant features of a situation, resulting in a lack of stable grounding for one's will. This ambiguity is often linked to situational factors.
4 The experience of strong global ambivalence toward an object makes it difficult to deal with it.[15] When Paul loves and hates Paula, it is more difficult to cope with her than when he is ambivalent only about her spontaneity with its advantages and disadvantages.
5 Finally, absorption occurs when the combination of ambivalence intensity, changing evaluations, and ambiguity creates a state of passivity that undermines agency, making it even more difficult to manage and resolve USTA. Together, these features can overwhelm a person's capacity for resolution, threatening their integrity – even outside an intellectualist or perfectionist framework – and leading to profound suffering. And they can make escaping strong ambivalence and achieving coherence particularly difficult.[16]

9.7 Mastering Ambivalence

We want to end this paper with a short outlook concerning how cases of unmastered ambivalence might still – in light of all the difficulties – be transformed into cases of mastered ambivalence. Mastering ambivalence is not the same as resolving it. As Coates argues, in some cases it can be more integer to stay ambivalent than to resolve the ambivalence. Mastering ambivalence requires a differentiated and balanced understanding that integrates ambivalence into a sufficiently coherent web of attitudes. In particular, mastering ambivalence might require that the person adopts a second-order attitude toward their ambivalence: They mindfully see their own ambivalence "from the outside" and accept it as ambivalence. They do not over-identify with the two sides of the ambivalence, nor try to push the ambivalence away. What Frankfurt demands of all cases might be true at least of cases of mastery of ambivalence. This process is unified by an affirmation of one's abilities, mental states, and cognitive processes, recognizing the value of sustained ambivalence for a well-functioning life.

Let us give shape to the idea of mastering ambivalence. Mastering ambivalence can involve overcoming the mentioned five challenges: (1) the high-value gap, (2) diachronicity, (3) ambiguity, (4) global ambivalence, and (5) absorption.

1 **Softening the high-value gap** requires strengthening emotional independence from the positively and negatively evaluated features of a situation. Here, a mindful dis-identification with both options is crucial. To do so, one needs to affirm oneself, and life itself, in a stronger and deeper way than one affirms both options. This enables the person to become more independent from the positively and negatively evaluated features of the situation.
2 **Overcoming diachronicity** involves developing a meta-cognitive perspective that allows for the simultaneous recognition of conflicting evaluations. Stability can be fostered by grounding attitudes in deeper, more enduring foundations rather than transient fluctuations.
3 **Addressing ambiguity** requires clarifying one's understanding of the situation and understanding and potentially reducing conflicting expectations. One can either reduce the ambiguity or understand and accept it mindfully.
4 **Transforming global ambivalence into local ambivalence** helps by differentiating between different aspects of one's situation. For example, consider the context of therapeutic support for individuals experiencing suicidal thoughts. Individuals might at first be overwhelmed by their strong desires to live and to die. The therapeutic practice of motivational interviewing, where clear reasons for living and for dying are articulated, helps to get a clear, organized, and calm picture of one's situation.
5 **Overcoming absorption** involves gaining emotional and cognitive distance. It is crucial to adopt an external view of one's own perspective and to situate oneself within the broader context of existence.

By systematically addressing these aspects, ambivalence can be integrated into a coherent framework, fostering a more balanced and resilient stance.

To visualize this more concretely, consider Sophie in the second variant – this time in a better state. Anna survives, and while Sophie cannot forget the loss of Betty, she manages to maintain warmth and responsible love for her remaining child. Years after Betty's death, she still wakes up at night, haunted by memories and painful regret. She remembers Betty's vivid will to live, her joy, and she feels pangs of self-accusation for not having been able to save her. Yet, after hours of reflection, she recalls that the situation was a true dilemma and that she did everything she could. She accepts her limitations and does not judge herself as incapable of well-functioning agency.

Sophie acknowledges her deep bond with both her deceased and surviving daughters. Though she experiences moments of sorrow and regret, she remains capable of caring for Anna with warmth and responsibility, offering her reassurance when Anna herself struggles with self-accusations over her sister's death. When Sophie finds herself overwhelmed by painful memories, close friends remind her of what she already understands in clearer moments – that the loss was neither her fault nor Anna's. Their support helps her distance herself from the paralyzing weight of guilt, preventing her from poisoning her relationship with Anna. They help her separate the tragedy of the dilemma from her own motivations, capacities, and actions.

In this way, Sophie comes to understand her needs and emotions as a mother, affirming the painful ambivalence as a natural outcome of deeply rooted affective, cognitive, and motivational attitudes in a dilemmatic situation. She can affirm her agency even as she profoundly rejects the dilemma itself, which continues to cause her suffering. She may have mastered ambivalence to a significant degree – perhaps even to the point of affirming her life as a whole despite the tragedy and its lasting pain. She may still experience intense emotional ambivalence, but she navigates it with coherence.

From our organically coherentist perspective, this higher degree of mastery over ambivalence corresponds to a stronger interconnectedness and mutual support among implicitly affirmative attitudes. In her actions, she fosters well-being – for both herself and her daughter. In her feelings, she experiences implicit affirmation in moments of happiness and satisfaction. In her thinking, she upholds ideas of good motherhood and the meaning of care. A fundamentally life-affirming stance – one that does not deny the darkness, tragedy, or harm she has endured – aligns closely with her attitudes of care, reinforcing coherence at a deep level. After all, the acceptability of ambivalence depends on one's ability to manage it effectively. The deeper attitudes toward oneself and toward life that are implicit in the five ways of mastering ambivalence can also serve as a preparation for mastering potential future cases of USTA.

Of course, the masterability of ambivalence has limits. There are cases in which ambivalence is impossible or at least very difficult to master. For instance, there are cases in which ambivalence is less related to a specific object and instead represents an attitudinal trait that manifests across many or all options, things, people, etc. One can think of a person who is nearly always ambivalent about basically everything. In light of their lack of any "islands of wholeheartedness", their motivation and joy of living might be weakened tremendously. As discussed earlier, a certain degree of deep-rooted affirmation of life – of power of joy – is necessary for mastering any challenge, such as instances of USTA. Another case where ambivalence is very hard to master is this: If ambivalence is connected with a heterogeneous state of personal development – meaning that different aspects of the personality vary significantly in maturity and differentiation – it becomes challenging to achieve a coherent attitudinal balance.

This is because the less mature aspects of the personality are unable to fully comprehend or integrate the more developed ones. For example, imagine a variation of Sophie's case. In this case, Sophie is intellectually mature, but – due to having been neglected in her childhood – not mature in an emotional way. Against this background, she is not able to bring about the emotional states that would fit what she might understand intellectually. Thus, mastering any ambivalence would be very hard for her.

9.8 Conclusion

In this paper, we argued that ambivalence is harmful to the extent that it manifests USTA. In Section 2, we defined USTA and provided examples to flesh out this thesis. We then explored why and how USTA is harmful, agreeing with Harry Frankfurt that ambivalence could threaten a person's integrity. However, we also acknowledged the valid critiques of Coates and Maiese, as discussed in Section 3. To address these points, we reconsidered the concepts of ambivalence and integrity in Sections 4 and 5. We proposed a conception of integrity that appeals to organic coherence that is structured by affirmative attitudes. We then demonstrated that ambivalence, specifically in the form of USTA, posed a threat to integrity when both were understood in the broader, coherentist, and non-perfectionist terms we outlined in the previous sections. This showed why it is exactly cases of USTA that are harmful – they threaten the overall organic coherence and affirmability that are central to integrity and that are crucial for being a well-functioning agent. At the same time, this showed why certain cases, even of strong ambivalence, are acceptable and can even be rational – these are cases where the ambivalence is mastered by being coherently integrated into one's web of attitudes.

Notes

1 Frankfurt holds that ambivalence is inherent to inner states in independence of contingent circumstances, while Coates largely discusses ambivalence in dilemmatic situations.

2 Coates tries to pinpoint this conflict: Both Coates and Frankfurt agree that there are cases in which ambivalence can have positive instrumental value and that ambivalence, "in some sense is not necessarily self-defeating in the sense that it always leaves the ambivalent agent worse off". But Frankfurt would even count such cases as a threat to rational agency, while Coates (2023, p. 108) would not.

3 Even Coates mentions that long-persistent ambivalence can damage psychological health, and, in such cases, it can be "instrumentally good, that the agent is *wholehearted*" (Coates, 2023, p. 71).

4 According to the system-psychological account of Bateson and Watzlawick, the resulting relation can't be described in terms of linear causality. The relation is

merely a growing interdependence of dilemma-creating communication habits of some persons on one side and contradictory mental attitudes and communication strategies of another person, which may show symptoms of schizophrenia, on the other side.

5 Frankfurt's account of ambivalence is presented in detail in René Baston's and Sanja Dembić's chapter "Philosophical Perspectives on Suicidal Ambivalence" in this book (Chapter 2).

6 Identification with mental states independent of reflection can be understood as the integration of these states into a functional order of orientations, motivations, and desires. This process does not necessarily require explicit acceptance but rather a state of openness and functional integration. For example, a person may instinctively feel satisfaction when helping others or playing music without consciously identifying these actions as part of their identity. This natural alignment of desires and actions integrates these behaviors into their identity, fulfilling their need for a meaningful life.

7 Note that our account leaves it open that only some, but not all, kinds of ambivalence require identification.

8 For more formal analysis, organic coherence can be understood in terms of constraint satisfaction. Constraints are fitting conditions imposed by mental elements like beliefs, goals, values, and affective, motivational, and practical attitudes on other mental elements like beliefs and goals. A particular constraint satisfaction is a fitting relation between two elements of mental life. Viewed holistically, coherence maximization is a process of balancing conflicting constraints to achieve an integrated mental structure. Paul Thagard (2000) applies this concept in his theory of explanatory coherence, arguing that the formation of beliefs and practical attitudes functions as a dynamic network. In this network, mental attitudes are interconnected through positive or negative relationships, and the system strives to maximize coherence by minimizing contradictions and reinforcing consistency, density of interconnections, and mutual support. The degree of coherence between these elements depends on how well they satisfy each other's constraints. For technical details, see Thagard, 2000, p. 15ff. As Thagard (2000, p. 277) argues, this broad account of coherence might even be consistent with Catherine Elgin's equilibrium-based approach (cf. Elgin, 2017).

9 The idea is that there is a compulsion from coherence conditions that constrains possible directions and ranges of our affirmation, free motivation, and will. Considerations similar to Frankfurt's concept of volitional necessity are reflected in Alan Gewirth's examination of a generic coherence principle (Gewirth, 1978) and in concepts of evaluative identity and motivational necessity in Hausen (2015).

10 Similarly, Coates understands Nietzsche's ideas on will "as offering us a reductive account in terms of the functional roles that our underlying drives and affects play in structuring our behavior" (Coates 2023, p. 81).

11 A counterfactual acceptance that is necessary for integrity may be described as an affirmative attitude a person not only could, but would have under fitting conditions.

12 Coates mentions Agamemnon's treating of his beloved daughter like an animal as self-betrayal. For staying wholehearted, he pays the price of "betraying an inner element of what he was" (Coates, 2023, p. 132).

13 Dilemmas may be described as situational ambivalence; see our other chapter in this volume (Chapter 3). There is a difference between mastering a dilemma and mastering ambivalence. In mastering a dilemma and a related inner ambivalence, the dilemma or situational ambivalence can be resolved, while inner ambivalence is staying.

14 When dilemmas cause high emotional ambivalence which result in DID, this may be considered as an unfortunate output of organic coherence-maximization under hostile circumstances.

15 For an explanation and discussion of global ambivalence, see our other paper in this volume (Chapter 3).

16 Those mentioned features are vividly present in the experience of the installation *endegutallesgut* (2023) by artist Selin Acarbaş. The environment with some aesthetic diverse, ambiguous objects causes together with a storm-like sound an absorbing atmosphere. The objects evoke highly ambivalent associations, including subconscious shifts between conflicting impressions – hope and healing juxtaposed with the sensation of painful torture, the expansiveness of a poetic landscape with the oppressive sense of being trapped in a cave. The impression of another part of the installation oscillates between the pure, enlightened beauty of a Zen-like stone fountain and the disturbing image of black blood, flooding the bottom. The installation's overall impression seems to balance on a sharp ridge between hope and unbearable pain, an absorbing ambivalence with open end.

References

Bateson, G., Jackson, D. D., Haley, J., & Weakland, J. H. (1956). Toward a theory of schizophrenia. *Behavioral Science, 1*(4), 251–264.

Bleuler, E. (1911/2014). *Dementia praecox oder Gruppe der Schizophrenien* (Unchanged New Edition). Psychosozial-Verlag.

Coates, D. J. (2023). *In Praise of Ambivalence.* Oxford University Press.

Elgin, C.Z. (2017). *True Enough.* MIT Press.

Frankfurt, H. G. (2004). *The reasons of love.* Princeton University Press.

Gewirth, A. (1978), *Reason and Morality*, University of Chicago Press.

Hausen, F. (2015). *Wert und Sinn – Apriorische Hermeneutik des Tuns und Fühlens in der Spur Max Schelers.* Traugott Bautz Verlag.

Kwapil, T., Edmundson, M., Hernández, L., Kemp, K., Rbeiz, K., Clark, H., Bathery, A., Raulin, M., & Barrantes-Vidal, N. (2022). Schizotypal ambivalence is associated with schizophrenia-spectrum and borderline personality traits in young adults: Converging results from three interview studies. *Journal of Research in Personality*, 101, 104312.

Maiese, M. (2016). Dissociative identity disorder and ambivalence. *Philosophical Explorations*, 19(3), 223–237.

Thagard, P (2000). *Coherence in Thought and Action*, MIT Press.

Watzlawick, P., Beavin Bavelas, J., & Jackson, D. D. (1967). *Pragmatics of human communication: A study of interactional patterns, pathologies, and paradoxes.* W. W. Norton & Company.

10 Circles of Thought

When Ambivalence Threatens Our Agency

Sanja Dembić

Does ambivalence threaten our agency? In this chapter, I distinguish between two "faces" of ambivalence and argue that one of these faces threatens our agency. This has implications for the discussion of suicidal ambivalence, as it highlights a particular way in which these cases can be problematic and raises the question of how the person should respond. I explore Ruth Chang's (2009) idea that agents can *create* reasons for acting, rather than merely *responding* to their reasons for acting in cases of suicidal ambivalence.

The chapter is structured as follows. In Section 10.1, I reconstruct the debate about the value of ambivalence by focusing on the views of Harry Frankfurt and Justin Coates. Frankfurt argues that ambivalence necessarily threatens our agency, while Coates denies this. I reconstruct the main arguments for their views. In Section 10.2, I introduce what I call the two "faces" of ambivalence and argue that one of these faces threatens our agency even if one accepts Coates' view of ambivalence. I also highlight the implications of this view for the discussion of suicidal ambivalence. In Section 10.3, I explore the option of creating reasons to act, as opposed to responding to the reasons one already has to act, and discuss this option for the cases of suicidal ambivalence.

10.1 The Value of Ambivalence: Frankfurt versus Coates

The philosophical debate on ambivalence has been largely shaped by Harry Frankfurt and Justin Coates, both in terms of the concept of ambivalence and its value (see Chapter 2). Let me first reiterate the main points on the concept of ambivalence before turning to the question of value.

As discussed in several chapters of this book, there is no consensus on what it means to be ambivalent. According to some philosophers, to be ambivalent is "to be torn between competing courses of action, knowing that by pursuing one, one will have to give up on the other" (Coates 2017,

DOI: 10.4324/9781003616221-14

p. 419). In what follows, I draw on the conditions for being ambivalent as described in Chapter 2 of this book:

Amb S is ambivalent about whether to φ or to ψ if and only if:

1 φ-ing and ψ-ing are mutually incompatible (at time *t* or within a relevant period of time).
2 S has the desire to φ and the desire to ψ.
3 S *identifies* with their desire to φ and their desire to ψ in the sense that S has the *second-order volition* to φ and the second-order volition to ψ, i.e., S has the desire that both their desire to φ and their desire to ψ be effective (Frankfurt 1988)[1] or
3* S *cares deeply* about φ-ing and about ψ-ing, in the sense that
   a S *identifies* to a significant degree with their desire to φ and their desire to ψ.
   b By not φ-ing or not ψ-ing, S would be failing to honor an important aspect of their practical identity, i.e., who they are (Coates 2022).

Applied to cases of suicidal ambivalence, these views imply that S is ambivalent about whether to die by suicide or live on if and only if S has the desire to die by suicide and the desire to live on and (a) S has the desire that both their desire to die by suicide and their desire to live on be effective or (b) S regards both their desire to die by suicide and their desire to live on to have some authority to move them to action and by not dying by suicide or by not living on S would be failing to honor an important aspect of S's practical identity (e.g., their values and commitments).

What does it mean that something "threatens our agency"? One way of understanding this might be something like this: Ambivalence (necessarily) threatens our agency only if, in cases of ambivalence, some necessary condition of what it is to be a well-functioning (e.g., sufficiently rational and autonomous) agent is (necessarily) not met. On this view, the following aspects seem to be two sides of the same coin: considering something as a threat to one's agency and considering something as a necessary condition for our well-functioning agency. Thus, the question of what constitutes (a threat to) our agency can be approached from two sides. One approach aims first to identify the necessary conditions of our well-functioning agency and then to assess whether, in some cases of ambivalence, our agency is threatened. Another approach aims first to identify cases of ambivalence in which our agency is threatened and then to assess what conditions are necessary for our agency to function well.

Let me now turn to the question of the value of ambivalence. As discussed in Chapter 2, whereas Frankfurt argues that ambivalence necessarily threatens our agency, Coates argues that it does not. Their main overall arguments can be reconstructed as follows. According to Frankfurt (1988; 1992; 2004), ambivalent agents are necessarily *not unified* as agents and *not wholehearted* in their decisions. However, in his view, being wholehearted in one's decision and being unified as an agent are hallmarks of well-functioning agency. Therefore, ambivalence is necessarily a threat to well-functioning agency.[2] In contrast, Coates (2017; 2022) argues that being wholehearted in one's decision and being unified as an agent are not necessary conditions for well-functioning agency. What is necessary, however, is for the agent to be *normatively competent* in the sense of being able to respond adequately to their normative reasons (and to exercise that ability). In Coates' view, ambivalence may indicate that the agent is exercising their normative competence, and therefore, ambivalence does not necessarily threaten our agency.[3]

Coates does not explicitly address the nature of reasons. In the following, I will use the standard view of normative reasons for acting, which is as follows (e.g., Scanlon 1998; Raz 2009; Parfit 2011): A fact (or alternatively, a true proposition) gives us a normative reason to φ when it *counts in favor* of φ-ing. A normative reason for φ-ing is a *pro tanto* reason for φ-ing which is to say that it can be outweighed by a *pro tanto* reason against φ-ing. If an agent has *sufficient reason* for φ-ing, then she is justified in φ-ing. If S has *decisive reason* (or most reason) for φ-ing, then S should φ (Kiesewetter 2017). The action of φ-ing can be "adequate" or "inadequate" in the sense that it corresponds or does not correspond to the type of response which ones' normative reasons support.

I will now take a closer look at Frankfurt's (1) argument from wholeheartedness and (2) argument from unification, as well as Coates' counterarguments to them.

(1) *Wholeheartedness.* Frankfurt's argument from wholeheartedness can be reconstructed as follows:

1 S is a well-functioning agent only if S is wholehearted in their will.
2 S is wholehearted in their will if and only if there is an unequivocal answer to the question of what action S commits themselves to "without reservation" (Frankfurt 1988, pp. 165), which in turn means that S does so "in the belief that no further accurate inquiry would require him to change his mind" (Frankfurt 1988, p. 169).
3 If S is ambivalent about whether to φ or ψ, then there is no unequivocal answer to the question of what action S commits themselves to without reservation.
4 S is ambivalent about whether to φ or ψ only if S has the desire that both their desire to φ and their desire to ψ be effective (where φ-ing and ψ-ing are mutually incompatible).

Therefore, if S is ambivalent, S does not meet the requirement of wholeheartedness for well-functioning agency.

Coates (2022) discusses Frankfurt's argument from wholeheartedness and argues against premise (1). In his view, wholeheartedness cannot be a condition for well-functioning agency because there is nothing intrinsically valuable about wholeheartedness (or the freedom to have an undivided will; Coates 2022, p. 131). In some cases, one should not be wholehearted in one's decision. He uses the example of Agamemnon to illustrate this point. Agamemnon must decide whether to sacrifice his daughter Iphigenia to Artemis so that she will let the Greek warships sail to Troy (to rescue his sister-in-law Helen from Sparta). Whatever he does, he fails either as a father or as a king and brother. Agamemnon decides to kill Iphigenia. Regardless of whether he should have done so, Coates argues that the way Agamemnon's action can be criticized precisely because he does not maintain his ambivalence:

> Agamemnon takes "the easy way out" and unequivocally resolves his will by simply dissociating himself from what had, until just a few moments prior, been a central aspect of his practical self. [...] Agamemnon carries it out with a brutal and single-minded efficiency that would not be possible for a man who was still torn between his duties to his people and his duties to his child.
>
> (Coates 2022, p. 127)

In Coates' view, Agamemnon's action of killing his daughter should have been infused with ambivalence and the fact that he didn't is "his failure to continue seeing his love for Iphigenia as having guiding authority" (2022, p. 129). In the face of tragic dilemmas, well-functioning agency requires the agent to maintain ambivalence (Coates 2022, p. 131), because the agent has *normative reasons* to be ambivalent.

(2) *Unification.* Frankfurt's argument from unification can be reconstructed as follows:

1 S is a well-functioning agent only if S is unified as an agent.
2 S is unified as an agent only if S is practically consistent.
3 If S is ambivalent about whether to φ or ψ (and S believes that they cannot do both φ and ψ), then S is practically inconsistent (something like the intention consistency requirement).[4]
4 S is ambivalent about whether to φ or ψ only if S has the desire that both their desire to φ and their desire to ψ be effective (where φ-ing and ψ-ing are mutually incompatible).

According to Frankfurt (1988, p. 165), ambivalence consists essentially in having a divided will in the sense of condition (4) and well-functioning agency requires that the agent be unified in the sense of being practically consistent. Therefore, if S is ambivalent, S does not meet the requirement of unification for well-functioning agency.

Coates (2022) discusses Frankfurt's argument from unification as well and argues against premise (3). He states that neither his nor Frankfurt's view of ambivalence requires

> that the ambivalent agent *intend* [sic] to act on each of the inner motives that pull her in incompatible directions. What ambivalence requires instead is that an agent is genuinely motivated by psychological states that are part of her innermost practical self to act in distinct yet incompatible ways. But of course, this is consistent with the agent intending only to act on one of those motives when the time for acting finally arrives. Thus there is nothing about ambivalence per se that guarantees this kind of irrationality.
>
> (Coates 2022, p. 111)

So, basically, Coates is arguing that the intention consistency requirement does not apply to the psychological states that are necessarily involved in ambivalence, whatever they may be exactly. It only applies to intentions.

Coates (2022, p. 111) argument that Frankfurt's own view is not threatened by the intention consistency requirement is convincing only if Frankfurt's second-order volitions are indeed not intentions. But it is not entirely clear how second-order volitions relate to desires on the one hand and intentions on the other. Frankfurt himself is not explicit about this. There are at least three options: (1) second-order volitions are a subset of *desires* (related in a special way to other desires that the agent has); (2) second-order volitions are intentions, because they determine the person's will; and (3) second-order volitions are *sui generis*, because they are determinations of the person's will but are not identical to intentions. If second-order volitions are understood as in (1), then it is plausible to assume that they need not be consistent in the way that intentions need to be, since they are merely evaluative with respect to the other desires of the agent. If they are understood as in (2), then the intention consistency requirement obviously applies to second-order volitions. If they are understood as in (3), then it is unclear whether the intention consistency requirement applies, because the question arises as to what exactly the difference between second-order volitions and intentions is supposed to be.

In sum, Coates offers some compelling counterarguments to Frankfurt's view that ambivalence necessarily threatens our agency. Moreover, his arguments are based on the sensible view that well-functioning agency requires the agent to respond adequately to their normative reasons. In the next section, however, I will argue that the matter is somewhat more complex.

10.2 The Two Faces of Ambivalence

In this section, I will argue that there are two faces of ambivalence and that a version of the second face necessarily threatens our agency. In light of this, I will argue that responsiveness to reasons is not sufficient for well-functioning agency. What is also required is for the agent to form and maintain stable intentions. The discussion will highlight one particular way in which cases of suicidal ambivalence can be problematic.

(1) *Residual Ambivalence.* The first face of ambivalence I will call – following Swindell Blumenthal-Barby (2010, p. 29) – "Residual Ambivalence". The structure of this type of case is the following:

i S has the desire to φ and the desire to ψ.
ii φ-ing and ψ-ing are mutually incompatible (at time *t* or within a relevant period of time).
iii S cares deeply about φ-ing and about ψ-ing (in Coates' sense).
iv S *intends to φ*, but does *not intend to ψ*.

In such a case, the agent typically decides to perform one course of action and forms the relevant intention (and follows through with it if the world cooperates) even though the agent still cares about and is "drawn" to the other course of action, i.e., has some desire (but not the intention) to perform it.[5] This is the type of case that Coates (2022) offers as a counterargument to Frankfurt's view: The agent decides to φ, but has some residual ambivalence about ψ. Here, ambivalence is not necessarily a threat to our agency.

(2) *Live Option Ambivalence.* The second face of ambivalence I will call "Live Option Ambivalence", and it has the following structure:

i S has the desire to φ and the desire to ψ.
ii φ-ing and ψ-ing are mutually incompatible (at time *t* or within a relevant period of time).
iii S cares deeply about φ-ing and about ψ-ing (in Coates' sense).
iv S does *not form (or maintain) a stable intention to φ/ψ*, in the sense that
  a S switches between intending to φ/ψ and not intending to φ/ψ.
  b S switches between intending to φ and intending to ψ.

In such a case, the agent is not only drawn toward mutually incompatible courses of action, but does not "make up her mind", i.e., does not form or maintain a stable intention in one way or the other (or will, in Frankfurt's terms). This type of case is not necessarily a threat to our agency either. Ambivalence can be instrumentally valuable, because it can indicate what is important to us or what we care about, and it can be intrinsically valuable if it is an adequate response to our reasons. As Coates (2022) puts it, whether ambivalence threatens our agency depends on whether it indicates that we are exercising our ability to respond adequately to our normative reasons for acting.

However, there are at least two ways in which cases of Live Option Ambivalence can develop over time, and one of them threatens our agency even if we respond adequately to our reasons. Before elaborating on that, let me illustrate the two faces of ambivalence with an example. Suppose Angel is deeply in love with two different people, Chris and Taylor. Suppose that both Chris and Taylor reciprocate Angel's love and that all of them care deeply about monogamy. Chris and Taylor tell Angel that she has to decide, and Angel excludes being with neither Chris nor Taylor as an option. Angel is ambivalent about being with Chris or being with Taylor.

Now, imagine the following two scenarios:

1 *Residual Ambivalence:* Angel decides to have a relationship with Chris. Angel still cares deeply about being with Taylor, but she does not call into question her decision to be with Chris. In this case, Angel does not consider having a relationship with Taylor a live option, even though Angel is still drawn to being with Taylor.
2 *Live Option Ambivalence:* Angel decides to have a relationship with Chris. However, not only does Angel still care deeply about being with Taylor, but she also calls into question her decision to be with Chris. In this case, Angel still considers having a relationship with Taylor a live option.

We can imagine several versions of the second case: Angel could drop the intention to be with Chris and just reconsider the choice, or Angel could form the intention to be with Taylor instead. In any case, the main point is that Angel is *reconsidering the decision* and thus withdrawing from the decision she has already made or the intention she has already formed.

These types of cases are typically associated with different emotions. In the first scenario, it is easy to imagine that Angel is sad about not being in a relationship with Taylor and that she is going through a period of grief. This seems perfectly reasonable, since her decision to be in a relationship with Chris meant that she had to give up something else that was very important to her, namely being in a relationship with Taylor. Since Angel sees being in a relationship with Taylor as a lost option, she grieves this loss.

In the second scenario, the most prominent emotion is typically not sadness or grief, but regret. Regret involves "the preference that things should have been otherwise than they were in the respect that occasions regret" (Wallace 2013, p. 6). If Angel regrets her decision to be in a relationship with Chris, then Angel now prefers that she had decided differently at the time of her decision to be with Chris. Regret may lead Angel to reconsider whether to be with Chris or to consider being in a relationship with Taylor a live option.

Of course, reconsidering a decision is not in itself problematic. The ambivalence and regret Angel feels after deciding to be with Chris may indicate, for example, that being with Taylor is more important to her than she initially thought or that Taylor is the right person for her. In this case, the ambivalence would be instrumentally valuable because it would help Angel evaluate her reasons adequately and make the right decision after all. We can also imagine that some back and forth might be rational because it is a difficult decision to make.

However, there is a version of Live Option Ambivalence that is rationally problematic (even if the agent is responding adequately to her reasons), namely when the back and forth just never stops (and the situation is such that the agent has to make a decision). Taking into account the fact that there is a temporal dynamic to ambivalence, we can distinguish at least two ways in which Live Option Ambivalence can develop over time:

2a *Live Option Ambivalence Resolved*: The agent eventually forms a stable intention to φ/ψ (and the case may turn into one of Residual Ambivalence).
2b *Infinite Live Option Ambivalence*: The agent reconsiders her decision endlessly and never forms a (stable) intention to φ/ψ.[6]

For example, if Angel eventually stops reconsidering her decision and forms a stable intention to be with either Chris or Taylor, then her Live Option Ambivalence is resolved (and may turn into a case of Residual Ambivalence). But if Angel just keeps switching between the intention to be with Chris and the intention to be with Taylor, then her ambivalence at some point becomes, all things considered, irrational, even if she has sufficient reason to be with Chris and sufficient reason to be with Taylor.

The literature has identified several rational problems with endlessly reconsidering one's decision about what to do, even when one has sufficient reasons for both actions. Let me mention two:

a *Opportunity Costs:* Deliberation and decision-making are constrained by time and effort, and there are opportunity costs to endless reconsideration. This is to say that the time and effort spent reconsidering a decision could have been used for other valuable things, such as acting, gathering additional information, or deliberating about a different issue. At some point, the cost of further deliberation outweighs the expected benefits and the continued reconsideration becomes irrational (Simon 1990; Bratman 1987; Gigerenzer & Todd 1999).

b *Infinite Regress of Deliberation and Paralysis of Action:* Rational agents should not be constantly reconsidering all their decisions because doing so would make deliberation impractically infinite (Harman 1986). Moreover, an agent who always asks, "Should I reconsider?" before acting would never actually act which would lead to a paralysis of action (Broome 2013).

If endless reconsideration is irrational, then rational agents must have stopping rules for deliberation (Bratman 1987). Various criteria have been proposed: For instance, reconsideration should stop when the costs outweigh the expected benefits (Simon 1990) or when it is motivated by short-term impulses (Holton 2009) and reconsideration is required when new strong reasons emerge, or the agent recognizes a serious mistake in their prior reasoning (Harman 1986; Bratman 1987). This suggests that rational agency does not only require that the agent responds adequately to their reasons for or against φ-ing or ψ-ing but also that the agent eventually stops deliberating and forms and maintains a stable intention. In other words, practical rationality (or well-functioning agency) necessarily involves forming stable intentions (at least when the stakes for forming an intention are sufficiently high).

Several philosophers have pointed out that intentions are not just beliefs about what one will do (e.g., Bratman 1987; Holton 2009), but *commitments* that guide and structure future practical reasoning and action. The point of practical reasoning is to decide on and commit to a course of action. Without such a commitment, there is no authority to guide action. In light of this, further rational problems of Infinite Live Option Ambivalence may emerge. For example, if, after careful deliberation and based on good reasons, Angel decides to have a relationship with Chris, then Angel should stick to her decision unless she is confronted with new strong reasons. However, in order to form, maintain, and follow through with her intention to be with Chris, it is necessary for Angel to give up her option to be in a relationship with Taylor. Thus, if Angel does not intend to give up her option to be in a relationship with Taylor, she fails to meet an instrumental requirement of practical rationality (not intending an action that is believed to be a necessary means to another action that one intends to do). Being ambivalent, in the sense of endlessly conceiving the alternative as a live option, is therefore a threat to our rational agency.

This has implications for cases of suicidal ambivalence. Some cases of suicidal ambivalence are easily recognized as rationally problematic, for example, cases in which

a A person dies by suicide, but has decisive reason to live.
b A person lives on but has decisive reason to die by suicide.
  But in the light of the discussion in this section, there is also a third problematic case which we should not neglect:
c A person lives on, has no decisive reason either way, but has sufficient reason to live on and sufficient reason to die by suicide, and is infinitely live option ambivalent about what to do.

Now, such a state may still be better than immediately intending to die by suicide and, in some sense, even psychologically "functional". Nevertheless, it remains rationally problematic (and in some sense "dysfunctional"). So the question arises: How should the agent rationally respond to such ambivalence? There is no easy answer to this question, but in the following section, I will explore one option available to the agent, that of *creating* reasons for acting, rather than merely *responding* to reasons for acting.

10.3 Suicidal Ambivalence and Creating Reasons

What should a person do who is ambivalent about whether to die by suicide, in the sense of Live Option Ambivalence? In light of Coates (2022) view, the person should exercise their ability to respond adequately to their reasons by evaluating their normative reasons and deciding what to do on the basis of their reasons (see also Chapter 2). Their normative reasons will include reasons for dying by suicide (e.g., to escape suffering, feelings of hopelessness, burdensomeness, or loneliness); reasons for living on (e.g., to be with loved ones; to care for family members); reasons against dying by suicide (e.g., fear of dying); and reasons against living on (e.g., the expected continued suffering and feelings of hopelessness, burdensomeness, or loneliness). Ideally, the person will have decisive reason for one course of action and will be able to decide on that course of action. After careful deliberation, the person should resist unnecessary reconsideration and should not reconsider their decision unless compelling new reasons arise.

This is, of course, a highly rationalized view of the matter, and it is clear that people faced with suicidal ambivalence may be under such emotional distress that it reduces their ability to exercise their normative competence as described. Nevertheless, the ideal view can be used to argue that the person should decide as rationally and autonomously as possible, and if acute emotional distress reduces the agent's rationality and autonomy, then other people should help her get into a position where this obstacle is removed.[7]

But what if the person after careful deliberation concludes that she has no decisive reason either way, but has sufficient reason to live on and sufficient reason to die by suicide, and becomes infinitely live option ambivalent about what to do? In this case, it seems that the person has exhausted her rational options (assuming that she has considered all relevant reasons), because there are no more reasons to consider – her reasons have run out – but it is irrational to stay infinitely live option ambivalent about what to do.

However, there might be a further rational option, namely that of *creating* normative reasons for action. Ruth Chang (2009) challenges the traditional (externalist) view that normative reasons are exclusively given by facts that count in favor of some action and are simply there to be "discovered" by the agent. In contrast, Chang (2009, p. 245) argues for a hierarchical voluntarist view, according to which it is possible for the agent to actively "create" normative reasons through an act of will when the agent's reasons have run out.[8] How? By a volitional act of *commitment*:

> Commitments, as I understand them, are the volitional activity of taking something to be a reason by putting one's very self behind the consideration. By putting our very self behind some consideration, we can endow that consideration with the normativity of a reason. A commitment is that in virtue of which that consideration is a will-based reason. We thus 'create' reasons by engaging in an activity of willing that is their ground. Willing is something over which we have direct volitional control since it just is the exercise of direct volitional control. So will-based reasons, unlike given reasons, are creatures we make, not discover.
>
> (Chang 2023, pp. 17)

For example, when faced with a choice between two options, such as becoming a philosopher or a trapeze artist, the agent may, after careful consideration, conclude that she has sufficient reason for both actions, but no decisive reason for one. Chang (2009, p. 257) argues that at this stage the agent can simply – by a volitional act of commitment – *take* any consideration that counts in favor of one of the options as a reason for choosing that option. For example, "you might take the challenge of understanding a difficult philosophical problem as normative for yourself, thereby giving yourself a voluntarist reason to choose the philosophical career" (Chang 2009, p. 265). In doing so, the agent *creates*, by an act of will, a normative reason that may give her the additional *pro tanto* reason to give her the decisive reason to become a philosopher. The point is that the agent can take any consideration that counts in favor of one of the options as a reason for choosing that option, even if that consideration is irrelevant to the choice.

Let's assume for the sake of argument that Chang's voluntarist view is correct.[9] How exactly can such a view help when one's reasons have run out? Won't the unresolved problem of what to do just reappear on a second level? Because the question arises: Which option should I create reasons for, to become a philosopher or to become a trapeze artist? Since I have sufficient reason for both options, but no decisive reason for one of them, it seems that I also have sufficient reason to create reasons for both options, but no decisive reason for one of them. But then, it seems that the agent has not made a lot of progress in solving her problem of what to do.

The voluntarist could respond as follows: The position of the agent is not the same, because the agent's perspective on her normative situation has shifted: from responding to reasons to creating reasons. The situation is not one in which the agent faces the question: What normative reasons are there for me to discover and respond to? Rather, the situation is that the agent is free to create whatever distinctive rational identity she wants to create (within the limits of her given externalist reasons; Chang 2009, p. 265). In light of this new perspective, the agent can create reasons that can make it true that the agent has decisive reason to choose one option over the alternative. The important point is to realize that "you have an opportunity to make yourself into the kind of agent for whom there are stronger reasons to fly under the big top [trapeze artist] than to sit at home contemplating the nature of reasons [philosopher]" (Chang 2009, p. 259). However, there is no guarantee that this shift in perspective will give the agent a rationally determined solution to her problem of what to do. But for some cases of ambivalence, it might.

What does this imply for cases of suicidal ambivalence? How can this shift in perspective be applied to cases of suicidal ambivalence? Recall that it has to be a case where the person, in their view, has sufficient reason to die by suicide and sufficient reason to live on, but no decisive reason either way. Consider, for example, a person who has terminal cancer but who also has loved ones for whom they care deeply. On the one hand, she wants to suffer as little as possible and not die a slow and painful death and believes that the only way to ensure this is to die by suicide; on the other hand, she wants to spend as much time as possible with her loved ones. She endlessly switches between forming the intention to die by suicide and the intention to live on.

The shift in focus – from responding to reasons to creating reasons – could be described as follows. The person may realize that she doesn't want to be a person whose identity is determined by her pain and suffering and conclude that the only way to avoid this is to continue doing things that have nothing to do with her pain and suffering, such as spending time with her loved ones. It's not that she suddenly realizes that the reasons given by the fact that she values spending time with her loved ones outweigh the reasons given by the fact that she disvalues suffering and dying a painful death. Rather, she realizes that she has the opportunity to make herself into a person whose identity is not determined by pain and suffering. By committing herself to creating this identity and spending time with her loved ones, she creates reasons to live on.

But notice that this freedom to create reasons goes both ways. For example, the person may just as well realize that she wants to be a person whose identity is determined by autonomy and conclude that the only way to avoid a substantial loss of autonomy is to reduce the progression of pain and suffering. Again, it's not that she suddenly realizes that the reasons given by the fact that she disvalues suffering and dying a painful death outweigh the reasons given by the fact that she values spending time with her loved ones. Rather, she realizes that she has the opportunity to make herself into a person whose identity is determined by autonomy. By committing herself to creating this identity and reducing the progression of pain and suffering, she creates reasons for dying by suicide.

Before concluding, I would like to point out a potential problem with this view which concerns its applicability. Resolving suicidal ambivalence by creating reasons requires that the agent be able to create reasons for living or dying by suicide by making commitments. However, in many cases of suicidal ambivalence, the person is experiencing severe psychological distress (e.g., due to some mental illness) and feelings of hopelessness and burdensomeness. It is reasonable to assume that in many of these cases the person is simply unable to make a stable commitment. But then they do not have the option of creating reasons for the resolution of their suicidal ambivalence. An alternative view might be that even people who are experiencing severe distress do in fact engage in "creating reasons", but that they are guided or at least influenced by their current mood (tunnel vision, absorption, sudden mood swings, overstimulation) and perhaps simply biased.[10]

In response, the voluntarist might argue as follows: It may be true that the person is unable to make stable and normatively weighty commitments in the face of severe psychological distress. But abilities and commitments come in degrees, and there may be fluctuations in the person's mental condition. The person may be able to commit to certain things that carry little normative weight (e.g., to cherish certain moments) when she is in a relatively good state, and the person may be able to develop her ability to make commitments over time. It may also be that chance is involved and the person experiences something new that suddenly enables her to make a weightier commitment (e.g., she meets someone new). Probably not all cases of suicidal ambivalence (that are problematic) can be resolved, but we should use whatever degree of freedom we have to see if we can.

10.4 Conclusion

In this chapter, I have reconstructed some arguments about the value of ambivalence and argued that there is a way in which agents can be ambivalent that necessarily threatens rational agency. I have also explored the idea that agents can create reasons for acting in cases of suicidal ambivalence.

According to a reasons–responsiveness view of rational agency, rational agents should respond adequately to their normative reasons for or against an action. On Coates' (2022) view of ambivalence, an agent is ambivalent about two mutually incompatible courses of action only if the agent desires to pursue both options and cares deeply about them, but knows that by pursuing one option, they will have to give up the other. Wholeheartedness is not a necessary condition for rational agency, because an agent may have sufficient reason for both options, and it is possible for the agent to intend only one of the options even though they are ambivalent about what to do. In such a case, the agent may experience the first face of ambivalence which I call, after Swindell Blumenthal-Barby (2010), "residual ambivalence".

However, there is a second face of ambivalence that threatens rational agency, which I call "infinite live option ambivalence". This is the case when an agent endlessly alternates between intending two mutually incompatible courses of action (but has to make a decision). These cases are rationally problematic, even if the agent has sufficient reason for both options, because at some point the opportunity costs outweigh the expected benefits of further deliberation, leading to an infinite regress of deliberation and a paralysis of action.

This highlights a type of suicidal ambivalence that can be problematic and is easily neglected: A person lives on, has no decisive reason either way, but has sufficient reason to live on and sufficient reason to die by suicide, and is infinitely live option ambivalent about what to do. I have explored Chang's (2009) voluntarist approach to reasons, according to which an agent is able to create reasons (when their given reasons have run out) by making a commitment at will. Although there may be limits to its applicability, and there is no guarantee that an agent can resolve their suicidal ambivalence by creating reasons at will, it is another option that the agent may have to deal with an infinitely difficult situation.

Notes

1 Frankfurt (1992, p. 105) modifies this condition to: "Identification is constituted neatly by an endorsing higher-order desire with which the person is satisfied"

where satisfaction "is a matter of simply *having no interest* in making changes". Swindell Blumenthal-Barby (2010, p. 26) interprets Frankfurt slightly differently and argues that "identification" and "willing" (wanting a desire to be effective) are two different things.

2 Other authors (Velleman 1989; Bratman 2007; Korsgaard 2009) argue similarly that ambivalence necessarily threatens autonomy, because it threatens the agent's coherence or their diachronic stability.

3 Other authors who object to the view that ambivalence necessarily threatens autonomy or rationality are, for example, Velleman (2002), Marino (2011), Gunnarsson (2014), Razinsky (2016), Brunero (2021), and Feldman and Hazlitt (2021).

4 Intention consistency requires, roughly, that you do not intend to φ and to ψ in such a way that you believe that you cannot do both φ and ψ.

5 I take *deciding* to be a mental action that leads to the formation of an intention (and "decision" can be used for both the mental action of deciding and the result of that action, the formation of an intention). Forming an intention does not require a prior decision, but for the sake of clarity I will focus on cases where intentions are formed by a prior decision.

6 Swindell Blumenthal-Barby (2010, p. 29) calls this "paralyzing ambivalence".

7 It is beyond the scope of this chapter to develop this argument. The point is simply that even if we cannot normatively expect people experiencing suicidal ambivalence to deliberate about whether to die by suicide in this rationalized sense, it does not follow that we should not aspire to this ideal (to increase rationality and autonomy as much as possible).

8 The view is "hierarchical" because Chang (2009) does not assume that there are no externalist reasons at all. She just argues that not all of the agent's reasons are externalist reasons. Chang (2023, p. 16) emphasizes that this is what distinguishes her view from an existentialist view such as Sartre's.

9 For a development and defense of the voluntarist view, see Chang (2009; 2013; 2020; 2023).

10 I thank Martin Weichold for pointing this out.

References

Bratman, M. E. (1987). *Intention, Plans, and Practical Reason*. Harvard University Press.

Bratman, M. E. (2007). *Structures of Agency: Essays*. Oxford University Press.

Broome, J. (2013). *Rationality Through Reasoning*. Wiley-Blackwell.

Brunero, J. (2021). Instrumental Rationality: The Normativity of Means-Ends Coherence. *Ethics*, *132*(1), 243–248. https://doi.org/10.1086/715282

Chang, R. (2009). Voluntarist Reasons and the Sources of Normativity. In D. Sobel & S. Wall (Eds.), *Reasons for Action* (pp. 243–271). Cambridge University Press.

Chang, R. (2013). Commitments, Reasons, and the Will. In R. Shafer-Landau (Ed.), *Oxford Studies in Metaethics* (Vol. 8, pp. 74–113). Oxford University Press.

Chang, R. (2020). Do We Have Normative Powers? *Aristotelian Society Supplementary, 94*, 275–300.

Chang, R. (2023). Three Dogmas of Normativity. *Journal of Applied Philosophy, 40*, 173–204. https://doi.org/https://doi.org/10.1111/japp.12626

Coates, D. J. (2017). A Wholehearted Defense of Ambivalence. *The Journal of Ethics*, *21*(4), 419–444.
Coates, D. J. (2022). *In Praise of Ambivalence*. Oxford University Press.
Feldman, S. D., & Hazlett, A. (2021). Fitting Inconsistency and Reasonable Irresolution. In D. Gatzia & B. Brogaard (Eds.), *The Philosophy and Psychology of Ambivalence: Being of Two Minds* (pp. 131–146). Routledge.
Frankfurt, H. G. (1988). *The Importance of What We Care About*. Cambridge University Press.
Frankfurt, H. G. (1992). The Faintest Passion. *Proceedings and Addresses of the American Philosophical Association*, *66*(3), 5–16. https://doi.org/10.2307/3130658
Frankfurt, H. G. (2004). *The Reasons of Love*. Princeton University Press.
Gigerenzer, G., & Todd, P. M. (1999). Fast and Frugal Heuristics: The Adaptive Toolbox. In G. Gigerenzer, P. M. Todd, & T. A. R. Group (Eds.), *Simple Heuristics That Make Us Smart* (pp. 3–34). Oxford University Press.
Gunnarsson, L. (2014). In Defense of Ambivalence and Alienation. *Ethical Theory and Moral Practice*, *17*(1), 13–26. https://doi.org/10.1007/s10677-013-9464-x
Harman, G. (1986). *Change in View: Principles of Reasoning*. MIT Press.
Holton, R. (2009). *Willing, Wanting, Waiting*. Oxford University Press.
Kiesewetter, B. (2017). *The Normativity of Rationality*. Oxford University Press.
Korsgaard, C. M. (2009). *Self-Constitution: Agency, Identity, and Integrity*. Oxford University Press.
Marino, P. (2011). Ambivalence, Valuational Inconsistency, and the Divided Self. *Philosophy and Phenomenological Research*, *83*(1), 41–71. https://doi.org/10.1111/j.1933-1592.2010.00459.x
Parfit, D. (2011). *On What Matters* (Vol. 1). Oxford University Press.
Raz, J. (2009). Reasons: Explanatory and Normative. In C. Sandis (Ed.), *New Essays on the Explanation of Action* (pp. 184–202). Palgrave-Macmillan. https://doi.org/10.2139/ssrn.999869
Razinsky, H. (2016). *Ambivalence: A Philosophical Exploration*. Rowman & Littlefield Publishers.
Scanlon, T. M. (1998). *What We Owe to Each Other*. Harvard University Press.
Simon, H. A. (1990). Bounded Rationality. In J. Eatwell, M. Milgate, & P. Newman (Eds.), *Utility and Probability* (pp. 15–18). Palgrave Macmillan UK. https://link.springer.com/chapter/10.1007/978-1-349-20568-4_5
Swindell Blumenthal-Barby, J. S. (2010). Ambivalence. *Philosophical Explorations*, *13*(1), 23–34.
Velleman, J. D. (1989). *Practical Reflection*. Princeton University Press.
Velleman, J. D. (2002). Identification and Identity. In S. Buss & L. Overton (Eds.), *Contours of Agency* (pp. 91–123). Cambridge.
Wallace, R. Jay (2013). *The View from Here: On Affirmation, Attachment, and the Limits of Regret*. Oxford University Press.

Part 4

Ethical Implications of Suicidal Ambivalence

11 Ambivalence and Paternalistic Suicide Prevention

Michael Cholbi

11.1 Introduction

A wide body of research indicates that it is normal for persons considering suicide to be ambivalent regarding their choice to die. A study conducted by Kovacs and Beck (1977) found that about half of all suicidal individuals report ambivalence about their choice. Other scholars have concluded that ambivalence *nearly always* occurs among suicidal individuals. For instance, Harris et al. (2010) found that 94 percent of those with past suicide attempts underwent an "internal suicide debate" prior to their attempt, and the suicidologist Edwin Shneidman has proclaimed that ambivalence is the sole cognitive state present in almost every case of suicide (1996). A recent comprehensive scoping review of research on suicide ambivalence indicates that although different researchers conceptualize 'ambivalence' differently, ambivalent suicidal feelings and behaviors are common before, after, and in the midst of suicidal acts (Teismann, Seibert, and Forkmann, 2024). Hence, while it may be hyperbole to conclude that ambivalence is "the single most important psychological concept in our understanding of suicide" (Evans & Farberow, 1988, p. 12), overlooking suicidal ambivalence would result in an inadequate understanding of the psychology of suicide, as well as undermine the effectiveness of efforts to prevent suicide.

Yet suicidal ambivalence is also relevant to addressing the *ethics* of suicide prevention, particularly if suicide prevention is justified paternalistically. Paternalistic justifications of suicide prevention hold that in preventing suicide, we may prevent a person from harming themselves by ending their lives prematurely. Paternalism can take a wide variety of forms, but the version that has the greatest number of defenders is *weak* paternalism, which holds that it can be legitimate to interfere with a person's choices only if those choices will defeat their ultimate ends (Dworkin 2020).[1] According to weak paternalism then, suicide prevention measures may be justified, despite an individual not consenting to

DOI: 10.4324/9781003616221-16

them, because the individual would in fact be defeating their own ends by ending their lives prematurely. Weak paternalistic interference thus aims to prevent an individual from doing what is harmful or contrary to their interests as the individual themselves conceives of those interests.

That suicidal individuals are so often ambivalent about this choice could be taken as relevant to justifying suicide on weak paternalistic grounds because it indicates that suicidally ambivalent individuals have an *unsettled will* regarding whether they stand to benefit from hastening their own deaths. It is seemingly unobjectionable to prevent someone from ending their lives if they themselves are not rationally convinced that they ought to end their lives, for if a person who is ambivalent about hastening their deaths nevertheless ends their life due to suicide, they do so without their own full rational consent. In a weak paternalist spirit then, preventing an ambivalent person from ending their lives seems to accord with their own considered rational judgment about their ends or interests rather than acting in opposition to that judgment.

My purpose here is to consider whether this reasoning is in fact sound and, in particular, whether the fact that suicidal persons often appear ambivalent about ending their lives speaks in favor of paternalistic suicide prevention. My conclusion is that ambivalence's role in suicide prevention is more equivocal than is suggested by this reasoning. For even to the extent that ambivalence can be reliably identified, it is not a condition meaningfully correlated with any rational deficiency, and even when suicidal ambivalence occurs in conjunction with conditions such as depression, it does not necessarily provide us additional reason to prevent suicide.

I begin in Section 11.2 by summarizing how philosophers have come to deploy the notion of ambivalence and offer what I call 'the Basic Argument' for the conclusion that suicidal ambivalence makes paternalistically motivated suicide prevention more morally defensible. Sections 11.3–11.5 raise challenges to this argument. In Section 11.3, I argue that there is no incompatibility between ambivalence and having a settled rational will, nor will suicidal ambivalence provide straightforward evidence regarding whether a person's choice to die reflects a settled will or not. As such, suicidal ambivalence itself does not readily ground the conclusion that a person's will is unsettled with respect to their choice to die, a conclusion that might otherwise license paternalistic interference with a person's suicidal plans or actions. Sections 11.4 and 11.5 consider different strategies by which it might be shown that, because ambivalent suicidal individuals are likely to be led to choose to end their lives irrationally, it is therefore more morally defensible to interfere in ambivalent suicidal choices than non-ambivalent ones. In Section 11.4, I consider (and reject) the possibility that the irrationality in question stems from ambivalence itself resting on a deficiency in their capacity for rational deliberation, a deficiency that renders the choices of ambivalently suicidal individuals less than fully *consensual*. Section 11.5 takes up the more promising possibility that ambivalence lends support to paternalistic suicide prevention because the conditions commonly associated with suicidality (e.g., depression) bar suicidal individuals from engaging fully with the entirety of the evidence that bears on their decision regarding whether to end their lives. In this respect, such decisions are likely to be *ill-informed*. This second defense of the Basic Argument is more promising than the defense appealing to deficiencies in rational judgment, but is not unproblematic, in my estimation. I thus identify several drawbacks to this argument. In my conclusion, I cast doubt on the common intuition that the stakes of suicide with respect to an individual's well-being are sufficiently great that we have strong reasons to prevent ambivalent suicide.

To be clear, it is not my claim that ambivalence is irrelevant to the moral justification of preventing suicide. Rather, I conclude that its relevance is not as straightforward as it appears. For at least some instances of ambivalence are merely apparent, and even when suicidal ambivalence is genuine, it often betokens no shortcoming in rationality that would justify paternalistically motivated prevention measures.

11.2 The Nature of Ambivalence and the Basic Argument

Before examining the significance that suicidal ambivalence has for the ethics of suicide prevention, we had best clarify the notion of ambivalence at issue. As observed earlier, the empirical literature on suicidal ambivalence contains different understandings of this notion. Popular understandings of ambivalence are similarly inexact, sometimes treating indecisiveness or weakness of will (the failure to act in accordance with one's prior decisions or commitments) as emblematic of ambivalence. Philosophers who have sought to clarify the notion of ambivalence typically begin from the platitude that ambivalence is simply seeing one and the same thing with opposing attitudes (Razinsky 2016). For our purposes, however, the focus falls principally on *volitional* ambivalence, ambivalence regarding incompatible options for choice and action. Volitional ambivalence occurs when an individual confronts a choice among options that cannot, as a matter of fact, all be selected or pursued, and the individual finds that the reasons in favor of any one of the respective options do not decisively support that option over the others. As best as the volitionally ambivalent agent can tell, none of the choice options available to them is uncontroversially superior to any other, so in choosing any one option, important considerations will be left frustratingly unaddressed or excluded. When ambivalent,

> we feel as if we are unable to proceed without giving up something of significant value. In other words, the ambivalent agent experiences her practical conflict as one in which there will be some significant value remainder no matter how she chooses.
>
> (Coates 2022, p. 9)

That any choice the agents make will generate a value remainder or 'cost' indicates that ambivalence responds to perceived practical dilemmas, choice situations in which every option available to an individual invariably forces the agent to neglect rational considerations that would serve as decisive reasons in the absence of equally powerful considerations that support alternative options. Volitional ambivalence will often arise because different and seemingly incommensurable considerations speak in favor of options that are metaphysically incompatible. For the volitionally ambivalent individual, their available options are equally attractive or, at the very least, "stand on a par" (Chang 2017). Understandably, they may wish that the landscape of choices available to them were tidier and less complicated and thereby feel anguish prior to choice and regret afterward.

Why might the fact that a suicidal agent is ambivalent about whether to live or to die lend moral weight to trying to prevent such a suicide on paternalistic grounds, i.e., on the grounds that the agent is irrationally choosing to do what is not in their best interests? Ambivalence suggests that an individual finds themselves with an *unsettled will* with respect to some choice. In such cases, undertaking a drastic measure, such as shortening their lives via suicide, would seem to lack the individual's full endorsement. While choices that are non-ambivalent, i.e., in which the individual unequivocally endorses the chosen option, merit others' respect, high-stakes ambivalent choices may not. For if we have grounds for thinking that, absent the relevant ambivalence, an individual would unreservedly endorse continuing to live, then we ought to prevent them from ending their life via suicide. In so doing, we purport to act on behalf of their more rational, non-ambivalent self that would reject suicide. These insights can be captured and extended in the following *Basic Argument:*

1 A person is ambivalent concerning some choice if, no matter which option available to them they choose (or would choose), they view having to forego other options as involving a value remainder in which important considerations or concerns associated with the foregone options are neglected.
2 If a person is ambivalent regarding some choice, then whichever option they choose (or would choose) lacks their full rational endorsement.
3 If a person's choice lacks their full rational endorsement and the option they chose (or are most likely to choose) is likely to be harmful to them,

then others have greater moral permission to interfere with that choice on paternalistic grounds.

4 Conclusion: There is greater moral permission, on paternalistic grounds, to interfere with the choices of an ambivalent suicidal agent than with the choices of a non-ambivalent suicidal agent.

The Basic Argument implies that a suicidal agent who exhibits ambivalence is, morally speaking, a more appropriate target of paternalistic interference (presumably, interference meant to extend their life) than a non-ambivalent agent, one for whom their choice to end their lives is such that they perceive no meaningful value remainder associated with the option they intend to forego, namely, continuing to live.

The remainder of this chapter will be devoted to assessing the soundness of the Basic Argument. I will conclude that while ambivalence can be relevant to the moral defensibility of suicide prevention and may sometimes provide us a reason to prevent suicide on paternalistic grounds, the Basic Argument does not succeed in establishing a general *presumption* that, because a suicidal individual is apparently ambivalent about that choice, others thereby have a stronger moral basis for trying to prevent their suicides.

11.3 Ambivalence, Rational Endorsement, and the Will

Premise (3) of the Basic Argument is one that many anti-paternalistic moral philosophers will take issue with. However, I propose that premise (3) be accepted *arguendo* for the moment so as to focus on premise (2):

> If a person is ambivalent regarding some choice, then whichever option they choose (or would choose) lacks their full rational endorsement.

How, we might ask, does ambivalence indicate that a choice lacks an individual's full rational endorsement? The most straightforward answer appeals to the intuition that ambivalence bars a person's will from being settled, and having an unsettled will means that a person does not genuinely endorse, or endorse to a sufficiently strong degree, their choice. However rational the deliberation may have been that leads to this choice, the choice is in some way inauthentic, not a 'full-on' choice of the kind we make when we are not ambivalent. The worry, in the case of suicidal ambivalence for example, is not with the quality of the choice but with whether suicide really has been chosen by the agent. Paternalism toward the suicidally ambivalent agent is thus warranted because their choice is in some way counterfeit.

But this justification of premise (2) misses the mark. For a person may be ambivalent regarding a choice despite the option they choose having their full rational endorsement and despite their will being fully settled concerning the choice at hand. A person can, after all, decide on some option and fully commit to it even while recognizing that the foregone options are sufficiently appealing that important values or considerations will go unaddressed. Choices about whether to leave one's native country, whether to quit a job, or whether to pursue onerous treatment for a chronic illness are sufficiently complex that whatever we choose, the appeal of foregone options is likely to continue to resonate with us. Not all of our choices are 'clean' of evaluative *residue*; despite having persuaded ourselves of the wisdom of one option as against others, we do not thereby become oblivious to the appeal of what we did not choose. The presence of such residue does not mean that we did not judge the option we chose as best according to whatever standards we applied. It simply means that choosing the best option does not silence the appeal of alternatives, and sometimes, we settle a practical question regarding competing options while still 'feeling the tug' of the foregone option. In these cases, we are ambivalent even though our wills have been settled and the option we select has our full rational endorsement. There is nothing particularly remarkable about this, in my estimation. As Coates observes (2022, p. 19), it is entirely possible to be *certain* about what one should do and still be ambivalent, and being ambivalent does not entail wavering in one's commitment to what one *has* chosen. Indeed, there can be prudential value in not wavering in the face of one's ambivalence. A field general who, having chosen to command his forces to attack rather than retreat, has good instrumental reason to persevere with his choice even if that choice was one made ambivalently (e.g., aware that an attack could lead his forces to suffer many casualties).

Ambivalence is thus compatible with a person's will being settled, so in the case of suicidal ambivalence, we cannot therefore assume that it entails an unsettled will, and as such, ambivalence on the part of suicidal individuals does not render interference with their suicidal choices more morally justifiable. Premise (2) thus requires a different rationale if the Basic Argument is to be sustained.

Those sympathetic with the Basic Argument may concede the logical compatibility of ambivalence with having a settled will but respond that surely ambivalence is at least *evidence* of an unsettled will. A suicidal individual who exhibits ambivalence has, in many instances, presumably not made up their mind concerning whether to die or whether to continue to live. Evidence that a suicidal individual is ambivalent about their choice may thus be sufficient to strengthen our rationale for paternalistically motivated interference, even allowing that such ambivalence is consistent with their having a settled will.

While more plausible, this rationale for premise (2) faces considerable practical obstacles. Let us call a *harrowing decision* a decision in which an individual's will is settled despite their being ambivalent about that choice. As I proposed earlier in this section, harrowing decisions are commonplace. How though are third parties to differentiate a harrowing decision from one which is merely ambivalent? In other words, what evidence should sway us that another's choice not only is ambivalent but also reflects an unsettled will, as opposed to the former alone? Here, I believe that epistemic obstacles are formidable, and we certainly should not blithely assume that evidence of ambivalence is also evidence of an unsettled will.

A principal challenge in this regard is that the same evidence that supports our attributing mere ambivalence to an individual will often equally well support attributing to them a harrowing decision. When a friend informs us that they have broken up with their long-term romantic partner, saying, "it was a hard decision and I'll have trouble getting over them, but I'm glad it's over," shall we view them as simply ambivalent—after all, they report a kind of longing for the relationship to continue—or ambivalent yet resolute in their will? Our evidence does not straightforwardly differentiate between these. Sometimes, we make difficult choices and succeed in not 'looking back,' directing our attention to the options we have chosen and largely forgetting about the foregone option(s). But some difficult choices are not like this: Having chosen X, a person may immediately have 'chooser's remorse,' fixating on the road not taken. An individual making a difficult choice may therefore give every appearance of having an unsettled will. We may mistake a person seeming 'torn' by some choice she has made (or is considering making) with her being undecided about it. The primary evidence that they are simply ambivalent—feeling torn, seeing a great deal of merit in two incompatible options, etc.—is *also* compelling evidence that their choice is (or was) harrowing.

So too in cases of suicidal ambivalence, I contend. Should a mental health professional whose patient outlines a well-developed plan to end their lives but also expresses anxiety about their ability to carry that plan out, sadness about the lost life opportunities death will bring, and worry about the impact of their death on loved ones, view the patient as ambivalent and uncertain about their choice—that is, as having an *un*settled will—or as having made up their mind but still cognizant of the considerations that speak against the choice they have made to end their lives, i.e., as making a harrowing decision to end their own life? The state of the patient's will may well be opaque despite the abundance of evidence that they are ambivalent. Ultimately, only the patient is likely to be able to decipher whether they are ambivalent yet resolute versus ambivalent and wavering, and I am not confident that even suicidal individuals themselves will always be able to tell the difference. After all, feeling torn is likely to be characteristic of choices regarding whether to continue to live versus whether to die. We human beings have an instinctual fear of death and struggle to make sense of the biographical significance of our own deaths (Solomon et al. 2015) That death is irreversible can add to the sense of being torn about choices regarding hastening one's death. Hence, a person who is not in fact unsettled regarding their own prospective suicide may nevertheless labor under ambivalence (i.e., they may be anxious, sorrowful, or grief-like regarding the prospect of their own deaths). Indeed, the choice to end one's life via suicide is paradigmatically intricate, and the fact that there is so often an 'internal debate' within the minds of suicidal individuals underscores how fraught suicidal decision-making is. All the more, 'being torn' with respect to death hastening choices is equally likely to indicate rationality than any *deficiency* in rationality. An individual who approaches us indicating an interest in suicide who did *not* give some evidence of being ambivalent, whether or not this means their will is settled, is likely to be seen as irrational inasmuch as they are taking a weighty decision too lightly. Although the final stage of suicidal action (formulating a plan to cause one's death) is often impulsive, it is typically preceded by significant rumination about choosing to die. Suicide is rarely undertaken lightly; for virtually all suicidal individuals, it presents itself as a difficult choice, and were it not at least a harrowing choice, we might doubt that the individual is fully grasping the gravity of the choice at hand. But again, we cannot infer being unsettled from ambivalence, i.e., from a sense of feeling torn, since being torn is also strong evidence that an individual is making a harrowing ambivalent choice.

Mere ambivalence does not entail an unsettled will. And the uncertainty we face in differentiating mere ambivalence from harrowing decisions should undermine our confidence in identifying suicidally ambivalent individuals whose wills, being unsettled, give us greater license to interfere with their choices on behalf of their interests. So these rationales do not point the way to greater license for paternalistically interfering with choices to die.

At this point, defenders of the Basic Argument may offer a different tack. Perhaps the basis for concluding that ambivalence gives greater license to interfere in suicidal choices is that there is likely to be something deficient about the agent's rational endorsement of those choices. Let us now consider two general defenses of this claim.

11.4 Ambivalence and Deficient Rational Judgment

Recall premise (2) again:

> If a person is ambivalent regarding some choice, then whichever option they choose (or would choose) lacks their full rational endorsement.

The previous section considered rationales for premise (2) that, with respect to the choice to end one's life, assert that when undertaken with ambivalence, such choices do not deserve the respect that non-ambivalent choices to end one's life do because they are not full-fledged choices reflecting a settled will on the part of the agent. A different tack is to allow that such choices are genuine choices, but doubt that such choices rest on the agent's *rational* endorsement.

For instance, defenders of the Basic Argument may maintain that, especially in cases where an individual is ambivalent but nevertheless chooses to end their life, the appearance of having a settled will wherein a person has rationally decided to die is misleading. If the best explanation of why they have concluded that suicide is in their best interests is that they suffer from some sort of deficiency in reason, a deficiency that is responsible for their not consenting to what might prove effective suicide prevention measures, then interfering with their choice to die would have solid 'weak' paternalistic credentials: The ambivalent suicidal individual who chooses to end their life is making some sort of error, an error that militates in favor of our interfering with that choice (and subjecting to unwanted intervention measures). A person ought not (we might think) risk their own lives if, as a matter of fact, were they more rational, their ambivalence would resolve itself in a pro-preservation rather than pro-suicide direction. We may therefore act paternalistically to prevent them from taking such a risk. What then is the deficiency we might assume is present in genuine suicidal ambivalence?

Historically, many philosophers have taken a dim view of ambivalence. Dating back to Plato, such philosophers have proposed that the ideal human self is unified, with its motives and reasoning anchored around, and motivated by, a consistent, coherent set of aims or concerns. Such unity, according to these views, should be a goal of human life. For in the absence of such unity, our lives are less likely to be autonomous (a self torn by competing options, etc., cannot be governed in a coherent way, much in the way that a political sovereign cannot rule by issuing contradictory legal directives); meaningful (if a meaningful life is one we can affirm, then ambivalence entails that we cannot fully affirm our lives); or successful (ambivalence must lead to self-defeating patterns of action over time). More recently, Harry Frankfurt (1988) has argued that a self driven by ambivalence cannot enjoy the "wholeheartedness" that comes from identifying with a "real self" free of competing motives or concerns.

No doubt there is something appealing about the unified self, about living a life free of ambivalence. Ambivalence is troubling and vexatious, and so we should sympathize with the yearning to be rid of it. Still, that ambivalence, of the sort that is so commonly observed among suicidal persons, indicates a lack of rational capability such that the choice to end one's life manifests a form of rational incompetence is a suspect claim. Even though we might prefer not to face choices where the competing considerations do not decide unambiguously among our options, when we do face such choices, this is not evidence of any lack of rational capability on our part. As Coates (2022) argues (persuasively, in my estimation), ambivalence is not at odds with rational capability or "normative competence." One dimension of normative competence is *deliberative*. A normatively competent individual is able to appreciate how various considerations speak for or against different courses of action available to them, able to draw conclusions about what to do in light of those considerations, and able to form intentions to act on the basis of these conclusions. Yet there is no reason to think that ambivalence reflects, or contributes to, deliberative *in*competence. A person facing ambivalence can be attuned to how those facts speak for or against the options available to them and be ready and willing to act on the basis of the conclusions they might draw concerning what option those facts uniquely support. But none of this represents a fault or deficiency in the capabilities that define deliberative competence. In the case of suicidal ambivalence, a person can grasp how those facts are relevant to their choice to continue to live and be ready and willing to act on whatever conclusions they might draw from those facts. The 'trouble,' such as it is, need not reside in the ambivalent suicidal agent; the trouble resides instead in the facts themselves, to wit, that they do not align such that there is a uniquely favored option between continuing to live and opting to die.

The case for ambivalence, whether concerning suicide or some other practical matter, reflecting deliberative incompetence, is not compelling. To suppose otherwise is to adopt an extremely controversial metaethical stance. Ambivalence might betoken incompetence if the world was normatively constituted such that each choice presented to us could in fact be resolved by navigating the equivalent of a decision tree where no matter the path we follow, we arrive at a single uncontroversial practical terminus: *the* choice that we have decisive reason to pursue as against alternatives. But I see no reason to believe that the world is practically organized in this way, nor that ambivalence can (in principle) necessarily be dissolved away through further rational inquiry or deliberation. A number of philosophers have argued that at the very least, the world is not *morally* organized in this way. Sometimes, we face genuine moral dilemmas in which no matter how we act, we will be unable to honor all the morally relevant facts that bear on our choices and actions, resulting in an unsettling moral remainder (or perhaps even entailing that it is in fact impossible for us to do *the* morally right thing) (Williams 1985, Tessman 2017). But if this is true of the moral domain, it is likely equally true of the practical domain writ large—that ambivalence often indicates not a deficiency in us, but a fissure in the logic of the practical domain wherein our everyday assumption that there is always a uniquely and decisively correct choice available proves erroneous. This does not, of course, obviate the need to choose and act in such situations. Yet it does suggest that, perhaps tragically, our hope for a rationally tractable world will sometimes be thwarted (Cholbi 2016).

Preventing suicide using measures that do not have the individual's consent on the supposition that the individual's ambivalence betokens a rational deficiency that leads them to choose against their best interests is, I contend, not a morally justified strategy. This defense of premise (2) therefore fails. Let us now turn to a final defense that calls into question the rationality of suicidal choice under ambivalence.

11.5 Ambivalence and Deficiencies in Evidence

Coates identifies a third dimension of normative competence, a dimension where ambivalent suicidal individuals appear to come up short. In addition to being able to deliberate on the basis of considerations they recognize as relevant to some choice, a normatively competent agent must also be able to 'latch onto' all the considerations that logically bear on some choice. This *recognitional competence* is separable from the deliberative competence we emphasized in Section 11.4. After all, an individual can deliberate (and act) well in light of the considerations they recognize as relevant to a choice, but be unable to appreciate that certain considerations are in fact relevant to the choice in the first place. This can result in choices that are, in a sense, rationally rendered but ultimately irrational, in the way that (say) a person who is unaware that the clear liquid in the glass before them is petrol instead of gin might then form the misguided intention to drink the liquid. This intention reflects their deliberative, but not recognitional, competence.

In the case of suicidal ambivalence in particular, we might appeal to the conditions commonly associated with suicidality to infer that suicidal ambivalence is likely to flow from recognitional incompetence. Many suicidal persons have affective disorders such as depression or mania, conditions whose symptoms can include an inability to engage with evidence logically relevant to a choice. Depression, for example, is associated with anhedonia and pessimism. As a result of such symptoms, depressed individuals can struggle to recognize positive aspects of their lives or futures; that is, the individual ignores, downplays, or overlooks considerations that can (or would) contribute to their lives going well. This state is akin to evaluative tunnel vision, where the depressed individual sees all and only the bads of life and struggles to perceive its goods. As Richard Brandt (1975) once emphasized, conditions like depression often involve individuals being preoccupied with present suffering while 'discounting' the goods their lives could contain in the future. When depression occurs among the suicidally ambivalent, then we could reasonably expect that the ambivalence—again, wherein the individual sees reasons in favor of living and in favor of dying but neither is rationally decisive—occurs because depression leads to a kind of deficiency in recognitional competence in that depressed individuals are unable to perceive legitimate reasons to stay alive, tend to discount the possibility of a desirable future, etc. In the absence of depression, we would thus predict that the individual would not be ambivalent. Rather, with the pessimism, etc., associated with depression having abated, the individual will no longer be ambivalent, and having had their capacity for recognitional competence restored, they will conclude that there are instead decisive reasons to live rather than to die. All the more, they will reach this conclusion on the basis of a full, rather than partial, engagement with the evidence relevant to that choice.

When suicidally ambivalent persons are recognitionally incompetent, then this provides a reason to subject them, even absent their consent, to suicide prevention measures on paternalistic grounds. Such persons are suffering from a rational deficiency that leads them to erroneously think that suicide is at least attractive enough to be on an evaluative par with continuing to live. In subjecting them to such measures, we would therefore be acting in their interests as their more fully rational self would perceive it, preventing a suicide that is effectively *misinformed.* This reasoning in particular lends support to what we might call a 'speed bump' approach to paternalistically motivated suicide prevention. In preventing a nonconsenting person's death due to suicide, we slow their decision-making down, giving them adequate time to appreciate the reasons for continuing to live that conditions such as depression conceal from them. The 'speed bump' approach is thus an example of 'soft' paternalism, designed to ensure that agents' choices are made in an adequately informed way, as in John Stuart Mill's famous example of stopping a person about to unwittingly cross a rickety bridge. A soft paternalist approach may thus recommend that we place a 'speed bump' in front of a suicidal individual to afford them access to evidence crucially relevant to their choice as to whether to live or die, evidence that might not otherwise be available to them. In so doing, we make it possible for them to make this decision when their recognitional normative competence has been restored to them.

In my estimation, this 'speed bump' approach is morally superior to the approach considered in Section 11.4 (that ambivalence indicates a deliberative incapacity). For one, it does not appeal to the dubious hypothesis that ambivalence itself is *prima facie* irrational. Rather, it appeals to a hypothesis specific to suicidal ambivalence and the mental conditions associated with it. The 'speed bump' approach also expresses greater respect for the rational agency of suicidal agents. Informing someone (or enabling someone to become informed) about a body of evidence relevant to some important choice they face does not embody disrespect for them as rational choosers. The person about to take a swallow of petrol, falsely believing it to be gin, is not disrespected if we call out a warning to them to that effect. And if the passage of time is sufficient (because the symptoms of depression, etc., will tend to lift) to allow individuals to access evidence in favor of continuing to live that they are unable to access during their ambivalent moments, putting a 'speed bump' in front of them, preventing their suicidal act *now* so that they may be better positioned *later* to make a rational decision in this regard, our delaying them does not disrespect them as rational agents.

These merits notwithstanding, the 'speed bump' approach to preventing suicide in ambivalent agents is not without its difficulties. First, the problems identified in Section 11.3 linger: We need adequate evidence that an individual is unsettled about whether to live or to die as opposed to having decided to die but still feeling 'torn,' in ways that are natural and understandable given our common anxieties about death. The 'speed bump' approach is also not applicable to individuals who, in a rationally informed way, have resolved their wills and opted to die but still feel the tug of continuing to live, i.e., those who are making a harrowing choice to end their lives.

Second, keep in mind that any paternalistic justification of suicide prevention is *welfarist* at its root, alleging that preventing a person from premature death due to suicide is good for them or in their best interests. The 'speed bump' approach is open to the criticism that it rests on assumptions that may not hold true of all suicidally ambivalent individuals—and when they do not hold, slowing down a person's path toward suicidal action may actually be worse for them than not doing so. The approach predicts (a) that suicidal ambivalence resolves over time and (b) that it resolves in a pro-preservationist direction such that previously ambivalent individuals opt to continue to live. But (a) and (b) clearly do not hold true of every suicidal individual. Some suicidal ambivalence is chronic rather than momentary, and some ambivalent individuals ultimately resolve their ambivalence by opting to die. And when either (a) or (b) does not hold, acting paternalistically by inserting the proverbial 'speed bump' in the way of a person considering suicide does not respect the settled rational will of an individual. Delaying a person from acting on their intention to engage in suicide also has costs to their welfare that should not be overlooked. For during the period of delay, the suicidal person may undergo significant suffering that may well be greater in magnitude than whatever gains in welfare would-be intervenors hope to provide them by compelling them to live. Imagine an individual who is suicidally ambivalent for a long duration (a decade, say, due to chronic depression). Suppose further that at each point where the individual edges toward suicidal action, others prevent them from so acting, reasoning that delaying them will result in their coming to see that suicide is not in fact in their interests. During the decade of 'speed bumping,' such an individual may undergo intense suffering, and the greater this suffering, the greater the probability that they did not benefit on balance from having been subjected to repeated paternalistic interventions. When this occurs, the paternalistic interventions have actually *undermined* their lifelong well-being, in opposition to the very rationale behind paternalism in the first place. This highlights a point often overlooked in discussion of the ethics of paternalism: Many cases of paternalism are *not* like Mill's bridge crosser, who presumably is not harmed by being delayed in order to inform them of the dangers of the bridge. Yet the harms associated with paternalistic interventions must themselves be taken into account when justifying paternalism.

The other difficulty with the 'speed bump' approach is primarily philosophical and emerges when we consider how suicidal ambivalence can unfold over time. The approach operates on the principle that ambivalence lends greater moral support to paternalistic suicide prevention efforts when and because that ambivalence resolves itself by affording individuals better access to the reasons that logically bear on their decision as to whether to end their lives. We may capture this thought with the slogan 'rational resolution trumps ambivalence.' But this slogan has implications that proponents of the 'speed bump' approach may hesitate to accept.

Consider the following scenario: S has concluded (competently, with the full complement of their rational capacities, etc.) that it is in their best interests to die. However, S wavers in their willingness to engage in suicide, perhaps thanks to a strong instinctual fear of death. The slogan 'rational resolution trumps ambivalence' implies that those responsible for treating S, etc., should disregard S's current unresolved (albeit ambivalent) will in favor of S's past resolved will. In other words, they should not aim to prevent S's suicide because in the past S had a resolved will that had decided in favor of suicide. To make this possibility more vivid, suppose that S had signed an advance directive in the past. In the usual cases of psychiatric advanced directives, an individual authorizes their being subjected to suicide prevention measures, in effect asserting, "if I (later) indicate or entertain an intention to engage in suicide, you may use these measures to stop me." But S's psychiatric advance directive was *not* pro-preservationist: In a moment of non-ambivalent lucidity, S directed their doctors, etc., to not interfere if their later self wavers in their intention to end their lives. S's directive in effect announces, "if I seem to waver in my future suicidal plans, don't stop me!" Thus, while the slogan 'rational resolution trumps ambivalence' justifies preventive measures designed to prevent an ambivalent suicidal agent from ending their life on the basis that their later non-ambivalent self would not find in their best interests to do so, it also *bars* preventive measures to stop an ambivalent person's suicide when their past rationally competent self found suicide to be in their best interests.

My suspicion is that many supporters of the 'speed bump' approach would find this result—in effect, that their slogan sometimes bars the introduction of 'speed bumps' so as to keep the road toward suicide clear for agents with settled rational wills—to be deeply unpalatable. But it is difficult to see how they can resist this result in a principled way. If having a settled will, even when ambivalent, *ceteris paribus*, determines whether we may paternalistically prevent a person's suicide, then the relative temporal order of a settled versus an unsettled will looks irrelevant. That a suicidal person's will was once settled but is now unsettled should be viewed in the same light as a suicidal person's once having been unsettled but now having a settled will. The (rational) settling of one's will settles the matter, irrespective of when the settling takes place.

The only way to avoid this seemingly unpalatable implication is to revise the aforementioned slogan, making it conditional on what the agent chooses: 'rational resolution trumps ambivalence *only when the resolution is pro-preservationist*.' But this revised slogan embraces a significantly more controversial moral proposition than has been assumed in the dialectic to this point. Rather than the 'weak' paternalist thought that paternalism can be justified when agents are acting against their best interests but fail to recognize this due to a lack of information, a deliberative incapacity, etc., the revised slogan can only get its warrant from a 'strong' paternalist claim, to wit, that ending one's life is by its nature an irrational objective, so that only when one resolves suicidal ambivalence in favor of continuing to live is one's will *rationally* settled. In other words, to resist the unpalatable conclusion, we must believe that others are entitled to decide not merely whether a suicidal person is being rational but to subject them to their own beliefs about what the substantively rational choice is. The paternalistic actor thus justifies their preventive efforts not on the basis that this is what the suicidal individual would prefer were they more rational, but on the basis that continuing to live is what the actor prefers *for them*, regardless of whether the individual would prefer this when more rational. This represents, in my estimation, a significantly more disrespectful stance toward the suicidal individual as a rational agent.

This suggests that a defensible 'speed bump' approach must treat the phenomena of ambivalence consistently and not encode a pro-preservationist bias. My reasoning does not, of course, refute this approach. Its significance lies instead in illustrating that respect for a person's settled rational will does not have uniform implications for suicide prevention undertaken on paternalistic grounds. It can, as the 'speed bump' approach shows, speak in favor of such prevention. But so too can it speak against paternalistic prevention efforts.

11.6 Conclusion

Ambivalence (practical conflict that cannot be resolved 'costlessly' or without normative remainder) is apparently common in suicidal ideation. But this fact does not lend unambiguous support for preventing suicide on paternalistic grounds. Some ambivalent choices reflect a settled will, and in many cases, a settled will can be confused with being merely ambivalent. More generally, ambivalence is not *per se* a sign of practical rationality or agential deficiency of the kind that would license acting against a suicidal person's wishes by subjecting them to suicide prevention measures. While the 'speed bump' approach, in which prevention is warranted in order to provide individuals more time to better appreciate the reasons that bear on their choice of whether to continue to live, has merit, it too faces practical and theoretical challenges. In terms of the Basic Argument, it may well be sound, but only in a limited range of cases of actual suicidal ambivalence.

Note that I have not argued that ambivalence should be ignored when thinking about when and how to ethically engage in suicide prevention. But I have argued that ambivalence *as such* does not raise any 'red flags,' either for or against suicide prevention, because ambivalence is independent of rational capacity. The central question that clinicians and others responsible for preventing suicide in specific individuals ought to entertain is not 'is this person ambivalent toward the possibility of suicide?' but 'is this ambivalent agent rationally competent to make the determination regarding whether ending their life is in their best interests?'

Still, some may hesitate to accept my conclusions because of the *high stakes* involved in choosing suicide. They may hold that when a choice is weighty enough, we should treat ambivalence as a reason to prevent someone from making a regrettable choice. Thus, even despite the reservations I have highlighted regarding how ambivalence supports suicide prevention, we should nevertheless *err on the side of caution* given the magnitude of the harms that an irrational suicide results in (Pabst Battin, 1996, p. 141; Cholbi 2002)

Here too though we should doubt the force of the argument. For one, while the stakes of suicide are high, the risks at issue are not only on the side of choosing to die. As noted in Section 11.5, in certain very dire situations, an individual may stand to lose a great deal by being compelled to stay alive against their wishes. In those situations, preventing a person's suicide because we are erring on the side of caution amounts to treating as relevant the risks associated with choosing to die prematurely while treating as *irrelevant* the risks associated with continuing to live. That is untenable.

Similarly, my opponents might appeal to the notion that death is irreversible; if we rely on 'err on the side of caution,' we can prevent a person from subjecting themselves to a death that is not in their best interests and cannot be remedied or undone, but failing to prevent a person from dying due to suicide on a given occasion does not mean that they cannot subsequently choose to end their lives. In erring on the side of caution then, we give appropriate weight to the fact that death's harms cannot be addressed, but the harms of living on can be, including by means of suicide. But this does not convince either. A person who is non-consensually subjected to suicide prevention efforts may also be subject to irreversible harms. A person who (for instance) is made to live on but who in one year's time opts for suicide has presumably been subjected to a year of low (or even negative) quality of life. Like the harm of death, this year cannot be given back to them or the harm undone.

We should also question the moral intuition on which this appeal to the stakes of death rests. It supposes that high-stakes choices give others more moral right to interfere with our choices on paternalistic grounds, but this is far from obvious. Many choices others make that have similarly high stakes as the choice to hasten one's death (e.g., choices to marry or to rear children) deserve our respect even when they are made 'ambivalently.' Is the choice to end one's life exempted from the demand to respect individuals' choices, even when they exhibit ambivalence? On the contrary, we might think. High-stakes choices are *precisely* those that call for humility and deference from others, in no small part because the stakes are highest for the person whose choices they are. This is why most of us would find being treated paternalistically with respect to life's 'big decisions' (whether and who to marry, what career to pursue, etc.) more objectionable than being treated paternalistically with respect to more mundane matters (our daily dietary choices, say). Paternalism arguably is harder to justify when the stakes of a choice are high, in which cases choice related to suicide appear to deserve far *greater* respect than normal. After all, such choices (like all high-stakes choices) are the ones where we mostly want our own agency to be decisive in shaping our lives (Cholbi 2013, Cholbi 2017)

I conclude then that the Basic Argument overstates the ethical relevance that ambivalence has for suicide prevention justified by paternalistic considerations. Far more caution is therefore in order when invoking ambivalence in our reasoning about suicide prevention.

Note

1 Strong paternalism, in contrast, countenances paternalism when the paternalistic actor believes the individual's ends are themselves mistaken or irrational.

References

Brandt, R. (1975). The morality and rationality of suicide. In Perlin, S., ed., *A handbook for the study of suicide*, Oxford University Press, pp. 66–76.

Chang, R. (2017). Hard choices. *Journal of the American Philosophical Association, 3(1)*, 1–21.

Cholbi, M. (2002). Suicide intervention and non-ideal Kantian theory. *Journal of Applied Philosophy, 19(3)*, 245–259.

Cholbi, M. (2013). Kantian paternalism and suicide intervention. In Coons, C., and Weber, M.E., eds., *Paternalism: Theory and practice*, Cambridge University Press, pp. 115–133.

Cholbi, M. (2016). The denial of moral dilemmas as a regulative ideal. *Canadian Journal of Philosophy, 46(2)*, 268–89.

Cholbi, M. (2017). Paternalism and our rational powers. *Mind 126(501)*, 123–153.

Coates, D.J. (2022). *In praise of ambivalence*. Oxford University Press.

Dworkin, G. (2020). Paternalism. In Zalta, E., ed., *Stanford Encyclopedia of Philosophy* (available at https://plato.stanford.edu/entries/paternalism/)

Evans, G., & Farberow, N. L. (1988). *The encyclopedia of suicide. Facts on File.*

Frankfurt, H. (1988). Identification and wholeheartedness. In Schoeman, F.D. ed., *Responsibility, character, and the emotions: New essays in moral psychology*. Cambridge University Press, pp. 27–45.

Harris, K.M., McLean, J.P., Sheffield, J., & Jobes, D. (2010). The internal suicide debate hypothesis: Exploring the life versus death struggle. *Suicide and Life-Threatening Behavior, 40(2)*, 181–192.

Kovacs, M., and Beck, A.T. (1977). The wish to die and the wish to live in attempted suicides. *Journal of Clinical Psychology, 33(2)*, 361–365.

Pabst Battin, M. (1996). *The death debate: Ethical Issues in suicide*. Prentice-Hall.

Razinsky, H. (2016). *Ambivalence: A philosophical exploration*. Rowman and Littlefield.

Shneidman, E. (1996). *The suicidal mind*. Oxford University Press.

Solomon, S., Greenberg, J., and Pyszczynski, T. (2015). *The worm at the core: On the role of death in life*. Random House.

Teismann, T., Siebert A.M., and Forkmann, T. (2024). Suicidal ambivalence: A scoping review. *Suicide and Life Threatening Behavior 54(5)*, 802–813.

Tessman, L. (2017). *When doing the right thing is impossible*. Oxford University Press.

Williams, B. (1985). *Ethics and the limits of moral philosophy*. Fontana.

12 Ambivalence and Medical Aid in Dying

Brent M. Kious

12.1 Introduction

Often when people make momentous decisions—choices that may dramatically affect the course of their life and which seem to involve considerable risk—others want some reassurance that those decisions reflect what they really want. The decision to receive medical aid in dying (MAID) is particularly momentous and is also accompanied in many jurisdictions by strong safeguards to verify that the patient's request is fully autonomous. In Oregon, which legalized physician-assisted dying in 1997, the Death with Dignity Act includes a number of procedures that ensure that request is genuine. The law requires a patient to make three total requests: initially, one in writing and one verbally and, then no sooner than 15 days later, another verbal request (Oregon Death with Dignity Act, 1994). Oregon also allows the patient to rescind the request at any time and for any reason; it stipulates that the patient should clearly have decision-making capacity that is not compromised by their illness or any intercurrent conditions and that the patient should have the opportunity to make an informed decision that incorporates knowledge of their diagnosis, prognosis, alternative interventions, and the potential risks and consequences of taking the medications. Similarly, in the original version of Canada's MAID law, persons whose natural death was reasonably foreseeable (those with a terminal illness) were initially expected to adhere to a 10-day waiting period (An Act to amend the Criminal Code and to make related amendments to other Acts (medical assistance in dying), 2016), though this requirement was later removed. Canada still obliges applicants whose natural death is not reasonably foreseeable to wait 90 days before their request is honored, at least in most cases, and requires MAID providers to explicitly give the applicant the opportunity to withdraw their request prior to the procedure (Government of Canada, 2025).

The requirement that requests for MAID be authentic is particularly important for individuals requesting MAID for irremediable psychiatric

DOI: 10.4324/9781003616221-17

illness, which is currently possible in the Netherlands, Belgium (Deliens & van der Wal, 2003), Luxembourg, and Switzerland (Dyer, White, & García Rada, 2015), and may also be possible in Canada in the next few years (Reuters, 2024). Because psychiatric illnesses often directly affect multiple dimensions of decision-making, including knowledge, reasoning, motivation, and desire, and because they frequently also contribute directly to suicidal ideation, it is especially likely that a person who requests MAID for a psychiatric illness may not have done so authentically. In such a case, providing MAID would mean imposing a significant and nonconsensual harm. In contrast, if the request was made in a fully informed, rational, voluntary, and ultimately *autonomous* fashion (Beauchamp & Childress, 2013), the impermissible harm that would ordinarily be involved in MAID is transformed into a permissible benefit (Kleinig, 2010).

This concern about psychiatric MAID is amply demonstrated in a recent case from Germany, where MAID is legally ambiguous; a law criminalizing it was struck down by the Constitutional Court, though no replacement law has yet been enacted (Buchholz & Zimmermann, 2024). On July 12, 2021, Christoph Turowski, a German physician, provided an injection of lethal medication to a 37-year-old veterinary student, "Isabell R.", who had sought his assistance in dying because of severe and unremitting depression (Buchholz & Zimmermann, 2024). The process through which she received MAID was somewhat chaotic. After an initial attempt in which she ingested potentially lethal pills that Turowski prescribed, Isabell became violently ill, did not die, and was psychiatrically hospitalized. After her release from the hospital, she contacted Turowski again, and he arranged to meet with her at a hotel, where she ultimately administered the lethal injection to herself. She quickly died.

The case came to trial because of concerns that Isabell had not made a fully autonomous decision. Turowski was ultimately convicted of manslaughter and sentenced to three years in prison. Critical to this verdict was the fact that the overseeing judge felt that "The central prerequisite for immunity from prosecution … is the voluntary decision to die by suicide … ". The judge felt that voluntariness was not manifest in Isabell's case, as her choice did not reflect "permanence and inner strength." Although she had initially sought Turowski's support and had met with him on several occasions, her desire to die clearly fluctuated:

> At times, the student insisted that the defendant help her die, at other times she declared that she had returned to life. Two days before her death, she wrote to the doctor: "Thank you, Dr. Turowski, I will stay alive and would therefore like to cancel the appointment on Monday." The next day, she explained that after the failed suicide attempt, she

> couldn't risk it again. Shortly afterward, she added: "But if I dare, I'll get in touch again." And: "Sorry for the constant back and forth."
> (Bischoff, 2024)

According to another source,

> On the morning of her death, the woman wrote messages to Turowski in which she expressed doubts about the planned suicide, only to confirm it again minutes later. "The lady struggled with herself," states the presiding judge. "Didn't that concern you?" "It is in our nature that we weigh every decision," says Turowski. He calculated that the woman was in favor of suicide in 95 percent of the many messages to him and only against it in five percent.
> (Indo New York, 2024)

These commentaries suggest that the central concern in Isabell's case—the concern leading to Turowski's conviction—was that she was *ambivalent* about MAID, where her ambivalence indicated that her request was not fully voluntary and thus not autonomous. The connection between ambivalence and voluntariness is intuitively appealing. In what follows, however, I will argue that the connection is often spurious. I begin by outlining what I take ambivalence to be. I consider and ultimately reject coherentist accounts of ambivalence, according to which it is a matter of alignment between first-order desires and second-order desires. I suggest that ambivalence can be a matter of the relationship between first-order desires, and I distinguish between what I will call "weak ambivalence" and "strong ambivalence." I then argue that even strong ambivalence does not vitiate voluntariness and is compatible with fully autonomous decisions. Ultimately, I argue that the apparent ability of ambivalence to undercut voluntariness and autonomy is driven by other factors that impair autonomy more directly, but which are often indirectly associated with ambivalence.

12.2 What Is Ambivalence?

12.2.1 Ambivalence versus Related States

In ordinary English discourse, the term "ambivalence" is used in various ways. In this book, different chapters explore different definitions and characterizations of ambivalence. For the purposes of this chapter, I take the following ideas to be central. First, ambivalence is in some sense a matter of wanting different and incompatible things. We do not suppose that someone is ambivalent if they want only one thing or if they want many things but all of them are aligned. Any account of ambivalence we adopt should capture intuitions that it is a matter of being both for and against a particular option or set of options; that it involves a tension between positive and negative attitudes toward those options; and that for the ambivalent person, it is at least frequently unclear to them what they "really" or "most" want. As Ekstrom has indicated, the ambivalent person has "mixed feelings" about what to do (Ekstrom, 1993).

Second, it must be the case that although ambivalence can be a barrier to action, it is still compatible with action, at least in most cases. If ambivalence is invariably incompatible with action—perhaps because it involves a sort of Buridan's ass problem where choice is impossible because there is nothing to differentiate the options—it is presumably rare and not terribly interesting.

Moore et al. (2022), following Rorty (2014), helpfully distinguish several psychological states that are close kin to ambivalence. When an agent is *uninformed*, she does not know enough to make a choice, often because she does not know enough to form a preference. Imagine that Sally has been diagnosed with breast cancer, and her oncologist says that she has two options for chemotherapy, A and B, but does not give her any information about their comparative merits or demerits. Sally might describe herself as "ambivalent," but if she knew more about how A and B compare with respect to things that matter to her, she would have a clear preference.

Another related phenomenon is *vacillation*. Often, even psychologically typical individuals find that their preferences change over time, sometimes rapidly. Consider how some of my own preferences changed just yesterday. In the morning, I thought that I should watch my cholesterol more closely and so should stop having a big chunk of cheddar cheese each evening for a snack. But once evening rolled around, I started to have the usual cravings, saw the cheese in the refrigerator, and vacillated: my preferences changed, and I came to care a good deal more about eating the cheese than I did about controlling my cholesterol. Today, though, in the clear light of morning, I regret my decision, and I am back to caring more about controlling my cholesterol. It is worth noting here that the kind of vacillation I am describing is akin to *akrasia* or weakness of will (Davidson, 2001): I made a rule for myself about my behavior but then, exposed to temptation, changed my preferences, and thus ceased to follow the rule. Other kinds of vacillation could be more mundane and reflect our response to new information rather than volitional perturbations *per se*. You might have thought initially that you liked a particular political candidate, but then when you learned more about her policies, you decided that you did not, but then learned even more about the other candidate and changed your mind again, and so on. We see vacillation in the sense of *akrasia* as problematic for agency (at least, it is something we often strive to overcome), but vacillation understood as diachronic ambivalence as relatively unobjectionable and sometimes even laudable.

A very different sort of "ambivalence" is (local) *apathy*[1], wherein the individual does not have any strong preferences for any options. Apathy can occur, unproblematically, when we lack any of the basic drives that might help us discern between options. Suppose, for instance, that your partner asks whether you want to order Thai food or Indian food for dinner, but you have just eaten a huge chunk of cheese, and so you are not even remotely hungry. Then, you are likely to be locally apathetic: you may want neither Thai food nor Indian food (nor any other food) and so seem "ambivalent"—but really, apathetic—regarding which is selected.

Moore et al. (2022) describe "true ambivalence" as a matter of feeling torn between two or more incompatible options. Ambivalence in this sense is a matter of *painful* "indifference," where indifference, in their classification, is a matter of having incompatible preferences with respect to some option or competing preferences with respect to incompatible options. Although the distinctions made by Moore et al. (2022) seem largely correct, I would differ in one respect: I see little reason to suppose that the truly ambivalent person *necessarily* feels torn. Requiring this seems to artificially limit ambivalence to momentous decisions, wherein the agent feels strongly about each of the options available and has a lot invested in the outcome. Similarly, it seems to require that ambivalence is a source of distress, though it is not obvious why we should think so. Accordingly, I will use the term "ambivalence" in roughly the way that Moore et al. (2022) would be inclined to use "indifference": ambivalence is a matter of having, at the same time (i.e., *synchronically*), incompatible preferences (desires, valuations, conative attitudes) with respect to some option, or competing preferences over incompatible options. Either definition would, though, satisfy the desiderata we laid out at the beginning of this section: someone who is ambivalent in the sense of indifference frequently *can* make a choice, but also seems to have been both for and against the option in question and to have had mixed feelings about what she should do, whether or not she feels "torn." Centrally, she may not have known what she "really" wanted.

With these distinctions in hand, it is worth noting that it is unclear whether Isabell, from the case mentioned earlier, is exhibiting genuine ambivalence or some other volitional inconsistency, such as diachronic ambivalence (vacillation) or even *akrasia*. She was observed to have had variation over time in her expressed preferences: sometimes she indicated that she wanted to go ahead with MAID, and sometimes she indicated that she did not. But these observations are consistent with many different explanations. This is not, I should hasten to add, to say that if she was experiencing something like diachronic ambivalence, it would have been more compatible with autonomy. Diachronic ambivalence could be antithetical to autonomy, too.

12.2.2 Coherentism

The idea that ambivalence is (or can be) a matter of having conflicting preferences between incompatible options has been rejected by some scholars. In his work on free will and personhood (Frankfurt, 1988, 1999), Harry Frankfurt has argued that ambivalence really operates at the level of second-order desires or desires about what we should want or will (see Chapter 2). Frankfurt suggests that there are two ways a person can be ambivalent. In some cases, she has two conflicting first-order desires and has not yet decided which of these she wants to constitute her will—that is, to be effective in guiding her action. In this sort of case, her ambivalence is a matter of "failing to constitute her will." While (to use Frankfurt's famous example) she wants to use heroin and wants to be sober, she does not yet want to want either heroin or sobriety. This is similar to Moore's *indifference*, but not exactly the same. Ambivalence *qua* indifference probably often involves reflection on what one really wants and, thus, involves an attempt to constitute one's will, but does not necessarily do so, since one can have conflicting preferences without thinking about them as conflicting preferences or trying to adjudicate between them. In contrast, Frankfurt localizes ambivalence in the *attempt*, whether successful or not, to form a second-order desire and to resolve the competition between competing first-order preferences.

In Frankfurt's other sort of case, the ambivalent agent's second-order desires are themselves in conflict. Then, she might (at the first level) want to use heroin and want to be sober and also (at the second level) want to want to use heroin *and* want to want to be sober. Justin Coates largely agrees with Frankfurt's claim that ambivalence requires more than first-order conflict, since he thinks that ambivalence essentially involves a conflict "internal" to one's sense of agency (Coates, 2017). This requires some second-order desires as well as recognition of one's first-order desires as in some sense "one's own." Frankfurt's and Coates's accounts of ambivalence are *coherentist* (Ekstrom, 1993) because they posit that ambivalence is a failure of good agential functioning, where good agential functioning involves some measure of coherence across the hierarchy of one's desires (one wants to be sober and wants to want to be sober, and so on).

While we should concede that it captures two ways of being ambivalent, I see coherentism as too demanding.[2] First, coherentists must say that creatures that lack self-reflective capacities cannot be ambivalent when they are indifferent in the sense of Moore et al. (2022) or even ambivalent in their sense. But this is counterintuitive; it seems natural to suppose that my dog is ambivalent when she wants to pick up two different toys but cannot do both. Nor is the problem limited to creatures that are constitutively incapable of reflecting on their own mental states. Coherentism also implies that we cannot properly say that a person is ambivalent who is so severely distressed that self-reflection is inaccessible to them and who is torn between two options—e.g., *I want to die,* vs. *I am afraid to die.*[3] I also think it is possible that coherentism overestimates the amount of self-reflection that even ordinarily self-reflective agents do. In my experience, the question of whether a first-order desire that I am experiencing is one I want to act on or not rarely even comes up; this only happens when, for some reason, I experience some challenge to that desire. Admittedly, the presence of a conflicting desire can be one such challenge. But even then, I suspect that much of our deliberation is not about which desire we want to have, but rather about *which of the competing options is better.* Consider an example. I am trying to choose which pizza to order: pepperoni or Italian sausage. I want both but cannot have both. I might even feel torn. I think most of us would be inclined to say I am ambivalent, but it would be very strange if my deliberation focused on the merits of the desires themselves, as opposed to the relative merits of pepperoni and Italian sausage.

Something similar is true if we think of agential coherence as involving *identification* with a desire. I suspect that the question of whether a desire is really mine or not rarely comes up, except in cases where the desire is especially challenging in some way—e.g., it interferes with many other desires, or is morally questionable, or seems initially to have been imposed on us by outside forces. As I noted earlier, I like cheddar cheese and often wish that I did not, but I have never wondered whether the desire for cheese was really mine or not (if only I *could* disown it!), and I still think I can be ambivalent about eating cheese.

12.2.3 Weak and Strong Ambivalence

If we accept, as against coherentism, that ambivalence can be a matter of first-order conflict only, then one further distinction needs to be made. We have said that a person is ambivalent if she has competing preferences regarding incompatible options. But the competition between desires can be more or less fierce. I recently went to a conference in Hawaii, and before I went, I said to a colleague that I was ambivalent about going. Of course, it was no great struggle for me to go (it was Hawaii, after all). The issue was that though I mostly wanted to go, I was also a little reluctant to take time away from family and to sit on a plane for six hours. I would propose that we call this kind of ambivalence "weak." If someone is weakly ambivalent regarding an action, they have competing, incompatible desires regarding that action, but these desires differ greatly in strength, so that one is clearly motivationally effective (though its motivational superiority may only be evident after some time).

In contrast, we might say that a person has "strong" ambivalence if she has two or more *strongly competing* desires, where two or more desires are strongly competing if and only if they are similar in strength, *and* each of them would be motivationally effective if left to its own devices. So, for example, we might say that I am strongly ambivalent if, when asked by my department chair to head some committee, I both strongly want to head the committee (to avoid displeasing my chair, whom I fear) and strongly want not to head the committee (because I know it will get in the way of writing, which I enjoy). That at least one of the competing desires would individually be motivationally effective is important. Imagine that I very weakly want to eat chocolate ice cream and very weakly want to eat vanilla ice cream, but neither of these desires would lead me to eat ice cream on its own. Here, I do not think we would usually call this a case of ambivalence; it is better described as a case of local apathy.

The distinction between weak and strong ambivalence is important because only strong ambivalence poses a potential threat to autonomy. Weak ambivalence is common: it is often the case that when we strongly want X, we also weakly want not X (or Y, where Y is incompatible with X). In contrast, when a person is strongly ambivalent and wants both X and not X, and each of those desires is potentially motivationally effective, and the difference in strength between these desires is not readily discernible, there is a live question about what the person *really* wants, and thus a live question about whether a choice rooted in one of these desires is "really hers."[4] We could even imagine that when two desires are strongly competing, it is sometimes possible that one is actually somewhat weaker and thus does not reflect what the agent most wants, but can still, almost as a matter of luck or because of environmental factors, determine what she does. In Isabell's case, we might imagine that even though Isabell *really* wanted to live, her desire to die was quite strong and happened to interact with some subtle influence imposed, if only unwittingly, by Dr. Turowski. Indeed, I take this to be one of the fears behind his conviction: that he somehow colluded with Isabell's weaker desire so that it won out over the stronger.

While the distinction between weak and strong ambivalence is ethically significant, it is likely that the division between them is not strict. If individual desires can be more or less strong, then the competition between two desires can be more or less fierce. This implies that ambivalence can be a matter of degree and thus that there are hard cases where it is unclear whether a person is weakly or strongly ambivalent. While this is a limitation of the view, since it means that it will be hard to determine in these cases whether the individual's autonomy is compromised (assuming only strong ambivalence compromises autonomy), I do not regard this limitation as lethal; it may simply also happen that an individual's autonomy, if it seems threatened by ambivalence, is uncertain.

12.3 Revisiting the Relationship between Ambivalence and MAID

12.3.1 The Argument from Authenticity

So far, I have suggested that ambivalence about momentous decisions such as MAID appears to be morally significant because we think it compromises a person's autonomy. In the following section, I want to lay out the argument for this claim in detail so that we can decide whether to accept it.

Here is what we might call the *argument from authenticity*:

a An individual should be permitted to undertake some momentous decision, wherein she is at high risk of harm if she has typical interests and goals, only if she does so autonomously.
b A decision (and the ensuing action) is autonomous only if the choice underpinning it is *authentic*.
c A decision is authentic only if it reflects an agent's *true* values, desires, preferences, etc.
d If an agent is strongly ambivalent, she does not have a true value, desire, or preference in the relevant domain.
e Therefore, if an agent is strongly ambivalent and she makes some decision, that decision is not authentic.
f Therefore, if an agent undertakes an action but is strongly ambivalent, her action is not autonomous.
g Therefore, if an agent undertakes an action but is strongly ambivalent, and if that action involves a momentous decision, then she should not be permitted to undertake it.
h MAID is a momentous decision.
i Therefore, if an agent requests MAID but she is strongly ambivalent, she should not be permitted to undertake MAID.

We should, however, reject the argument from authenticity, largely because of problems with premise (d). First, as coherentists might concede, an agent could be strongly ambivalent in my sense but still positively identify with one (or both) of her desires. She could, that is, be *autonomously ambivalent*. For instance, to use Sartre's example (2007), she might very much want to stay at home taking care of her mother and also very much want to go join the French resistance, but ultimately identify with the latter desire, wherein she sees it as the one she wants to guide her choices. In this case, she would be wholehearted in one sense even though she was strongly ambivalent, making it seem more likely that her decision was autonomous.

Similarly, as Marino argues (2011), ambivalence could sometimes enhance autonomy. The strongly ambivalent person may, if she is going to act, be forced to adjudicate between her competing desires, deliberating about how they are to be balanced. Suppose, to use Frankfurt's case, that Greg is addicted to heroin (and so wants to use heroin), though he also wants not to use heroin because it conflicts with many life goals. Finally, on reflection, he has aligned himself with the desire not to use heroin because he has thought carefully about what he wants to want to do. Of course, Coates and Frankfurt would both say that Greg is *not* ambivalent, as he has alignment between his second-order desire and one of his first-order desires. Unless we accept coherentism's conception of ambivalence, however, we should see cases like this as showing that (first-order) ambivalence is, if not exactly conducive to autonomy, then at least sometimes compatible with it.

Additionally, there is reason to suspect that many momentous decisions involve strong ambivalence that poses no threat to autonomy. Imagine that Marco needs to decide which college to go to, and he has been accepted by both Harvard and Yale (which are equally good schools that would serve his life goals equally well). This seems a momentous decision: it will significantly affect the course of his life. But Marco is ambivalent: he wants to go to Harvard, but he also wants to go to Yale. He eventually settles on Harvard, though for no reason he can give (perhaps he just picks). Should we doubt in any respect that his decision was autonomous? It does not seem so, and if we did say that his decision was non-autonomous, we should be forced to doubt the credentials of many other difficult, superficially respect-worthy decisions.

Moreover, there is a continuum between weak and strong ambivalence that is determined only by the relative strength of the desires involved. As we already observed, weak ambivalence does not even appear to threaten autonomy—if it did, very few decisions would be autonomous. Since the relative strength of a desire alone should not determine whether or not it is mine or whether decisions flowing from it are inauthentic (very strong desires can still be mine, and very weak desires can still be mine), there is no clear antecedent reason to think that strong ambivalence should threaten autonomy when weak ambivalence does not.

Finally, the strongly ambivalent person simply has multiple strong, potentially motivationally effective desires. In a scenario where there is only one such desire—i.e., the agent is not at all ambivalent—there is no question but that the resulting decision is autonomous. But if we reject coherentism, what about adding another strong, motivationally effective desire—a desire which could alone conduce to autonomous action—undercut autonomy? If, individually, each of the desires in question would be regarded as reflecting the agent's true desires, then having two such "true" desires should not entail that one (or both) of them is false. This would only follow if we assumed that, as a matter of psychological normality, an agent can only ever truly want one thing from a list of incompatible options, so that having two strong desires is psychologically abnormal. But, as yet, we have seen no reason to assume this.

12.3.2 Irrationality and Other Coherentist Problems

We might consider arguments other than the argument from authenticity for thinking that ambivalence undercuts autonomy. Coherentists like Frankfurt could regroup and argue that if an agent undertakes an action but is (strongly) ambivalent, then we need not respect her choice, because it is *irrational*, or because it is not *free*, or because she is *not fully a person* with respect to that choice. Frankfurt thinks that (strong) ambivalence is irrational: we cannot rationally want both X and not X, just as we cannot believe both P and not P (Frankfurt, 2004). Likewise, he argues that freedom of the will requires *forming* a will, where this involves achieving coherence between first- and second-order volitions; to have free will, for Frankfurt, is a matter of "having the will I want to have" (Frankfurt, 1971). For the same reasons, Frankfurt argues at length that true persons are those who form a will; if we act without willing (where this involves forming effective second-order volitions), then we act, at least temporarily, as mere "wantons." It is, admittedly, uncertain what the difference between these properties is, and indeed whether they are different from authenticity, but let us assume that the concepts track distinct though connected properties.

We should not too readily embrace these claims, however. As Coates has argued (2017), wanting both X and not X does not entail irrationality in any obvious way. Wanting two incompatible things is not irrational in the same way that believing P and not P is irrational, because, while it is impossible for both P and not P to be true, it is not at all impossible that X and not X are both worth wanting. Incompatible desires may simply be responsive to the complex evaluative terrain presented by the world, wherein few things are all good or all bad, there are many characteristics that might make a thing good (or bad), and it is surpassingly rare that we can get everything we want. In many cases, the values that speak in favor of alternative actions are incommensurable (Chang, 1997). Suppose that you need to choose between becoming a philosopher and becoming a banker or, to again borrow Sartre's example, that you need to choose between caring for your ailing mother and running off to join the resistance. These options are in most cases practically incompatible, but the things that speak in favor of each of them, the values which they serve, may also not be comparable on any shared metric. What makes philosophy a good thing to do is quite different from what makes banking a good thing to do; what makes caring for your mother a good thing to do is quite different from what makes supporting the resistance a good thing to do. As long as we have no single value or set of values with respect to which these alternatives can be weighed, the most we can say is that each promotes different values. This state of affairs may be regrettable in some sense, but it is not irrational.

Another important response to coherentist arguments is that in most contexts we do not assume that being strongly ambivalent is antithetical to having free will, nor to being a person. Most of us think that we can choose freely in a way that demands respect from others even if we have not formed second-order volitions. If I want chocolate ice cream and then buy some, we would ordinarily assume that my doing so was free, even if I did not think about whether I wanted to want chocolate ice cream. Similarly, and even more obviously, we do not always imagine that an individual loses claims to others' moral respect if they act wantonly. Even if we think that eating chocolate ice cream is usually bad for people and that people do not adequately consider whether they should want to eat ice cream, we would not assume that it would be appropriate to loiter at ice cream parlors haranguing would-be sundae consumers, treating them as though they are not in control of themselves. This is not, of course, to say that buying ice cream is similar in depth and gravity to receiving MAID; obviously, it is not. But the logical structure of the relationship between ambivalence and autonomy underlying these otherwise very different decisions is relevantly similar.

12.4 A Diagnosis

The troubles of the preceding arguments suggest that ambivalence itself does not actually compromise an agent's autonomy. Why, then, does it seem to? My diagnosis is this: ambivalence merely *appears* to undercut autonomy, and it does so because it often co-occurs with failures of practical rationality that really do affect autonomy.

There are a number of ways ambivalence can be associated with practical irrationality without itself *constituting* irrationality. Sometimes, the ambivalent agent may also be confused or agitated so that they are not thinking clearly. I recall, with some embarrassment, an occasion where I went shopping for ski boots. I was in a bit of a rush because of other time-sensitive obligations and was stressed about the fact that ski boots are so expensive. I had also not had a chance to research the various options, so I had not formed a settled preference. The features of the boots that were available to me were motivationally opaque; I did not have a clear sense of what mattered. I was torn: should I buy boots or not? If so, which ones? In the end, I ended up buying a pair of boots that were both ill-fitting and much more expensive than I wanted and regretted it as soon as I returned home. My decision was probably not a fully autonomous one, and I certainly chose poorly. This could be attributed to the fact that I was ambivalent. But I would suggest instead that my ambivalence was merely a symptom of other more serious problems: that I decided under pressure and was agitated and so made incorrect inferences on the basis of a poor understanding of inadequate information.

Another problem might be that the ambivalent agent is often subject to "external," ego-alien influences that independently threaten autonomy, such as coercion, undue influence, and manipulation. Consider Isabell's case again. While she may have been ambivalent, it is also true that she was struggling with depression, and depression itself often appears to undercut autonomy (Elliott, 1997; Rudnick, 2002). Indeed, the fluctuation in her desires may even indicate a sort of struggle between Isabell "herself"—what she would want were she not depressed or what she wants insofar as she is not depressed—and her depression, where the desires to which it gives rise do not reflect or constitute her good. Ambivalence itself may be a symptom of this struggle between the agent and those "external" influences. Imagine that a particularly sadistic terrorist tells you, quite credibly, that if you do not blind yourself with a hatpin, he will detonate a nuclear bomb in Manhattan. You are likely to be strongly ambivalent: you may think that you should accede to his demands—millions will die if you do not, including many people you care about—but also find it very hard to do so, since sticking a hatpin in your eye would fly in the face of your every instinct. Should you decide to blind yourself, you would not be acting autonomously. But here it is the terrorist's coercion, not your ambivalence, that undercuts your autonomy.

Note, too, that the content of the ambivalent person's competing desires seems to matter. We typically see ambivalence as threatening autonomy when the agent chooses something that is unconventional or controversial. Imagine that John has gangrene in one of his toes. If he does not get the toe amputated, he will die. He is ambivalent: he does not want to die, so he wants the amputation, but he *also* does not want the amputation, since he would like to keep his toe. Now imagine two variations on this case. In the first variation, John decides for the amputation, even though he does not want to lose his toe, and survives. In the second variation, John decides against the amputation, becomes sick, and dies. My intuition about these variations is rather different. In the first variation, there is no question but that John's decision is autonomous (*ceteris paribus*). Indeed,

John's decision is probably very similar to those of most persons who decide to get a life-saving amputation. But in the second variation, John's autonomy is definitely in question; at the very least, there is a higher bar for showing that he is autonomous. Of course, the difference between these cases is not the ambivalence itself, but the substance of what John chooses. In the first variation, he chooses something that is *prima facie* reasonable; in the second variation, he does not. Reaching briefly back to Isabell's case, it strikes me that we would have no doubts about the autonomy of her decision if she had opted *not* to receive euthanasia, despite her ambivalence.

To emphasize this idea, consider that we do not typically regard ambivalence as threatening autonomy where the agent's options are equally good (or equally bad). In many cases, there is no question about whether ambivalence undercuts autonomy, because all of the options subsumed by the ambivalence are reasonable. Again consider Marco's case: he must decide whether to go to Harvard or Yale, which are equally good. There is very little to distinguish them, and he wants very much to go to both schools. He is strongly ambivalent. Whatever he ultimately chooses, and even if his decision is made on the basis of the most trivial differences (he likes Yale's colors better than Harvard's, or visits a particularly charming coffee shop in Boston) or, indeed, even if he simply picks one of the schools arbitrarily, his decision is still (*ceteris paribus*) autonomous. Ambivalence over reasonably good options does not compromise autonomy.

These considerations imply that ambivalence is only a threat to autonomy where one or more of the agent's options is *prima facie* bad. Many of us are predisposed to assume that MAID itself does not reflect an agent's good, since dying is *usually* bad, so the bar for being convinced that it is really good for someone is usually quite high (Kim & Berens, 2023). This is especially true of MAID for a primary psychiatric diagnosis, where the antecedent likelihood that it is good for the person requesting it is very low. Conversely, ambivalence is much less problematic when MAID is more easily seen as good for the agent. Imagine that instead of having unremitting depression, Isabell had metastatic ovarian cancer that was clearly incurable and which would cause her very severe pain and physical incapacity for a year before she died from malnutrition. She requests MAID, but has the very same misgivings she expressed in the original case. Still, after extensive deliberation, she pursues MAID. I suspect many of us would see this case as less problematic and would hypothesize that our judgment is rooted in the idea that perhaps MAID is not always a good for persons with mental disorders.

12.5 Back to the Case and Some Conclusions

I have argued that there is an intelligible concept of ambivalence according to which it can involve only conflict between first-order desires with minimal reflection on those desires. If this sort of ambivalence is possible, then we can distinguish between weak ambivalence and strong ambivalence. Weak ambivalence involves a conflict between two motivationally dissimilar desires, while strong ambivalence, which is more troublesome, involves desires that are motivationally similar. Only strong ambivalence presents a *prima facie* threat to autonomy.

I argued further, however, that the effect of strong ambivalence on autonomy is not as deleterious as we tend to assume. Strong ambivalence is common and often does not appear to undermine autonomy. While in other cases it does appear to do so, this is because it is often correlated with other factors that really do undermine autonomy, such as succumbing to external influences, impairments in understanding and reasoning, and emotional distress.

Where does this leave us in thinking about Isabell and Dr. Turowski? Although many features of the case are troubling and cast the rightness of Dr. Turowski's decision to provide MAID into doubt, Isabell's ambivalence is not one of them. It was concerning that Isabell suffered from a depressive illness, of which suicidal ideation and suicidal behavior are common symptoms. The circumstances of the case raise serious doubts about whether she truly had decision-making capacity, and these were not allayed by Turowski's allegedly cursory examination of her psychiatric history. It is also reasonable to wonder whether Isabell's decision really reflected what was best for her: although her illness was severe, it may not truly have been treatment resistant, as her treatment history also appears to have been underexplored. It is conceivable that she could have recovered with better or more extensive treatment. Finally, some might worry that Turowski may have indirectly and inadvertently influenced her decision, rendering it independently non-autonomous. On the other hand, Turowski seems to have believed that Isabell's ambivalence was not serious, perhaps because he saw her lingering doubts about MAID as reflecting instinctive, natural fear of death, despite her considered judgment about what to do.

These remarks have implications for MAID more generally. Although ambivalence itself does not threaten autonomy, MAID physicians should still verify that their clients have resolved any strong ambivalence before providing MAID and, in particular, that they have carefully considered their reasons for receiving or rejecting MAID and decided to receive it. This is for both rhetorical and epistemic reasons. Epistemically, if the person requesting MAID appears ambivalent, we should have high uncertainty about the autonomy of their decision because it is relatively likely that other factors, such as agitation, confusion, impulsivity, or inadequate information, are also impinging upon their choice. From a rhetorical standpoint, ambivalence may signal to other professionals, legal authorities, and the general public that the MAID provider has not done enough to inform the requestor, to allow them to contemplate their options, or to evaluate the quality of their decision-making.

Notes

1 In psychiatry, we sometimes use the term "apathy" in a more global sense to detect a lack of drive or preference in many settings.
2 An alternative would be the development of a less intellectualistic conception of coherentism; see Chapter 9.
3 Unless they want to allow in some manner that the failure to form a second-order volition is ensured in cases where self-reflection is precluded or even in cases where the capacity for self-reflection is constitutively absent. Then, I have no disagreement with coherentists' account of ambivalence, since I would certainly allow that we can have higher-order ambivalence.
4 Note that one might be tempted here to adopt a coherentist account of authenticity, according to which a desire is really an agent's if and only if she reflectively endorses it. I reject this approach for the same reason I laid out earlier, namely that it is too demanding. There are many cases where we would say that a person really wants something even though there is no indication that she has done any reflection on that desire.

References

An Act to amend the Criminal Code and to make related amendments to other Acts (medical assistance in dying), R.S.C. c.3, (2016).

Beauchamp, T. L., & Childress, J. F. (2013). *Principles of Biomedical Ethics, 7th Edition*. New York: Oxford University Press.

Bischoff, K. (2024, April 8, 2024). Verdict against euthanasia assistant: Berlin doctor sentenced to prison for manslaughter. *Berliner Zeitung*. Retrieved from www.berliner-zeitung.de/mensch-metropole/urteil-gegen-sterbehelfer-haftstrafefreispruch-fuer-berliner-arzt-li.2203689

Buchholz, J., & Zimmermann, F. W. (2024, April 8, 2024). Doctor sentenced to three years in prison for manslaughter. *Legal Tribune Online*. Retrieved from www.lto.de/recht/nachrichten/n/540Ks223-lg-berlin-i-sterbehilfe-medizinstrafrecht-ethik

Chang, R. (1997). *Incommensurability, Incomparability, and Practical Reason*. Cambridge: Harvard University Press.

Coates, D. J. (2017). A wholehearted defense of ambivalence. *The Journal of Ethics, 21*, 419–444.

Davidson, D. (2001). How is weakness of the will possible? In *Essays on Actions and Events* (pp. 21–42). Oxford: Oxford University Press.

Deliens, L., & van der Wal, G. (2003). The euthanasia law in Belgium and the Netherlands. *The Lancet, 362*, 1239–1240. doi:10.1016/s0140-6736(03)14520-5

Dyer, O., White, C., & García Rada, A. (2015). Assisted dying: Law and practice around the world. *BMJ, 351*, h4481. doi:10.1136/bmj.h4481

Ekstrom, L. W. (1993). A coherence theory of autonomy. *Philosophy and Phenomenological Research, 53*(3), 599–616.

Elliott, C. (1997). Caring about risks: Are severely depressed patients competent to consent to research? *Archives of General Psychiatry, 54*(2), 113–116.

Frankfurt, H. G. (1971). *Freedom of the Will and the Concept of a Person, 68*(1), 5–20.

Frankfurt, H. G. (1988). Identification and wholeheartedness. In *The Importance of What We Care About* (pp. 159–176). Cambridge: Cambridge University Press.

Frankfurt, H. G. (1999). Autonomy, necessity, and love. In *Necessity, Volition, and Love* (pp. 129–141). Cambridge: Cambridge University Press.

Frankfurt, H. G. (2004). *The Reasons of Love*. Princeton: Princeton University Press.

Government of Canada (2025). Canada's medical assistance in dying (MAID) law. Retrieved from www.justice.gc.ca/eng/cj-jp/ad-am/bk-di.html

Indo New York (2024, February 19). Accusation of manslaughter: Has a Berlin doctor exceeded the limits of euthanasia. *Indo New York*. Retrieved from https://indonewyork.com/breaking/trial-accusation-of-manslaughter-has-a-berlin-doctor-exceeded-the-limits.html

Kim, S. Y. H., & Berens, N. C. (2023). Risk-sensitive assessment of decision-making capacity: A comprehensive defense. *Hastings Center Report, 53*(4), 30–43.

Kleinig, J. (2010). The nature of consent. In F.G. Miller & A. Wertheimer (Eds.), *The Ethics of Consent: Theory and Practice* (pp. 3–24). New York: Oxford University Press.

Marino, P. (2011). Ambivalence, valuational inconsistency, and the divided self. *Philosophy and Phenomenological Research, 83*(1), 41–71.

Moore, B., Nelson, R. H., Ubel, P. A., & Blumenthal-Barby, J. (2022). Two minds, one patient: Clearing up confusion about "ambivalence." *The American Journal of Bioethics, 22*(6), 37–47.

Oregon Death with Dignity Act, §127.800 Stat. (1994).

Reuters. (2024, February 1, 2024). *Canada to Delay Assisted Death Solely on Mental Illness Until 2027*. Reuters Daily Briefing. Retrieved from www.reuters.com/world/americas/canada-delay-assisted-death-solely-mental-illness-until-2027-2024-02-01/

Rorty, A. (2014). The ethics of collaborative ambivalence. *The Journal of Ethics, 18*, 391–403.

Rudnick, A. (2002). Depression and competence to refuse psychiatric treatment. *Journal of Medical Ethics, 28*(3), 151–155.

Sartre, J.-P. (2007). *Existentialism is a Humanism*. New Haven: Yale University Press.

Index

Made in the USA
Monee, IL
12 November 2026

cd8f6551-7a0a-4f8e-887f-faf812204e26R01